DATE DUE			

Paving the Way for Madam President

LEXINGTON STUDIES IN POLITICAL COMMUNICATION
Series Editor: Robert E. Denton Jr., Virginia Tech

This series encourages focused work examining the role and function of communication in the realm of politics including campaigns and elections, media, and political institutions.

TITLES IN SERIES:

1. *Governing Codes: Gender, Metaphor, and Political Identity,*
   By Karrin Vasby Anderson and Kristina Horn Sheeler
2. *Paving the Way for Madam President,* By Nichola D. Gutgold
3. *Maryland Politics and Political Communication, 1950–2005,*
   By Theodore F. Sheckels

Paving the Way for Madam President

Nichola D. Gutgold

LEXINGTON BOOKS

A division of
ROWMAN & LITTLEFIELD PUBLISHERS, INC.
Lanham • Boulder • New York • Toronto • Oxford

LEXINGTON BOOKS

A division of Rowman & Littlefield Publishers, Inc.
A wholly owned subsidary of The Rowman & Littlefield Publishing Group, Inc.
4501 Forbes Boulevard, Suite 200
Lanham, MD 20706

PO Box 317
Oxford
OX2 9RU, UK

British Library Cataloguing in Publication Information Available

Library of Congress Cataloging-in-Publication Data

Gutgold, Nichola D.
  Paving the way for Madam President / Nichola D. Gutgold.
      p. cm.—(Lexington studies in political communication)
  Includes bibliographical references and index.
  ISBN-13: 978-0-7391-1593-0 (cloth : alk. paper)
  ISBN-10: 0-7391-1593-6 (cloth : alk. paper)
  ISBN-13: 978-0-7391-1594-7 (pbk. : alk. paper)
  ISBN-10: 0-7391-1594-4 (pbk. : alk. paper)
  1. Women presidential candidates—United States. I. Title. II. Series.
HQ1391.U5G88 2006
973.09'9—dc22
[B]   2006011531

Printed in the United States of America

♾™ The paper used in this publication meets the minimum requirements of
American National Standard for Information Sciences—Permanence of Paper
for Printed Library Materials, ANSI/NISO Z39.48-1992.

This book is dedicated to my parents,

Nicholas and Julia DelBalso

who live on in my heart.

To my husband, Geoff, whose energy, kindness,

and optimism make life enjoyable and exciting.

And to our spectacular children—

Ian, whose wide smile, kind heart, and musical creativity make
him a treasure.

And to Emily Ann, whose crafty industriousness, warmth,

and wit make for a pleasurable companion.

I love you all.

Contents

Foreword
by Geraldine Ferraro

When I was campaigning as the vice presidential candidate in 1984, I told voters to remember that Eleanor Roosevelt was thirty-six before she was allowed to cast her first vote. Not only shouldn't she have been barred from choosing public officials, she should have been one. We no longer live in either-or situations; we can be whatever we choose to be. We can win Olympic medals and coach our daughters' soccer teams. We can walk in space and help our children take their first steps. We can negotiate trade agreements and manage family budgets. We can be corporate executives and also wives and mothers. We can be doctors and also bake cookies with our six-year-old future scientists. The choices are unlimited.

I was an elementary school teacher, a lawyer prosecuting criminals in the D.A.'s Office in Queens, a three-term member of Congress, vice presidential candidate, a candidate for the U.S. Senate, and am currently senior managing director of a global consulting firm. I'm also a wife, mother of three, and doting grandmother of seven almost perfect grandchildren. Like those profiled in this book and millions of other women, I have had to write my own script and blaze my own trail. This book shows the multidimensional lives of women who have paved the way in politics. I am proud to have been part of the changing history that has helped pave the way for the first woman president.

As I've said before, politics is not a spectator sport. I have enjoyed the rough and tumble of fighting for the things I care about. Let the lives of the women in this book inspire you to participate in politics and change history. The women profiled in this book have proven what Susan B. Anthony always knew: "Because our cause is just, we can not fail." Becoming president isn't an impossible dream for women. It isn't a matter of *if*, it is a matter of *when*.

Geraldine A. Ferraro, 2005

Acknowledgments

This book was such a fun and passionate project and I want to thank several people who were instrumental in its completion. Dr. Eugene Slaski, historian and former Pennsylvania State Lehigh Valley campus CEO read the book proposal and chapters as I finished them, and offered advice and considerable editing. Director of Academic Affairs, Dr. Roger Egolf, encouraged me to consider a new title for the book.

My former student, Dolores Hooper, a 2005 graduate of Penn State Lehigh Valley provided me with exceptionally good research assistance, as did students Richard Day and Jordan Isaac. The outstanding staff at the beautiful Margaret Chase Smith Library, Skowhegan, Maine, generously awarded me the Ada Laeke Research Grant so that I could visit and research. I especially wish to thank Angela Stockwell, who graciously hosted my visit, and who, as a former secretary to Senator Smith, provided a wealth of information. Thanks to Senator Elizabeth Dole, whose remarkable career has inspired me for over a decade now and who is always willing to help my latest project by answering questions and providing valuable speech manuscripts. My admiration is very deep. To Patricia Schroeder, with her wonderfully relaxed personality, who didn't mind when my Communication Arts and Sciences honors students, and my own two children piled into her office to meet her and interview her as part of the class's work on contemporary American orators. And to Bert Ramlow, her assistant, who is as warm and accommodating as could be. To Ambassador Carol Moseley Braun who graciously allowed me to interview her and to her assistant, Diane, who was responsive to last-minute scheduling changes. My special thanks to Series Editor Robert

E. Denton, Jr., Joseph Parry and the very enthusiastic and warm Katie Funk, editors at Lexington for their belief in and encouragement of the project. Molly Ahearn, Assistant Production Editor, was both pleasant and professional.

My very supportive campus—Penn State Lehigh Valley and especially Sue Snyder who encouraged me as only she can to write this book. And to our energetic and enthusiastic Chancellor and CEO Dr. Ann Williams, who is a fine example of a trailblazer herself. Thanks also to Marie Cocco of the Washington Post for her column about Geraldine Ferraro which started me thinking about this topic.

Thank you very much.

Introduction

Women and the American Presidency

"Never doubt that a small group of thoughtful, committed citizens can change the world: indeed, it's the only thing that ever has."[1]

President of the United States. The title evokes images of power, leadership, and tradition. It also brings to mind the male dominance that has been a part of the office since its inception. It has been more than twenty years since the only woman in United States political history, Geraldine Ferraro, has been a candidate on a major party ticket. It is astonishing that in America, a country heralded for its democracy, leadership has been so gender-skewed. The first question that comes to mind is: *why?* Children have been known to ask: "Mommy, how come the president is always a boy?" If you are the parent, grandparent, aunt, or uncle of a child who asks this question, what are you going to say? This is America, after all—"land of the free, home of the brave"—surely if a woman *could* be elected president, in this country, she would be. So, while you think of how you would answer the child who asks you this question, consider the progress the world has made in breaking the gender barrier in politics. The world—except for America—that is. Women are presidents and prime ministers all over the globe. In Ireland, Mary McAleese is president, and she succeeded Mary Robinson, Ireland's first woman president who is widely considered to be the best president the country has ever known. Even after leaving office, Robinson has been a high profile advocate for human rights.[2] In the Philippines Gloria Macapagal-Arroyo succeeded Corazon Aquino and in Nicaragua, Violeta Chamorro is president. Margaret Thatcher's impressive management of the United

Kingdom's role in the Falkland Island War demonstrated her leadership. As prime minister of Israel, Golda Meir maintained a difficult coalition at home, while negotiating abroad with the hostile Arab nations and with the United States. Mireya Mosoco leads Panama, and at the beginning of 2006 Liberia inaugurated Africa's first woman president. Chile elected the first woman leader in Latin America who didn't rise to power on her husband's reputation, and Germany has a new woman chancellor. In about thirty other countries women serve as president or prime minister.

A majority of Americans *say* that the country is ready to elect a woman president in 2008—and even more said they would vote for one. A Hearst Newspapers/Siena College poll showed in February 2005 that of the four women mentioned as possible candidates, Hillary Clinton, Barbara Boxer, Elizabeth Dole, and Condoleezza Rice, Clinton was the front runner with 53 percent of the vote. In a *New York Times* article titled "Who Says a Woman Can't Be President? We Do," Lynn Martin, former secretary of labor, states that what people *say* and what they *think* can often be wildly divergent. The chairperson for Deloitte and Touché Council on the Advancement of Women reported that in a poll conducted in 2000, 60 percent of Americans believe a woman will be elected president, and 83 percent believe a woman will be elected vice president in their lifetimes. But 16 percent said they would not vote for a woman; while that's an improvement over the 32 percent who felt that way in 1992, it is still too big a bloc to write off.[3] CBS News conducted a poll in February 2006 that found 92 percent of those polled said that they would vote for a woman for president if she were qualified.[4] In a Gallup poll conducted in 1955, 52 percent said they would support a woman for president. That number rose to 73 percent in 1975 and to 82 percent in 1987.[5] The increased support of those polled sounds like reason for enthusiasm, although former congresswoman and presidential candidate Pat Schroeder said bluntly, "I think people lie when they say they would vote for a woman."[6] While the polls continue to give promising news, perhaps the only polls that really count are the ones that voters go to on election day.

Laura Liswood, Secretary-General of the Council of Women World Leaders suggests that the reason to elect more women leaders is to offer different points of view, values, experiences, priorities, interests, and conditions of life. Theirs are not necessarily better, more noble, more important, but they are theirs.[7] Sidney Verba believes that women would bring a different personality into politics—one that valued compromise and conciliation rather than domination.[8] A woman president would give American politics better gender balance and would end the debate about whether or not a woman will ever be elected.

CONTRIBUTION TO THE GROWING LITERATURE

There have been many books that examine women's leadership and the women's movement; two themes that emerge in this book. Marie C. Wilson's *Closing the Leadership Gap: Why Women Can and Must Help Run the World* recounts her experiences as one of the founders of the White House Project, an organization dedicated to advancing women's leadership across all sectors, including the United States presidency. Gail Collins, in her work, *America's Women: Four Hundred Years of Dolls, Drudges, Helpmates, and Heroines* traces the lives of more than four centuries of women and shows the tension surrounding the expectations for women. Linda Witt, Karen M. Paget, and Glenna Matthews' *Running as a Woman: Gender and Power in American Politics* orients the reader about the challenges women candidates face. Catherine Whitney, et al., *Nine and Counting: The Women of the Senate* and Kim Fridkin Kahn, *The Political Consequences of Being a Woman* also bring attention to the experiences of female candidates. Kathleen Hall Jamieson's book, *Beyond the Double Bind: Women and Leadership*, offers insight into the unique constraints facing women candidates. Eleanor Clift and Tom Brazaitis tell the story of women angling for the White House and engage the reader with *Madam President: Women Blazing the Leadership Trail*. Robert P. Watson and Ann Gordon, editors of *Anticipating Madam President*, focus more specifically on the obstacles facing female presidential hopefuls. Brad Koplinski's book *Hats in the Ring: Conversations with Presidential Candidates* offers interviews with many presidential candidates. Mary S. Hartman edited a collection of interviews with powerful women, called *Talking Leadership: Conversations with Powerful Women*. In their own words, women leaders describe the situations they have faced in their quest for leadership equality. Maria Braden in *Women Politicians and the Media* examines the media's role in women politician's careers. Jo Freeman's *A Room at a Time: How Women Entered Party Politics*, chronicles how women have made progress slowly in the political process. In *American Women Speak*, editors Doris Earnshaw and Maria Elena Raymond offer the reader a collection of speeches and short biographies of nineteen women politicians. The introduction by Ruth B. Mandel of the Eagleton Institute of Politics at Rutgers University warns that "as a society, we must yet learn how to listen and really hear the varied voices of American women." In *American Political Rhetoric: A Reader* (fifth edition), editors Peter Augustine Lawler and Robert Martin Schaefer offer a chapter on gender as it relates to civil rights. In that chapter, Barbara Jordan's 1992 speech, "Change: From What to What" includes the hopeful wish that "what we see today is simply a dress rehearsal for the day and time we meet in convention to nominate . . . Madame President."[9]

Autobiographies by women politicians offer insights about their lives; *It's My Party, Too* by former New Jersey Governor Christine Todd Whitman, *24 Years of Housework and the Place Is Still a Mess* by Patricia Schroeder, Geraldine Ferraro's *Ferraro, My Story*, and Hillary Clinton's *Living History* offer readers firsthand experiences of the lives of women politicians. In *Lives of Their Own: Rhetorical Dimensions in Autobiographies of Women Activists*, Martha Watson describes the value of studying biography as a useful tool in scholarship. James Olney's *Studies in Autobiography*, offers a similar perspective on the advantage of studying autobiographies. Books that focus on the rhetoric of women leaders have been important in the effort to chronicle women's political progress, since, as Thomas Hollihan points out in *Uncivil Wars: Political Campaigns in a Media Age*, "politics *is* communication."[10] Brenda DeVore Marshall and Molly A. Mayhead, editors of *Navigating Boundaries: The Rhetoric of Women Governors*, offers insight into the challenges faced by five female governors. In *Governing Codes: Gender, Metaphor and Political Identity*, Karrin Vasby Anderson and Kristen Horn Sheeler examine the political identity of four contemporary female politicians. *The Rhetoric of First Lady Hillary Rodham Clinton: Crisis Management Discourse* by Colleen Elizabeth Kelley describes the unique rhetorical position of Hillary Clinton. Karlyn Kohrs Campbell's edited volume *Women Public Speakers in the United States* profiles many of the prominent women speakers of our time.

Deborah Alexander and Kristi Andersen surveyed voters to determine gender role attitudes among women candidates in an article titled "Gender as a Factor in the Attribution of Leadership Traits" in *Political Research Quarterly* in September 1993; Stephen Stambough and Valerie O'Regan asked whether the Year of the Woman in 1992 changed how women candidates are covered in the press in a chapter for a book called *Campaigns and Elections*, edited by Robert P. Watson and Colton C. Campbell. In the same volume, Gary Aguiar examined women's underrepresentation in elective office. Jane Blankenship and Deborah C. Robson unveiled a "feminine style" in women's political discourse in an exploratory essay in a *Communication Quarterly* article in 1995. Karlyn Kohrs Campbell discussed the phenomenon of 'hating Hillary' that has swept the nation in her 1998 article in *Rhetoric and Public Affairs*.

Paving the Way for Madam President invites the audience to relive the experiences of five women who aimed for the White House as well as the vice presidential candidacy of Geraldine Ferraro in 1984. Republican Senator Margaret Chase Smith, the moral voice of the Senate, brought attention for her 1964 presidential bid that took her all the way to the convention hall. In 1972, Democratic Congresswoman Shirley Chisholm touted her message of being "unbought and unbossed" in her groundbreaking presidential campaign. In 1988, outspoken Democratic Congresswoman Pat Schroeder made an exploratory bid that drew headlines in the end, for her tearful reaction during her withdrawal speech more than for her bid. In 1999, Republican Elizabeth Dole, who has since become senator from her home state of North Carolina, discovered that, despite her fame and long political career, it was hard to run against candidates George W. Bush and Steve Forbes who had unprecedented amounts of money, and in 2004 former Illinois Democratic Senator Carol Moseley Braun briefly brought an articulate, and the only female voice to the chorus of Democratic hopefuls. Their speeches are examined and press stories retold; through interviews with Pat Schroeder, Elizabeth Dole, and Carol Moseley Braun, the book offers insights for the next generation of women leaders.

WHY THESE FIVE WOMEN?

Margaret Chase Smith, Shirley Chisholm, Patricia Schroeder, Elizabeth Dole, and Carol Moseley Braun are chronicled in this book because they ran for major party nominations, and because as public figures are most widely acknowledged in the press for their presidential efforts. The time-frame of these five women's presidential aspirations—beginning in 1964, offers the reader a sizable, yet manageable length of history to examine. There have been other women presidential candidates, and a brief acknowledgment of their efforts is made here. Victoria Claflin Woodhull was the first woman to run for President of the United States. In the fall of 1872, a diverse group of radicals and reformers, calling themselves the Equal Rights party, had unanimously nominated Victoria Claflin Woodhull to run against a slate of candidates that included Ulysses S. Grant and Horace Greeley. At age thirty-four, stockbroker and entrepreneur publisher Woodhull would have been too young to take office if she did win, and as it turned out, she was jailed on election day, charged with sending illegal materials through the mail, under the newly passed Comstock Acts, and could not even campaign. On Election Day, voters sent Ulysses S. Grant to the White House.

Belva Ann Bennett Lockwood, protégé of Woodhull, and the first woman ever to practice law before the United States Supreme Court, ran for president in 1884 and again in 1888 on the Equal Rights Ticket. She didn't get very far, and on election day in 1884, Benjamin Harrison became president. In 1888 Grover Cleveland was elected.

In 1972 Patsy Mink, a Democratic Congresswoman from Hawaii, entered the race for president in January and used her strong anti-war reputation to make an impressive showing in the Oregon primary, finishing eighth. But even those who were active in Shirley Chisholm's presidential race in 1972 have a scant memory of Mink's presidential effort and her *New York Times* obituary from September 2002 fails to mention her presidential bid.[11] Some of the women who have made exploratory bids and those who have actually run for president are not recognized by many historians, rhetoricians, and political scientists, as well as the press. This book is a blend of biography and an examination of these women's speeches. Especially heavy on biography, the book strives to illuminate the lives of these women, since so often they are ignored in history books. As more women make bids for the presidency, more in-depth studies of their speeches and political experiences will be warranted. Like the five women who laid the groundwork for women and the United States presidency, this book aims to lay the groundwork for scholars to begin to understand their experiences and contributions.

In addition to the five women profiled extensively in this book, and Victoria Woodhull, Belva Lockwood, and Patsy Mink, the following women have made presidential bids: Leonora Fulani, ran for president in 1992 as a member of the New Alliance Party. She qualified for $2 million in federal matching funds. Three Democrats in 1996 ran for president: Heather Harder entered primaries in Arkansas, Ohio, Texas, Illinois, and New Hampshire and garnered 29,149 votes; Elvena Lloyd-Duffle entered primaries in Arkansas, Ohio, Oklahoma, and Texas and received 92,324 votes; and Caroline P. Kileen entered the New Hampshire primary and received 395 votes. Six Republicans also made bids in 1996: Susan Ducey entered primaries in Nevada and Texas and received 940 total votes; Ann Jennings entered the Arizona primary and received 304 votes; Joann Pharr entered the Arizona primary to win 125 votes; Mary "France" Le Tulle entered primaries in Nevada and Texas and garnered 940 votes; Georgiana H. Doerschuck entered the New Hampshire primary and won 154 votes; and Isabell Masters entered the Oklahoma primary and received 153 votes. In 1996 Mary Cal Hollis of the Socialist Party won 4,228 general election votes; Monica Moorehead of the Workers World Party received 28,336 general election votes; and Diane Beall Templin of the Reform Party received 1,947 general election votes. Vice presidential candidates have included Frances "Sissy" Farenthold in 1972 and Geraldine Anne Ferraro in 1984.[12]

GERALDINE FERRARO'S JOURNEY

"Guam Loves Gerry," "El Tiempo Es Ahora," even a poem: "The Republicans May Think They're Hot. But We Have Gerry and They Do Not."

The placards at the Moscone Center in San Francisco at the Democratic National Convention in 1984 summed up the euphoria over Geraldine

Ferraro's selection as the vice presidential candidate on the ticket with Walter Mondale. When she stood to speak, Ferraro exemplified the hopes and dreams of American women everywhere who want to be treated equally with men. The Democratic nominee, Walter Mondale, had been Attorney General of Minnesota and a Senator from Minnesota, and was Vice President from 1976 to 1980 in the Carter administration. Mondale and Ferraro challenged incumbent president Ronald Reagan and Vice President George H. W. Bush. In the convention hall, the excited audience welcomed the first woman in the history of America to be on a national ticket by chanting "Gerr-ee, Gerr-ee." It was history in the making, and in the faces of the throngs of audience members—many whom had brought their daughters and their granddaughters, the emotion was palpable. Geraldine Ferraro recounted the view from the podium: "As I looked out over the convention floor, I saw the faces of America: farmers, factory workers, young professionals, the elderly, business executives, blacks, whites, Hispanics, Native Americans, Asian-Americans, and women—so many women."[13] Dressed in a white suit, smiling broadly, Geraldine Ferraro began her speech:

> Ladies and gentlemen of the convention—ladies and gentlemen of the convention—ladies and gentlemen of the convention, my name is Geraldine Ferraro, I stand before you to proclaim tonight: America is a land where dreams can come true for all of us.

She continued and acknowledged her pride in being the vice presidential candidate and then, inadvertently described herself as "the daughter of an immigrant from Italy has been chosen—has been chosen to run for *President* in the new land my father came to love." She described her education from her family and from the schools she attended.

> If you work hard and play by the rules, you can earn your share of America's blessings. Those are the beliefs I learned from my parents. And those are the values I taught my students as a teacher in the public schools of New York City. At night, I went to law school. I became an assistant district attorney, and I put my share of criminals behind bars. I believe: If you obey the law, you should be protected. But if you break the law, you must pay for your crime.[14]

DAUGHTER OF AN ITALIAN IMMIGRANT

Geraldine Anne Ferraro was born August 26, 1935, in Newburgh, New York, the only daughter of Dominick and Antonetta Ferraro. Geraldine was the youngest, the only girl, and her parents adored her, especially after having suffered the loss of two of their sons who had died—one when he was only six days old and the other in a car accident at age three. Her father died unexpectedly of heart disease when Geraldine was only eight and her mother had to manage without him. Her mother's strength and determination to raise her children was an inspiration to Geraldine. Her mother strongly encouraged her to attend a private boarding school, Marymount School in Tarrytown, where she received a full scholarship and then went on to Marymount College. Upon graduation she taught school and also studied for a Fordham University law degree at night. Shortly after passing the bar exam, she married John Zaccaro, a real estate broker and they had three children, Laura, John Jr., and Donna. She kept her maiden name—Ferraro—out of respect for her mother, who had sacrificed, working as a garment worker to support the family. "Don't forget your name," her mother told her. 'Ferro means iron. You can bend it, but you can't break it.'"[15] When her children grew older, she practiced law in a private firm. Later she joined the Queens District Attorney's office, where she was chosen to head a newly created special victim's bureau, which dealt with sex and child abuse cases.

In 1978, Geraldine Ferraro entered a three-sided Democratic primary in the conservative and ethnic 9th Congressional district in Queens. She won and when she went to Congress in 1979 she joined the Congresswomen's Caucus. At the time, there were just eleven Democratic and six Republican women. Because of that she noted, "we remained a sprinkling of females in a male bastion, without the numbers to be a force." She was re-elected to two more two-year terms. During her three terms in the House, she championed the Equal Rights Amendment and sponsored the Women's Economic Equity Act. Her unabashedly liberal voting record frequently put her at odds with the Reagan administration.[16]

When Walter Mondale chose Geraldine Ferraro as his vice presidential candidate, the press rushed to raise questions such as How can a man and woman come to be seen as partners, or as a team rather than as a couple? Shouldn't a feisty, argumentative, "tough" woman be drawn in a man's suit when pictured next to a quieter, less animated man (in a woman's dress)? [Picturing Walter Mondale in a dress, to emphasize the opinion that he wasn't a strong male figure, was a frequent editorial cartoon strategy of the 1984 election.] Was a woman indeed "tough enough" to push the nuclear button? Did any woman have enough foreign policy experience? These questions were asked continually, and perhaps they were inevitable. That Ferraro, as a member of Congress, had "been confronted with more foreign policy questions than Ronald Reagan faced as governor" tended to get lost.[17] Judith S. Trent and Robert V. Friedenberg note that "there was very little the congresswoman could have said or done to have created a public persona favorable enough to refute the preconceptions of some Americans regarding the personal characteristics or attributes vice presidents are expected to possess.[18]

In 1992 she ran unsuccessfully in the Democratic primary for a Senate seat in New York. In 1994 President Bill Clinton appointed her United States ambassador to the United Nations Human Rights Commission. She served until 1996, then became host of CNN's "Crossfire," a political debate show, from 1996 to 1998. Her new cause has her speaking on behalf of research funding for multiple myeloma, the rare blood disease that kills half of those who are afflicted. Ferraro was diagnosed with the disease in 1998.

"I believe that in 2008, we are going to see a woman and perhaps women running for their party's nomination," she said. "I expect that we will see Hillary Clinton on [the Democratic] side and [Texas] Senator Kay Bailey Hutchison for the Republican nomination in 2008, and both of them will have established their bona fides in the United States Senate."[19]

Geraldine Ferraro had a star quality as a vice presidential candidate. When she burst on to the national scene, she was instantly in demand as a speaker around the country. She was especially in demand in the six states in 1984 that had women as candidates for the Senate: Maine, Oregon, Colorado, New Mexico, Virginia, and Minnesota. She became a very positive force for women that would encourage them to go to the voting booth in record numbers on Election Day.

Her campaign for vice president included challenging the president on his record on women. On the campaign trail in San Francisco, she said,

> Women are not better off with a President, an Administration, and a party united against the Equal Rights Amendment. When I take my oath of office for my second term as Vice President, I want to swear to uphold a Constitution that includes the ERA. Name a program that helps women. This administration has tried to slash it. Name a policy that treats women fairly. This Administration is against it. This Administration is for the gold standard for the economy and the double standard for women.[20]

Her debate on October 11, 1984, with Vice President George H. W. Bush was the toughest part of the 1984 campaign. She said, "It was the toughest because I had to prove that I could handle tough issues and I had to know what the issues were, and I was concerned about the foreign policy stuff."[21] Most press accounts reported that the debate was a draw, and that Geraldine was not "overpowered by her disdainful opponent."[22]

Her husband's financial dealings as a real estate broker in New York had been scrutinized in the press, in part because John Zaccaro was the main income earner in the family, but some critics thought it was also because they were an Italian-American couple. Insinuation that Geraldine

Ferraro's campaign finances were corrupt because she financed her first congressional campaign with family loans and the sale of property, and her decision not to reveal her husband's income on a congressional disclosure form were all fodder for the press. Her stance on abortion, as a Roman Catholic, drew the ire of the Archbishop of New York. About her position on abortion, Ferraro said, "I do not believe in abortion, I am opposed to abortion as a Catholic. I also feel very, very strongly about the separation of church and state."[23]

CHARACTERISTICS OF GERALDINE FERRARO'S COMMUNICATION STYLE

Geraldine Ferraro's speaking style exemplifies the phrase "a New York minute" with her quick rate of speech. "By the normal standards of public oratory, Mrs. Ferraro speaks much too quickly. A normal eighteen-minute speech gets compressed into twelve minutes by the time she has raced through it."[24] Her style is direct, animated, and even curt. She forcefully expresses what she believes, but she also interjects a colloquial and friendly greeting, with a twinkle in her eye, that takes the sharp edges off her direct statements. She brings to her speech energy and confidence, even a bit of ham. Her penchant for wisecracks and her attacks on Ronald Reagan during the 1984 campaign, (a typical role for vice presidential candidates), the short six-to-eight-second sound bites that got on the air "added up to a serial portrait of a hit person."[25] She is not shy and in fact often directly confronts her critics. Once she phoned the Archbishop of New York directly to explain her position on abortion. Her statements are often accentuated with slang phrases "Lemme tell ya" and "Lemme just say."[26]

The nomination of Geraldine Ferraro for vice president was a historic milestone and remains the most lasting achievement of the Mondale campaign.[27] Ronald Reagan and George Bush beat Walter Mondale and Geraldine Ferraro handily in November 1984, but the impact of Geraldine Ferraro's historic candidacy make her forever a pivotal figure in woman's road to the White House.

OBSTACLES IN WOMEN PRESIDENTIAL CANDIDATES' PATHS

Since no woman has won the presidency, the first question that comes to mind is: What are the obstacles preventing a woman from being President of the United States? There is no simple answer. Reasons why any candidate—male or female—fail to make it to the top are individual to the candidate and the circumstances of the campaign, however, there are two broad categories of obstacles that face a female president, sociological and structural.

SOCIOLOGICAL BARRIERS

Kathleen Hall Jamieson identifies several obstacles facing women in leadership—obstacles that are identifiable to the five women profiled. Jamieson explains that "binds draw their power from their capacity to simplify complexity."[28] The binds that Jamieson identifies include:

1. Womb/Brain: women can exercise their wombs or their brains, but not both;
2. Silence/Shame: women who speak out are immodest and will be shamed, while women who are silent will be ignored or dismissed;
3. Sameness/Difference: women are subordinate whether they claim to be different from men or the same;
4. Femininity/Competence: women who are considered feminine will be judged incompetent, and women who are incompetent, unfeminine;
5. Aging/Invisibility: as men age, they gain wisdom and power; as women age, they wrinkle and become superfluous.

And, Jamieson added a "latter-day" bind: women who succeed in politics and public life will be scrutinized under a different lens from that applied to successful men, and for longer periods of time.[29] Some of the dimensions of public life that seem especially difficult for women in politics include:

Absence of a legacy—because no woman has been President, there is no role model for a woman presidential candidate to emulate. The only role models are those who have tried, and this work attempts to offer readers an understanding of the efforts of five women presidential candidates. A derivative effect of absence of a legacy is the "first" phenomenon. That is, Margaret Chase Smith, Shirley Chisholm, Patricia Schroeder, Elizabeth Dole, and Carol Moseley Braun each has been described in the media as "firsts"—whether the first black woman to run for President, or the "first" woman elected to both the House and the Senate or the "first" woman elected to the House from her State or to serve on a committee, or the "first" woman who was the spouse of a presidential candidate to become candidate or the "first" black woman elected to the Senate. While each of these designations is true, and notable, and in fact is even done in this book, this repeated emphasis on their pioneering status accentuates each woman's "spectacle" factor.

Kristina Horn Sheeler referred to this phenomenon as the "pioneer" in a series of metaphoric clusters she assigned to women governors. The drawback
to the prestige as a pioneer, Horn Sheeler points out is that because of the
few women involved "their pioneering achievements can easily be chalked
up to the status as symbolic rather than serious leaders."[30]

Dutch communication scholar Geert Hofstede's observation of feminine and masculine cultures is especially important to the prospects of a
woman American president. Hofstede notes that "Femininity stands for a
society in which social gender roles overlap: both men and women are
supposed to be modest, tender, and concerned with the quality of life."
Masculinity, on the other hand, "stands for a society in which social gender roles are clearly distinct: men are supposed to be assertive, tough and
focused on material success."[31] The United States ranks relatively high on
measures of masculinity, ranking fifteenth out of fifty-three countries.[32]

GENDER SOCIALIZATION AND THE PRESIDENCY

The Barbie doll is perhaps the most antithetical item to a woman president.
Yet, Marie Wilson, president of The White House Project, an organization dedicated to advancing women's leadership, endorsed the creation
of President Barbie in 2000 and a reissued version in 2004 because she explains, "my grandchildren play with those dolls, and I'd rather them playing with this one."[33] Research has revealed significantly different patterns of
vocational development at work in adolescent boys versus adolescent girls.
In a study in the 1970s, it was concluded that girls who are choosing a career
are influenced by what they believe boys think is appropriate feminine behavior, and that girls do not feel rewarded by their peer groups for intelli-
gence and achievement.[34] Other studies conducted in the 1980s found that
in contrast to boys, girls are faced with decisions about how they will com-
bine family and work before choosing a career. Because of these conflicts,
girls have historically chosen lower prestige and more stereotypically feminine careers than have boys.[35] According to Danzinger, the career expectations of adolescent boys are greatly influenced by ability, academic achievement, and opportunity, while those of adolescent girls are influenced mainly
by class background and parental expectations.[36] McMahon and Patton
pointed out that career preferences are formed early in adolescence and, for
both girls and boys, are heavily influenced by gender role socialization, one
of the earliest and thus most powerful forms of socialization. The strength of
this socialization often creates a narrow, gender-based range of career op-
tions.[37] In the 1990s Carol Gilligan and Lyn Mikel Brown wrote about the
loss of adolescent girls' perception that they could achieve untraditional occupational goals and how parents could socialize their daughter not to lose

the confidence that they exhibited as young girls.[38] In 2002 Cary M. Watson echoed the importance of focusing on adolescent girls' development with respect to career goals by stating that gender, achievement level, age, and school environment are all factors that may influence an adolescent girl's career choice. He found the results of a study aimed at determining whether or not adolescent girls expected to achieve as much as adolescent boys. He discovered that adolescent girls actually eclipsed boys in their expectations of career choices.[39] This finding would seem to bode well for the concept of a woman president. Of equal importance then would be what girls see women accomplishing, whether it is in her own home or in the media; how girls see women seems paramount to a girls ability to envision a life of achievement for herself. Two Notre Dame political scientists, Christina Wolbrecht and David Campbell, studied the political aspirations of adolescent girls in twenty-seven nations. Girls in countries that had more women in elected office were more likely to envision themselves as voters, activists—and candidates—when they were adults.[40]

Karlyn Kohrs Campbell noted that women who came across as leaders were so unusual in America, that she termed it "oxymoronic," but with an increase of women in politics in America, United States voters would be able to recognize a woman leader as something possible.[41]

Media portrayals of women have long been scrutinized in terms of their contribution to viewers' concepts of themselves. Whether the portrayal of a woman president in films and television may help prepare for real-life women to pursue the highest office in the land is the subject of debate. Clift and Brazaitis contend that the evolution of pop culture in the media age brings that goal [of a woman president] closer with each passing year.[42] Seeing women in the role could help to desensitize the press and public about the idea. Joan Allen portrayed the vice president in the 2000 film "The Contender." In 1998, Joan Van Ark was a capable vice president in "Loyal Opposition: Terror in the White House." Glenn Close portrayed the able vice president in the blockbuster film "Air Force One" in 1997. In 2005 ABC-TV created a new show, "Commander in Chief" featuring Geena Davis as an independent vice president who takes over when the Republican president has a stroke. "Commander in Chief" was cancelled in 2006 due to low ratings.

For years, the White House Project, an advocacy group committed to advancing women's leadership, had been lobbying Hollywood to commission a television show about a woman president, and the organization is promoting the program "Commander in Chief" by encouraging people around the country to host a "White House Party" on the night of the premiere of the television program. According to the White House Project President, Marie C. Wilson, the show will change the perception of women as leaders and make the reality of a woman president possible.[43]

STRUCTURAL BARRIERS

There are three overarching structural barriers that prevent a woman from achieving success in presidential politics; her "outsider" status, the structure of our electoral system, and inability to raise substantial funding. A female candidate, given the fact that she has never won the presidency, makes her an outsider to presidential politics. No outsider has won the presidency since Jimmy Carter won in 1976. The "fifty-fifty" rule, adopted by both Democrats and Republicans ensures that men and women be equally represented on all nationally appointed party committees.

The structure of our electoral system creates difficulties for specific groups to mobilize, including women. Our legislative bodies are based on representation in geographic districts, instead of identity, interests, or ideology. The single member district favors candidates who represent a majority, not a minority of voters in a district, or at least a majority of the voters in the dominant party's primary. Ethnic groups could organize and elect one of their own when they were geographically concentrated—even then each new group took decades to crack the barriers of existing party leadership. Women are geographically dispersed, making it a challenge to capture the majority necessary to be elected. Women are more likely to win elections in multi-member districts, but these have not been common.[44]

The lack of significant fundraising mechanisms have also hindered women candidates. Advocacy groups are aimed primarily at helping women candidates raise the needed funds to be successful. Another goal of groups advocating for more women in electoral politics is never to quit until women make up fifty percent of politicians and when there are as many women running for president as men. The National Women's Political Caucus was formed in the 1970s to help women candidates run successful campaigns. The Caucus holds workshops that offer information about fund-raising, developing a platform, motivating volunteers, and obtaining media coverage. From 1976, the Caucus also has worked to further the appointment of women to public offices, especially to important policy-making posts. To achieve this goal, the Caucus, working with other women's groups, reviews the qualifications of hundreds of women and submits selected names and credentials to new administrations for consideration. Then, that group and others gave that most essential of campaign lubricants: money. Advocacy groups continue to support female candidates and there are several groups that are in existence today.

The White House Project is the best known advocacy group that is dedicated to educating the public about women's leadership and helping more women get elected to political offices, including the presidency. It was co-founded in 1998 by Marie C. Wilson, Laura Liswood, and Barbara Lee to change the political climate where women have a level playing field and can launch successful campaigns.[45] Ms. Wilson, former president of Ms. Foundation for Women, now devotes all of her time to heading the White House Project, with headquarters in New York. As White House Project president, Wilson has appeared on many national news programs such as *Good Morning America, CNN's Inside Politics, The News Hour with Jim Lehrer* and *CBS News*. In her appearances, Wilson reiterates the main goal of the White House Project, which is to raise gender equity in American politics.

One of the highest-profile initiatives of the White House Project was the Ballot Box initiative in 1998, a mock election featuring twenty women leaders. After over 100,000 Americans voted, the top five women contenders for the president were Hillary Clinton, Elizabeth Dole, Dianne Feinstein, Lt. Gen. Claudia Kennedy, and former New Jersey Governor and EPA Secretary Christine Todd Whitman. Initially the Ballot Box initiative was introduced in *Parade* Magazine, and then it was extended to an Internet site and five other magazines: *Essence, Glamour, Jane, Latina,* and *People*. Those who took part in the balloting were asked to pick a woman based on demonstrated leadership qualities, not political beliefs.

In 2000 and 2004 the White House Project was present at both the Democratic and Republican Conventions, building awareness for its mission. At the conventions, White House Project members spoke with party leaders, delegates, and media and women's leadership about the need to bring balance to our democracy. The group also sponsored forums featuring former United States Secretary of State Madeleine Albright and former astronaut Mae C. Jemison.

The Council of Women World Leaders is a network of current and former women prime ministers and presidents established in 1996 by Vigdis Finnbogadottir, President of Iceland (1980–1996) and first woman in the world to be democratically elected president, and Laura Liswood, Secretary General. The Council's mission is to mobilize the highest-level women leaders globally for collective action on issues of critical importance to women. Through its networks, summits, and partnerships, the Council promotes good governance and gender equality, and enhances the experience of democracy globally by increasing the number, effectiveness, and visibility of women who lead their countries. Mary Robinson, President of Ireland (1990–1997) and United Nations High Commissioner for Human Rights (1997–2002), serves as Chair of the Council. Another organization committed to women's leadership initiative is the Barbara Lee Foundation which is dedicated to cultivating women's full engagement in the American democratic process and promoting their participation at all levels of government. Founded by Barbara Lee, one of the founders of the White House Project, the organization has produced a comprehensive guide for women aspiring to be governors, called *Keys to the Governor's Office*.[46]

EMILY's List founded in 1985 by Ellen Malcolm and a group of "founding mothers" is a grassroots political network. The name Emily is an acronym for "early money is like yeast," since its main mission is to raise money to help elect pro-choice Democratic women to federal, state, and local offices. At the time it was founded, no Democratic woman had ever been elected to the United States Senate in her own right, no woman had ever been elected governor of a large state, and the number of Democratic women in the United States House of Representatives had declined to twelve.[47] The Women's Campaign Fund also supports pro-choice women, but it is a non-partisan political action committee, founded in 1974. The Women's Campaign Fund has helped over 2,000 women run for office in its over thirty-year existence.[48] Like EMILY's List, the Women's Campaign Fund provides women with resources early in their candidacy and is active in national, state, and local campaigns. WISH List (stands for Women in the Senate and the House) shares a similar mission with EMILY's List and the Women's Campaign Fund. The WISH List raises money to identify, train, support, and elect more Republican women leaders to public office at all levels of government, specifically targeting pro-choice Republican women. All these organizations hold events to benefit their chosen candidates, such as dinners, receptions, press conferences, and even smaller living room events. In 2003–2004, WISH recruited, trained, endorsed, and supported about 200 mainstream Republican women candidates.[49] Another PAC, American Women Presidents, is a bipartisan group whose goal is to elect female leaders founded by Mosemarie Boyd and Lawrence E. Moore, III. Like other political action committees promoting women candidates, such as EMILY's List and the WISH List, American Women Presidents endorses women running for elected offices in the political pipeline to the presidency and makes financial contributions to support their campaigns.

The National Organization for Women (NOW) PACs rely upon the members of the grassroots feminist organization through NOW's 550 local chapters that work with candidates for election at every level of government. In 1996 alone, NOW PACs endorsed more than 700 women's rights candidates throughout the United States.[50]

The League of Women's Voters, headquartered in Washington, D.C., is a nonpartisan organization that encourages active participation in government through voter information, civic participation, election and campaign finance reform, education, and advocacy. It works to get people involved in the democratic process at the federal, state, and local levels.

SISTERHOOD

Several of the women chronicled in this book had occasion to meet. Perhaps because of the few numbers of women in politics, they sought each other out at various points in their careers. Pat Schroeder addressed Congress in the 1990s fighting the Comstock Act, which was the cause of Victoria Woodhull's incarceration in the 1800s. Pat Schroeder also worked with Elizabeth Dole on initiatives involving women and children in the 1980s when Dole was Secretary of Transportation. Both Elizabeth and Bob Dole's involvement in the Glass Ceiling Initiative gave them opportunities to work with Congresswomen Schroeder and Chisholm. Shirley Chisholm was reportedly upset with Patricia Schroeder for dropping out of the presidential race as early as she did.

In her twenties, Elizabeth Hanford consulted Maine Republican Senator Margaret Chase Smith about what she could do to improve her career. In 1994 Elizabeth Dole was awarded the Margaret Chase Smith American Democracy Award. The first award was given to Margaret Chase Smith in 1992 and is awarded yearly to a person who has made a significant contribution to American democracy. Intentionally or not, this small group of trailblazing women crossed party lines to champion alike causes and to draw strength from each other.

As different as the five women are in this book—different races, different ages, different ideologies, different styles—there are more similarities. Each woman exhibited enormous patriotism, a true love for her country that gave her the energy and persistence to press on, even though the odds were against her. They each had the optimism to try and the courage to dare to move women a little further on the path to political equality. This book tells their stories—the obstacles they faced as well as the opportunities they helped create—for future generations of women.

NOTES

1. Margaret Mead. *Continuities in Cultural Evolution*. (New Haven: Yale University Press, 1964), 3.
2. John Horgan. *Mary Robinson*. (Niwot, Colo.: RobertsReinhart, 1998), 2.
3. Judy Mann. "Who Says a Woman Can't Be President? We Do." *New York Times*, January 29, 2000, 11.
4. www.cbsnews.com/stories/2006/02/03/opinion/polls/ (accessed February 7, 2006).
5. www.thewhitehouseproject.org/v2/press/2006/February/20060207-cbssundaymorning (accessed February 7, 2006).
6. Patricia Schroeder. Interview with Nichola Gutgold, March 24, 2005.

7. Laura A. Liswood. *Women World Leaders: Fifteen Great Politicians Tell Their Stories.* (San Francisco: Pandora, 1995), 131.

8. Sidney Verba. "Women in American Politics." In Louise A. Tilly and Patricia Gurin, eds., *Women, Politics and Change.* (New York: Russell Sage Foundation, 1990), 556.

9. Peter Augustine Lawler and Robert Martin Schaefer, eds. *American Political Rhetoric, A Reader*, 5th edition. (Lanham, Md.: Rowman & Littlefield, 2005), 332.

10. Thomas Hollihan. *Uncivil Wars: Political Campaigns in a Media Age.* (New York: Bedford/St. Martin's, 2001), 1.

11. Elisa Gootman. "Patsy Mink, Veteran Hawaii Congresswoman, Dies at 74." *New York Times*, September 30, 2002, 10.

12. The names of the women in this paragraph are listed on www.cawp.rutgers.edu which is the website for the Center for American Woman and Politics, Eagleton Institute of Politics at Rutgers, State University of New Jersey. (accessed June 22, 2005).

13. Geraldine A. Ferraro with Linda Bird Francke. *Ferraro: My Story.* (New York: Bantam Books, 1985), 23.

14. "Transcript of Speech by Rep. Ferraro Accepting Nomination." *New York Times*, 20 July 1984, A–14.

15. Ferraro with Francke, 17.

16. Biographical information came from: Geraldine A. Ferraro with Linda Bird Francke. *Ferraro: My Story.* (New York: Bantam Books, 1985), International Speakers Bureau Geraldine Ferraro, www.internationalspeakers.com (accessed June 23, 2005).

17. "Woman: Bold Move in Choice of Running Mate Holds Risk for Mondale." *Los Angeles Times*, 8 July 1984, 21.

18. Judith S. Trent and Robert V. Friedenberg. *Political Campaign Communication.* (Westport, Conn.: Praeger, 2000), 67.

19. www.cnn.com/2005/US/02/13/ccn25.tan.ferraro (accessed 17 February 2005).

20. Myra MacPherson, "Woman's Day; With Tears and Hope, Democratic Women Hail Their Heroine" Washington Post, July 19, 1984, D1.

21. Geraldine Ferraro. Interview with Nichola Gutgold. October 20, 1998.

22. Jane Blankenship. "Geraldine Ann Ferraro." In Karlyn Kohrs Campbell, ed. *Women Public Speakers in the United States, 1925–1936: A Bio-Critical Sourcebook.* (Westport, Conn.: Greenwood Press, 1994), 199.

23. Jane Perlex. "Ferraro the Campaigner." *New York Times*, 30 September 1984, 22.

24. Ibid.

25. Peter L .Goldman, Tony Fuller, and Thomas DeFrank. *The Quest for the Presidency 1984.* (New York: Bantam Books, 1985), 330.

26. Geraldine Ferraro. Interview with Nichola Gutgold. October 20, 1998.

27. Ted Widmer. *Campaigns: A Century of Presidential Races from the Photo Archives of The New York Times.* (London: DK Publishing, 2001), 307.

28. Kathleen Hall Jamieson. *Beyond the Double Bind: Women and Leadership.* (New York: Oxford University Press, 1995), 5.

29. Ibid., 16.

30. Kristina Horn Sheeler. "Marginalizing Metaphors of the Feminine." In Brenda DeVore Marshall and Molly A. Mayhead (eds.) *Navigating the Boundaries: The Rhetoric of Women Governors.* (Westport, Conn.: Praeger, 2000), 17–18.

31. Geert Hofstede. *Cultures and Organizations: Software of the Mind*. (London: McGraw-Hill, 1991), 14.

32. Ibid., 262.

33. Eleanor Clift and Tom Brazaitis. *Madam President: Women Blazing the Leadership Trail*. (New York: Routledge, 2003), vii.

34. Peggy Hawley. "What Women Think Men Think: Does It Affect Their Career Choice?" *Journal of Counseling Psychology*, 18, 193–199.

35. Jacqueline S. Eccles. "Why Doesn't Jane Run? Sex Differences in Educational and Occupational Patterns." In R. D. Horowitz and M. O'Brien (eds.) *The Gifted and Talented: Developmental Perspectives* (Washington, D.C.: American Psychological Association, 1985), 251–295.

36. N. Danzinger. "Sex Related Differences in the Aspirations of High School Students." *Sex Roles: A Journal of Research*, September 1983, 683–684.

37. Mary McMahon and Wendy Patton. "Gender Differences in Childrens' and Adolescents' Perceptions of Influences on Their Career Development." *School Counselor*, 44, 368–376.

38. Carol Gilligan and Lyn Mikel Brower. *Meeting at the Crossroads*. (New York: Random House, 1992).

39. Cary M. Watson. "Career Aspirations of Adolescent Girls: Effects of Achievement Level, Grade, and Single-Sex School Environment." *Sex Roles: A Journal of Research*, May 2002, 323–342.

40. Christina Wolbrecht and David E. Campbell. "Do Women Politicians Lead Girls to Be More Politically Engaged? A Cross-National Study of Political Role Models." A paper presented at the 2005 American Political Science Association Conference, September 1–4, 2005.

41. Karlyn Kohrs Campbell. "The Rhetoric of Women's Liberation: An Oxymoron Revisited." *Communication Studies*, 50 (1999), 138.

42. Clift and Brazaitis. *Madam President: Women Blazing the Leadership Trail*, xxv.

43. Email correspondence from Marie C. Wilson to Nichola D. Gutgold. September 2, 2005.

44. Wilma Rule. "Women's Under-representation and Electoral Systems." *Political Science and Politics*, 27: 4 P.S., December 1994, 689–692.

45. Marie C. Wilson, personal correspondence with Nichola D. Gutgold. December 1, 2000.

46. www.barbaraleefoundation.org (accessed June 24, 2005).

47. www.emilyslist.org (accessed June 19, 2005).

48. www.wcfonline.org (accessed June 19, 2005).

49. www.thewishlist.org (accessed June 19, 2005).

50. www.now.org (accessed June 24, 2005).

Margaret Chase Smith campaigned enthusiastically for the presidency. Courtesy of Arthur E. Scott, the Senate's first photo-historian.

1

Margaret Chase Smith
A "Quiet Woman"[1]

I would be pioneering the way for a woman in the future—to make the way easier—for her to be elected President of the United States. Perhaps the point that has impressed me the most on this argument is that women before me pioneered and smoothed the way for me to be the first woman to be elected to both the House and the Senate—and that I should give back in return that which had been given to me.[2]

The death of the President of the United States changed the world on November 22, 1963, as people everywhere plunged into mourning when an assassin's bullet claimed the life of President John F. Kennedy. John Kennedy was the first president to die in office since Franklin Delano Roosevelt died of a cerebral hemorrhage in 1945, and he was the first to be assassinated since William G. McKinley was shot in 1901. Maine Republican Senator Margaret Chase Smith had planned to make her announcement to run for President of the United States on December 5, 1963, but in deference to the memory of the slain president, she postponed her speech until January 27, 1964.

Even though America was still in a state of collective shock over the sudden death of its president, Republicans were eager to reclaim the White House after Richard Milhous Nixon lost to the charismatic and handsome young Massachusetts senator. President Kennedy, just a week before his assassination, called Maine Republican Senator Margaret Chase Smith "a very formidable public figure."[3] Several other prominent Republicans wanted to be the next president; the list included Ambassador Henry Cabot Lodge of Massachusetts, Governor William Scranton of Pennsylvania, Governor Nelson Rockefeller of New York, Governor George Romney

21

of Michigan, and Senator Barry M. Goldwater of Arizona. Nelson Rockefeller was considered a liberal candidate and Barry Goldwater was an ul-
traconservative. The choice of Senator Margaret Chase Smith would add a
moderate voice to the chorus of Republican hopefuls. In a speech delivered
at the Women's National Press Club on January 27, 1964, in Washington,
D.C., the slender and spry sixty-six-year-old New Englander, who had become well known for her integrity and character, explained her motivation
for seeking the United States presidency. Margaret Chase Smith com-
manded attention in her dark suit, a double strand of pearls around her
neck and her signature fresh red rose pinned to her lapel. The audience
wondered if she would announce that she would be in the race or not.
Even her closest assistant, Bill Lewis, didn't know how her speech would
end. "Sounding like a woman on the verge of saying no,"[4] reported *The
New York Times*, Senator Smith, who had served in the House of Representatives from 1940 to 1948 and was serving her third term in the Senate, said
she would, indeed, seek the presidency. She began the speech by identifying with the members of the press in her audience, and reminding them of
her own experience as a newspaper reporter. She stated:

> For more than a year now I have been receiving a steady flow of mail urging
> me to run for President of the United States. At first my reaction was that of
> being pleasantly flattered with such expression of confidence in me. I was
> pleased but did not take the suggestion seriously for speculation prior to the
> past year has been limited to vice presidential possibilities.[5]

When she began to discuss how she had been encouraged to run for
president, she offered the specific reasons her advisers and supporters
told her that she should run:

> In fairness to everyone, I concluded that I should make my decision [to run
> for President] before the end of January—and I have done so. It has not been
> an easy decision—either "yes" or "no" would be difficult. The arguments
> made to me that I should become a candidate have been gratifying. First, it
> has been contended that I should run because I have more national office ex-
> perience than any of the other announced candidates—or the unannounced
> candidates—with that experience going back to 1940 and predating any of
> the others. Second, it has been contended that regardless of what happened
> to me, should I become a candidate was not really important—but that what
> was really important was that through me for the first time the women of the
> United States had an opportunity to break the barrier against women being
> seriously considered for the Presidency of the United States—to destroy any
> political bigotry against women on this score just as the late John F. Kennedy
> had broken the political barrier on religion and destroyed once and for all
> such political bigotry. The argument contends that I would be pioneering the
> way for a woman in the future—to make her more acceptable—to make the

way easier—for her to be elected President of the United States. Perhaps the point that has impressed me the most on this argument is that women before me pioneered and smoothed the way for me to be the first woman to be elected to both the House and the Senate—and that I should give back in return that which had been given to me. Third, it has been contended that I should run in order to give the voters a wider choice—and specifically a choice other than that of Conservative or Liberal—to give those who considered themselves to be Moderates or Middle-of-the-Road advocates a chance to cast an unqualified vote instead of having to vote Conservative or Liberal. In this contention, it has been argued that this would give the voters a greater opportunity to express their will instead of being so restricted in their choice that many of them would not vote. Fourth, it has been contended that I should run because I do not have unlimited financial resources or a tremendous political machine or backing from the party bosses—but instead have political independence for not having such resources.[6]

Margaret Chase Smith laid out her arguments carefully. The arrangement of her arguments told of the character of the speaker: careful, thorough, practical, and reasonable. The language was not obscure or difficult to understand, yet she spoke in a soft voice that forced the audience to listen intently. Like a teacher describing a subject to students, she gave her audience a full explanation for her actions, in order to create clear understanding. She had come very far from her days with her knitting bag by her side as her husband shaped the laws of the nation as a congressman. The announcement was the high point of Senator Smith's presidential campaign.[7]

Smith's supporters knew that with the large number of contenders, her chances of winning were small, but if they knew their candidate at all, then they knew that she was going to make a wholehearted effort to win. *Time* magazine stated, "Many people shrug off the lady Senator's declaration as being something frivolously feminine. They don't know Maggie. Feminine she is, but not frivolous."[8] (The press took to calling Margaret "Maggie" when she ran for president).[9] In her announcement speech Smith clearly stated that she saw her run as a favor to future generations of women who would aspire to run for president and her long shot bid would give them confidence to know that other women went before them. Even though there is no doubt she was sincere in expressing her wish to help future generations, she may have unwittingly undermined her efforts, since she was repeatedly asked whether or not she was a "serious" candidate. Mentioning her goal to "break the barrier"—or what would later be called the "glass ceiling"—did not mean that Margaret Chase Smith didn't want to be president. Even though she couldn't win, her campaign wasn't only symbolic. What kind of woman would subject herself to the brutality of a national political campaign, when she knew she couldn't win? To understand what heritage and circumstances contributed to Margaret Chase

Smith's dedication to America as a model public servant,[10] a look at her life and family background is warranted.

NEW ENGLAND'S STRONG WORK ETHIC AND PRAGMATISM SHAPE A FUTURE LEADER

Margaret Madeline Chase was born in Skowhegan, Maine, on December 14, 1897, in the same house where her mother had been born. Margaret Madeline, named for her father's mother, was the oldest child of Carrie Murray, a seamstress, and George Emery Chase, a hotel headwaiter. When Margaret was just six months old, her parents moved to Augusta, Maine, where her father found work at the Hotel North Augusta. A beautiful baby, with dark wavy hair, rosy cheeks, and a wide smile,[11] she received a lot of attention from admiring customers and staff as she sat in the dining room of the hotel in her highchair. Her father's job didn't last a year, and to make ends meet the young family moved back to North Avenue, Skowhegan, with Carrie's parents where they lived until Margaret was five. By this time Margaret had a brother, Wilber, born in 1899, and then two more brothers—Roland Murray, born in 1901 and Lawrence—born in 1903, joined the family. George moved his family to Shawmut where he opened a barber shop. The small town afforded Margaret the opportunity to walk to a local shop and a post office. The Chases lived in a double tenement house, the other half of which was occupied by an alcoholic woman. When Margaret spied her tipsy neighbor staggering around outside, she would loudly announce: "There she goes again," as if Margaret were the voice of the town.[12] Even as a young child she displayed the pioneering spirit that would characterize her political career. She would tell Agnes, a pre-teenage girl hired by Mrs. Chase to care for the children that she didn't want to stay home all day; she wanted to "do things."[13] She enjoyed conversing with adults, rather than children, and she shared a close relationship with her mother, who admired Margaret's confidence and leadership traits. As the oldest child and daughter, Margaret became her mother's partner in caring for the house and the other children. They forged a lifetime bond that not only provided Margaret with the certainty that she was treasured and needed but also that she could be as capable and independent as Carrie.[14] Her father was strict and sometimes remote. He struggled to make a good living, and wasn't thrilled to be living in his father-in-law's home. He loved fishing, and because Margaret liked to wake early, the daughter and father shared fond memories of fishing together at Smithfield Pond, where the family spent many summer weekends without the extended family.

Early in 1903 at only eighteen months of age, one of Margaret's brothers, Roland Murray, died from pneumonia. Shortly thereafter, Mrs. Chase knew she was pregnant again. After two years in Shawmut and the death of a child, the Chases moved back to Skowhegan.[15] Another brother, Laurence Franklin, died when he was not quite three years old of dysentery.[16] These tragedies forced Margaret to grow up faster than she might have otherwise. She was anxious to make her own way in the world, and being the oldest child made her especially interested in assisting the family with finances, something that her younger siblings could not do. That Margaret was industrious and opportunistic was apparent early in life.

Margaret Chase earned average grades and was an ambivalent student at Lincoln and Garfield Elementary Schools. She didn't enjoy school where the provincial style of teaching, large class sizes, and "little or no thought given to science, music, art, literature, history or geography,"[17] made Margaret feel as though school was a necessary evil. When Margaret was almost twelve, her parents had another girl, Evelyn Mary. Three years later another sister, Laura, was born. By the time Margaret was thirteen she was earning extra money to contribute to family finances at Green's 5 and 10 cent store. This independent, mature behavior in such a young girl has been noted by several biographers and journalists, who make the argument that the twelve-year-old, who couldn't even reach the top of the shelf at Green's 5 and 10 cent store, wanted to earn her own keep. Certainly it showed that Margaret wasn't lazy, and she had the motivation to speak up and ask for a job, while other girls her age were probably content to restrict their activities to those of a typical childhood.[18] It also demonstrated that the New England tradition of pride in a job well done and working for the sake of work itself was ingrained early in Margaret. It was a work ethic that would be evident always in Margaret Chase Smith.

In high school, Margaret didn't find academics any more interesting than she did in grade school. She discovered that she was an excellent basketball player, and she gained attention and confidence playing basketball on the high school team in full, knee-length blue serge bloomers and pleated white middy blouses worn outside with large black silk ties.[19] While still in high school, Margaret took a job as a substitute telephone operator and the job suited her especially well.[20] She was asked by the town's night telephone operator, who knew that Margaret was looking for part-time work, if she would like to come in and learn how to be an operator. The operator wanted someone as a substitute so she could get out once in a while.[21] Margaret loved the job and all of its benefits—she found it interesting and fun to listen to other people's phone conversations and it was at that job that she met her future husband, Clyde Smith, a smooth-talking, recently divorced selectman in Skowhegan, who was twenty-one years her senior. Margaret, the high school girl and part time phone operator, was impressed with his suave voice and his sophisticated style and she wasn't the only person to think that Clyde Smith had a certain way about him. He was by many accounts a handsome, dynamic, articulate man.[22] When Margaret was seventeen, Clyde offered her a higher paying job than the telephone operator job. She accepted and became a part-time assistant to record tax assessments in the town books for the selectmen. Because she was still in high school, Clyde arranged for Margaret to take her typing and shorthand classes at night. For about six months during her high school senior year and the following summer, Margaret learned about real estate, taxes, and budgeting and observed the political process from a rare vantage point.[23] She enjoyed her work with Mr. Smith, because it was stimulating and she found local politics interesting. Her high school experience, mostly because of her involvement with the basketball team, gave her a sense of accomplishment. The basketball team, with Margaret as the team manager, and running center, took the state championship in her senior year. Margaret had formed warm and lasting relationships with her teammates. Through the critical years of adolescence, they had become a natural source of support and strength for each other and had provided a pivotal experience in young Margaret's life.[24] Her basketball team experience and a class trip to Washington, D.C., were the two highlights of Margaret's academic career. When Margaret graduated from high school in 1916, she was anxious to find a permanent job, since her job with the selectmen's office was about to end.

Recent high school graduate Margaret Chase briefly taught school at the Pitts School, a one room school four miles south of town. She disliked the work, especially since she didn't enjoy academics and had a difficult time inspiring her students. Before the school year ended, she left the teaching job for the New England Telephone Company where she worked in the business office. She also took on the coaching position at Skowhegan High School's girl's basketball team. Under her leadership, the team did very well and the local newspaper noted that the victories were due to the efforts of Coach Margaret Chase.[25]

In September 1918, Clyde Smith won a seat in the Maine legislature. His gift of eloquent public speaking became well known throughout the state. In one ceremony in honor of the Skowhegan World War I veterans, Clyde declared: "Medals that adorn the uniform tell of courage and endurance that braved the worst of the cause, but the most majestic and distinguishing decoration is the commonest one of them all, the Wooden Cross, and somewhere in the mysterious future, where the flowers bloom and the birds forever sing, the spirit of justice is solving their final reward, for the star that sets must rise again."[26] While Margaret admired Clyde's flowery use of language, in her own public speaking, she chose to be less abstract and more concrete in her word choice. In fact, they were opposites in their political styles. Clyde was a born politician—excellent at working a room and inspiring his audience with colorful language and romantic notions. Margaret, while very good with people, did not engage in flowery language or abstract ideas. She spoke in a matter-of-fact, no-nonsense manner that gave her credibility and stability. Margaret and Clyde's relationship was still important to both of them, although their careers were also requiring their full attention.

Margaret left the job at the telephone company and accepted a position as a stenographer at Skowhegan's weekly newspaper, the *Independence Reporter*. Margaret forged a close working relationship with the editor of the paper, Roland T. Patten, who found Margaret's work ethic indispensable. She moved up from stenographer to subscription clerk to Gal Friday and Roland Patten encouraged her interests in cultural activities and the community. Roland Patten's encouragement may be part of the reason that Margaret became interested in Sorosis, a literary and social group that met weekly. Margaret also was elected president of the Skowhegan Business and Professional Women's (BPW) Club. A result of World War I, the BPW enjoyed a large growth in membership. In the organization's hierarchy of goals, sisterhood, rather than political clout, was the primary objective. These "new women" were a limited edition, since many of their working friends were domestic or factory workers.[27] As president of the BPW, Margaret fostered the public speaking skills of the members by having them stand and speak about their own work and interests. She believed this would give the members confidence as well as a better idea of what was going on in Skowhegan.[28] Margaret also created and served as editor of *The Pine Cone*, a magazine for the BPW. Margaret's organization and leadership skills caught the attention of the leaders of the statewide organization of the BPW, and members of the organization encouraged Margaret to run for the state presidency of the BPW. In 1926 Margaret won the presidency of the statewide BPW by a large percentage. As BPW president, she traveled the state to visit clubs. She left little to chance and was a master of preparation and organization. In anticipation of having to use someone's name in a meeting, for example, she made sure that the name was in her notes, along with the exact words she wanted to use in introducing that person.[29] Margaret Chase was becoming a good politician and gaining recognition in her own right and with the influence of well-known Clyde Smith, the two were gaining a reputation as a powerful political duo.

It was not a surprise, when on May 14, 1930, Margaret Chase became Mrs. Clyde Smith. In a simple ceremony at her parent's home, the bride was attended by her sisters. Margaret and Clyde were married until Clyde's death, just one month short of ten years later, and they did not have children. Her marriage to Clyde Smith was the beginning of Margaret's political climb, and like most women in politics at the time, her entrance was by way of marriage. On his deathbed, Clyde Smith let his intentions be known: "My physician informs me that I am a seriously ill man, and that in his opinion even though I survive I may be physically unable to take an active part in congressional affairs for an indefinite time. All that I can ask of my friends and supporters is that in the coming primary and general election, if unable to enter the campaign, they support the candidacy of my wife and partner in public life."[30]

After conducting four campaigns in five months, Margaret Chase Smith succeeded her husband in representing Maine's Second District. She knew she could do the job. She said, "I had been close to my husband while he was in Congress. I knew everything he did, and through him I had been close to many of the Congressmen I had to work with now. So I just kept right on doing what I'd *been* doing. The only thing different was the voting."[31]

Early in her legislative career, Congresswoman Smith developed a strong interest in military issues. Her committee assignments did not make her interest in military issues easy to advocate. She was appointed to the Education and Post Office Committees. Senator Smith thought that these committees kept her from working on issues for which she held strong views. When Margaret Chase Smith gave her maiden congressional speech, it was in support of public nurseries and day care centers. Margaret Chase Smith ran for her second term in 1942 and again handily re-elected without having to face primary opposition. During World War II, she secured a seat on the House Naval Affairs Committee. She researched the negative effects caused by the rapid war build-up. More important, she almost single-handedly won permanent status for women in the military. Because of her efforts on behalf of nurses in the far Pacific during World War II and her fight to secure permanent status, Margaret Chase Smith earned great respect from women in the military for her unending support of their cause.[32] She handily won re-election in 1944 and 1946. One of her closest friends was noted journalist May Craig, who Margaret gave access to her office files, even when Chase Smith wasn't present. Her relationship with Craig came to an end when Margaret did not tell Craig about her plans to speak against McCarthy. Knowing that May admired and approved of Joe McCarthy, Margaret realized that May would be surprised by Margaret's speech. Her assistant, William C. Lewis, Jr., noted that not only was their disagreement on McCarthy a factor in the end of May and Margaret's alliance, but that many who thought May Craig was a mentor and a ghostwriter for Margaret would now realize that was not the case.[33] The political alliance with Lewis, which began in 1943, was similar to the one Margaret and Clyde had shared, although this time around, Margaret was in charge.[34] Bill Lewis served as Margaret Chase Smith's longtime executive assistant in the Senate and remained her loyal confidante and aide until his death in 1982. Following her successful eight years in the House, the opportunity to run for a Maine Senate seat came when Senate Majority Leader Wallace White resigned. Repeatedly, Margaret Chase Smith heard her colleagues and even friends say "The Senate is no place for a lady." Newspaper editorials debated the issue and despite her gender being an issue, Margaret Chase Smith beat the odds in 1948 when she soundly defeated the incumbent governor, Horace Hildreth; former governor, Sumner Sewall; and the Reverend Albion Beverage in the Republican primary for the United States Senate. She then went on to win the general election. It was about this time that Margaret wanted to be referred to as "Margaret Chase Smith" instead of "Mrs. Clyde Smith" and so she made an effort to reinforce with the press and public that she preferred to be called "Margaret Chase Smith." On January 3, 1949, poised and chic, fifty-year-old Margaret Chase Smith took her seat in the male bastion of American politics, the United States Senate. Senator Smith, elegantly dressed in a long-sleeved, black crepe dress with a three-strand pearl necklace and her signature fresh red rose on her lapel, looked every inch the experienced public servant she had become.

Two years into her first term, Senator Smith's fifteen-minute speech—perhaps more aptly called a sermon—titled the "Declaration of Conscience" delivered on the floor of the Senate on June 1, 1950, brought her national attention. Her now legendary speech also marked the beginning of the end for Senator Joseph McCarthy. The lone female in the Senate, Margaret Chase Smith stood to speak out against Senator McCarthy, when not one of her male colleagues had the courage. The reason for the rhetorical event occurred about four months earlier, when Senator McCarthy, in a routine speech, announced that he had in his hand a list of 205 Communists in the U.S. State Department. When her Republican colleague McCarthy first started to speak about the list of Communists he had, even Margaret thought that it was true. She wrote "At first, I will admit, I was impressed with what he was saying. 'That I hold in my hand a photo static copy' had a most impressive tone and ring of authenticity. It looked as if Joe [McCarthy] was onto something disturbing and frightening."[35] Fear of a worldwide Communist conspiracy had grown in the United States since World War II. The fear was fueled by the media, and *Newsweek* ran several articles that warned about growing Communist membership in labor unions.[36] Because she was a freshman senator and a Republican, Senator Smith was reluctant to speak up. Her bravery was fueled, however, by her moral character and her deep anti-communist beliefs. Senator Smith supported the Hatch Act of 1939, providing for the dismissal from government of any person who was a member of a party opposing the United States government. She also proposed a bill outlawing the Communist party. She asked McCarthy if she could see the document that proved the charges, and although he did show her the paper, Margaret did not think that it was relevant to his charges. Senator Margaret Chase Smith became the first member of the

Republican Party to openly condemn the reckless Wisconsin Republican senator. Unlike most Republicans, Chase Smith refused to remain silent as McCarthy's sensational charges gave rise to an anticommunist witch-hunt sanctioned by the Senate. In widely publicized public hearings, McCarthy bullied defendants under cross-examination with unsubstantiated and damaging accusations, destroying the reputations of hundreds of innocent citizens and officials. The "Declaration of Conscience" speech was Senator Smith's first major address and it was profound—because of its purpose, its style, and the speaker herself.[37] The address, her maiden speech on the floor of the United States Senate, co-authored by Bill Lewis, Jr., began with clarity, aimed to explain her concerns:

> Mr. President, I would like to speak briefly and simply about a serious national condition. It is a national feeling of fear and frustration that could result in national suicide and the end of everything that we Americans hold dear. It is a condition that comes from the lack of effective leadership in either the Legislative Branch or the Executive Branch of our Government. That leadership is so lacking that serious and responsible proposals are being made that national advisory commissions is appointed to provide such critically needed leadership. I speak as briefly as possible because too much harm has already been done with irresponsible words of bitterness and selfish political opportunism. I speak as simply as possible because the issue is too great to be obscured by eloquence.[38]

Margaret Chase Smith rebuked both Democrats and Republicans in her speech. Press reaction was mixed, but *Newsweek* featured Margaret on its cover and suggested that she could get the nod for vice president in 1952. While many of her senate colleagues, even Democrats, thought Margaret was right on target with her speech, they admitted that they would not have spoken up as she did because, for one reason, it would have killed their political careers. One supporter said to Margaret, when she asked why others had not spoken up: "My God, Margaret, that would be political suicide!"[39]

The "Declaration of Conscience I" speech can be credited for casting Margaret Chase Smith's destiny in national politics.[40] The negative result of the courageous speech by Senator Smith, however, caused her to feel the full brunt of McCarthy's vengeance. When McCarthy was asked why he never responded to her charges, he said, "I don't fight with women senators."[41] While McCarthy did not receive any action against him until years later, he dropped Margaret Chase Smith from a key investigation subcommittee, even though such action ran contrary to Senate tradition. By the end of 1951 Republican presidential hopeful George Aiken asked Margaret to be his running mate and she refused, stating "I appreciate the confidence that Senator Aiken expressed, [but] I am not a candidate. I am realistic enough to know that there is not even the remote possibility of such a thing happening."[42] The repercussions of her bravery against McCarthy in

1950 were still being felt by Margaret. At the 1952 Republican National Convention in Chicago, Margaret was not even a speaker. McCarthy also attempted to defeat Senator Smith during her 1954 re-election campaign. Refusing to be influenced by outside interests, the loyal voters of Maine returned their beloved Margaret Chase Smith to office.

In 1954, during a heightened period of Cold War tensions, Senator Smith organized and personally financed a trip to twenty-three countries in order to become better informed about conditions in the rapidly changing postwar world. During her travels, she met and conferred with leaders such as Winston Churchill, Konrad Adenauer, V.M. Molotov, and Charles DeGaulle. She visited Europe, the Middle East, and Asia in an effort to gauge the threat posed by the spread of Communism. The interviews and reports she filed for the CBS television program, *See It Now*, hosted by Edward R. Murrow, helped establish Senator Smith as a respected world leader in her own right. Her presence on national television increased her fame and showed a telegenic and worldly Margaret Chase Smith. The trip was only interrupted by the need for Senator Smith to return to Washington in December 1954 to vote on the censure of Senator McCarthy.

Despite Margaret's clash with McCarthy, she managed to gain appointments to two of the most powerful Senate committees, Armed Services and Appropriations. Among Senator Smith's varied interests was her commitment to medical research. In 1955, she sponsored groundbreaking legislation that committed the federal government to a vast program of support in this field. Senator Smith was also a strong supporter of the space program and served as a charter member of the Senate's Aeronautical and Space Sciences Committee. So active was Senator Smith in the United States Space Program that the director of NASA, James E. Webb said, "If it were not for a woman, Margaret Chase Smith, we never would have placed a man on the moon."[43] In 1956, Margaret Chase Smith drew national attention when she debated First Lady Eleanor Roosevelt on the CBS program, "Face the Nation." Invited by the women's division of the Republican National Committee, in response to CBS's wish that a Republican woman speak in support of President Eisenhower, Margaret, at first, simply didn't want to do it, partly because she didn't think televised political debates were either "constructive or informative."[44] She also did not think much of her own debating skills and thought that the Republican Party must have a "more effective" and "sharper" debater. But, when the National Committee asked again, noting that no other woman asked was willing to do it, Margaret relented and planned for the debate. Despite the newness of television as a political tool, Senator Chase Smith showed tremendous savvy in her preparation to make the most out of the communication interaction. Margaret Chase Smith wanted to have the opportunity to give a two-minute opening and a two-minute closing statement. Her reasoning was that she would be polite and courteous throughout the questioning, but the statements would give her a chance to state more firmly her stances. CBS denied the request for opening statements, but allowed closing statements. As Margaret Chase Smith considered her performance, she grappled, along with Bill Lewis, Jr., about her appearance. "This was staged like a scene," she reasoned, and she wondered: "What would I wear? How would my hair be styled?"[45] She decided to present herself as a contrast to Mrs. Roosevelt, and thus wore a simple black dress, a double string of white pearls, and her signature red rose on her lapel. She wore her white hair as she often did, with its usual soft waves. The contrast that Margaret Chase Smith aimed for was achieved. Margaret Chase Smith appeared striking and composed, her statements polite and controlled in contrast to the coat and hat-wearing Eleanor Roosevelt, whose voice was often high pitched; while she smiled, her delivery suggested that she was strident in her views, and she spoke longer than her allotted time, prompting the interviewer to raise his voice in an effort to move the debate along. Unlike the genial Senator Smith, who managed to forcefully make her point while remaining calm, Mrs. Roosevelt seemed agitated. Perhaps even more impressive than her insight about the visual nature of the relatively new television medium, was the insight that Senator Smith had about the potential impact that her closing statement would have in the debate. While she deeply admired Mrs. Roosevelt, and considered her a friend, their ideological differences would be summed up at the end of the debate when Margaret Chase Smith closed with:

> Democratic Presidents, together with leaders of our Allies chose Dwight D. Eisenhower to lead our nation to victory in World War II and to head up NATO to stop the spread of Communism. In fact, he was so good the last Democratic President asked him to be the candidate for President on the Democratic ticket. It is strange to hear Democratic leaders now accusing him of not being a leader. Why the difference? It is clearly the difference between principles and politics. They chose him on the nonpolitical basis of principle—they now attack him because he is not a partisan Democrat. Tuesday—Americans—whether Democratic, Republican, or Independent—will again choose principle instead of politics and elect Dwight D. Eisenhower."[46]

So angry was Eleanor Roosevelt at the end of the debate that she refused to shake Margaret's extended hand. Margaret reflected on what might have worked up Eleanor's ire: "What was surprising [about my closing statement] was my abrupt change in delivery. It was not the restrained, measured delivery in deferential tones—nor was it said with a smile. Instead it was a biting staccato."[47] Even though Margaret outshone Eleanor stylistically, both women were impressive in what mattered most—their knowledge of the issues. This *Face the Nation* program was the first ever to feature a woman—let alone two—and both Eleanor Roosevelt and Margaret Chase Smith made excellent spokespeople for their political parties.

In 1960, Senator Smith again made history when she soundly defeated her Democratic opponent Lucia Cormier. *Time* magazine featured both women on its September 5, 1960, cover, since the race marked the first time two women had ever vied for the same Senate seat. Margaret Chase Smith humorously described the situation: "I was so successful in the 1948 and 1954 elections in overcoming the campaign argument that "the Senate is no place for a woman," that I must have overdone it. For the Maine Democratic leaders concluded that their best chance to beat me was with a woman of their own—Lucia Cormier."[48] Margaret Chase Smith was dubbed the "silent candidate" in the media, since she refused to comment publicly about her opponent. Margaret was keenly aware that the campaign between two women could be sensationalized if they criticized one another. She said, "Both of us recognized that we had to guard against actions or developments that might reflect on women generally—on women in public office, women in politics. We wanted to avoid the slightest appearance of a clawing, scratching 'cat' fight."[49] It was not until 1986 that two women again sought the same senate seat.

MOVED TO RUN, SHE SAYS, BY REASONS NOT TO DO SO[50]

The files in Margaret Chase Smith's senate office, neatly labeled "Presidency" and "Vice Presidency" were getting thicker and thicker in the years since she had arrived in Washington, D.C. Senator Smith had been hearing suggestions that she should be a candidate for the vice presidency for more than a decade, but in 1963 the suggestions were coming in greater volume and from all fifty states. Bill Lewis said that she had come closest to getting the vice presidential nomination at the 1952 GOP Convention when the BPW Clubs started a drive in her behalf. They claimed 250 delegates were committed to vote for her and other delegates were falling in line, when the word came that General Dwight D. Eisenhower, the presidential nominee, had selected California Senator Richard M. Nixon to be his running mate.[51]

When Margaret Chase Smith announced her candidacy for president in 1964 at the National Press Club in Washington, D.C., where the Women's Press Club had gathered for a luncheon, she identified with her audience by reminding them that she began her career as a journalist. She said:

Many years ago I worked for the weekly newspaper in my hometown—the *Independence Reporter*—in a succession of a variety of jobs ranging from general reporter to circulation manager and some of them concurrently performed as can be done only on a weekly paper. . . . But it was when I did five

columns a week nationally for United Feature Syndicate for more than five
years that I felt a greater professional kinship with you. I learned what a
chore it was to produce seven hundred words almost daily.

Margaret enjoyed a warm relationship with the press. Perhaps because of
her experience as a reporter, she was sensitive to a reporter's need to get
information to be able to compose stories and tried to accommodate as
much as she could. Margaret was photogenic and often appeared on the
front page of many of the newspapers that ran stories. Making her announcement speech to an audience of reporters made sense, because not
that long ago, she worked in the newspaper business, too. She used her
experience in the press to create a suspenseful speech.

When Margaret Chase Smith laid out her argument "to run or not to
run" for president, it sounded like an oral "pro or con" list that someone
on the brink of a big decision draws up. Her arguments "pro" a presidential race, were that she had a dearth of political experience, her run
would break the gender barrier in politics, her candidacy would offer voters a moderate choice, since her ideology was less liberal than Rockefeller
and less conservative than Goldwater, and finally because she didn't have
a campaign war chest, she would be an independent politician. Her
speech was not celebratory or especially jubilant. Instead, it showed a
thoughtful politician who was interested in explaining her reasoning.

During her forty-five minute announcement speech, Margaret said that
one of her reasons for running was to "break the barrier against women
being seriously considered for the Presidency." Such a statement may
have made her bid seem symbolic. During her campaign she constantly
faced questions from the press that asked her if she was serious about becoming president. After the campaign, Margaret Chase Smith stated,"I
wouldn't have been in it if I hadn't been serious."[52] When she delivered
the speech, she cleverly wrote two speech endings; one that announced
her candidacy and one that didn't; and though the speech was distributed
to the audience ahead of time, the ending of the speech was not printed,
so they had no way of knowing what her decision would be until she finished her speech. Her reasons for "not" seeking the presidency were also
presented in her speech. She said:

> First, there are those who make the contention that no woman should ever
> dare to aspire to the White House—that this is a man's world and that it should
> be kept that way—and that a woman on the national ticket of a political party
> would be more of a handicap than a strength. Second, it is contended that the
> odds are too heavily against me for even the most remote chance of victory—
> and that I should not run in the face of what most observers see as certain and
> crushing defeat. Third, it is contended that as a woman I would not have the
> physical stamina and strength to run—and that I should not take that much
> out of me even for what might conceivably be a good cause, even if a losing

cause. Fourth, it is contended that I should not run because obviously I do not have the financial resources to wage the campaign that others have. Fifth, it is contended that I should not run because I do not have the professional political organization that others have. Sixth, it is contended that I should not run because to do so would result in necessary absence from Washington while the Senate had roll call votes—and thus that I would bring an end to my consecutive roll call—a record which is now at 1590.

Shortly after her presidential candidacy announcement speech, Margaret was interviewed on "Face the Nation," a CBS television and radio news program. In the interview, newsman Warren Duffee noted that:

In your announcement speech you stated that your campaign would be run on the remarkable premise that you had no organization, virtually no time to campaign, no money, that you did not intend to buy newspaper advertising space or TV and radio spots to any extent. Now this would appear to be a very unusual way to start a campaign. I am wondering if this response that you have gotten is going to bring in enough money for you to perhaps alter some of these austere foundations which you set forth originally.

Senator Smith responded firmly that she had no intention of changing her original plans. She stated:

I shall not alter my plans on the money because it would be so out of character for me. My Maine campaigns—my campaigns in the State of Maine—and, as you know, have increased my majorities each time. I have not spent money. I think the largest I every spent was in 1948, in my first election for the Senate, and both the primary and the election cost me less than $10,000. The offers of money have been very, very fine, and I am deeply grateful, but I want to go into the primary in New Hampshire in character.[53]

ON THE CAMPAIGN TRAIL

Margaret Chase Smith entered the New Hampshire primary behind Barry Goldwater and John D. Rockefeller who had previously announced their candidacies. The thrifty Margaret Chase Smith ran a low-key campaign, without receptions, parties, or campaign contributions. She even maintained her impeccable Senate attendance record by saying that her campaigning would be limited to times when the Senate was not in session. She did not have a campaign headquarters. Her motives ran deeper than a desire to save money. She didn't want to spend other people's money because she didn't want to owe them anything. Her high moral principles positioned her against the idea of "buying" votes or making a big, splashy, expensive showing. When she showed up on the campaign trail, that was what voters got—her and very little, if any, entourage. She told a young school girl as she campaigned that "What I am doing today may make you President some day."[54] She was quick to point out that she wasn't a feminist. She said, "I'm running on my record as a Senator, not a woman Senator," she said, "with more national office experience than any of the other announced candidates. I'm not a feminist."[55]

A unique expression of campaign support came in the form of a campaign song written by musicians Bucky Searles and Dick Nirenberg. The lyrics were:

> We want a woman in the White House, we want some hist'ry to be made. . . . To make the country hustle, give Uncle Sam a bustle, and make the Gen'ral Staff the ladies aid. We want a woman with some know-how. . . . Someone to carry on the fight. . . . She'd eliminate a war and be home again by four, she's a woman and a woman's always right. She has a secret weapon that would cast a peaceful spell. It's "Bingo" played by Hotline with Nikita and Fidel. Evacuate the Pentagon; On this we're standing pat. . . . But leave the building standing and we'll put in a laundromat. WE WANT A WOMAN IN THE WHITE HOUSE, someone who really knows the score. She would make the G.O.P. join the Democrats for tea. With a WOMAN IN THE WHITE HOUSE, and you know that it's the right house, with a woman President in Sixty-four.[56]

After only one week of campaigning, the *Bangor Daily News* stated that she could not win the presidency. Political columnist Lorin Arnold wrote that after traveling nearly one thousand miles on the campaign trail with Senator Smith, he was "persuaded she cannot win." He cited that although most of the people Senator Smith met were very impressed with her, they felt that "the presidency was no place for Senator Smith or any other woman."[57] Frequently the press suggested that although she was running for the presidency, she would settle for the vice presidency. Erica Falk and Kathleen Hall Jamieson note that according to newspaper coverage of Smith, even if she did well, the papers funneled her to the vice-presidency and not the presidency.[58] Her gender wasn't the only drawback that some critics saw. Senator Smith observed that her age had been noted in almost every news story about her candidacy. She said, "Since my candidacy was announced, almost every news story starts off: The sixty-six-year-old Senator. I declare, I haven't seen the age played up in the case of the men candidates." One reporter expressed concerns that Senator Chase Smith was menopausal, by stating, "The female of the species, undergoes physical changes and emotional distress of varying severity and duration which have an effect on judgment. Her cause is hopeless, and makes a travesty of the women's right's cause."[59] She also had a sharp response to an interviewer's query about whether or not she would be strong enough to endure an all-night crisis conference at the White House should she win the presidency. To that she replied, "I had some statistics gathered yesterday and they show women live seven years longer than men."[60] Two issues she did want played up in the media, however, were her main campaign issues of spending and foreign policy. During the first primary, Henry Cabot Lodge was the big victor in New Hampshire, winning 35.4 percent of the vote.[61] Frugal as her roots suggest, Margaret Chase Smith spent just $250 in New Hampshire. The second primary was in Illinois where Margaret Chase Smith received 30 percent of the vote, second after Goldwater. In Illinois Margaret only spent $85! Illinois was the best showing Margaret enjoyed in the presidential race, and Lewis V. Morgan, Jr., the director of Senator Smith's Illinois campaign, said that his analysis showed that Senator Smith won votes wherever she went. She visited private homes and other small gatherings, which gave observers the impression she was being received more like a favorite aunt from Maine than a politician.[62] The *Fort Worth Star Telegram* noted that "Smith Showing in Illinois Almost Overshadows Barry."[63] In the next primary, in Oregon, Senator Smith did not campaign due to travel costs and placed a disappointing fifth. Similarly, in the Massachusetts primary, Senator Smith placed fifth. The last primary before the convention was the California primary, and Margaret Chase Smith chose not to participate. She refused to participate in a "stop Goldwater" coalition started in California by Governor Rockefeller and Henry Cabot Lodge in an effort to unseat the likely nominee, Goldwater. Senator Smith did not want to involve herself in such action because she was running a "positive campaign" and was not interested in "stop movements."[64] By the eve of the Republican National Convention held in San Francisco in July, Arizona Republican Senator Barry Goldwater was just short of the number of delegates needed.

When she arrived at the airport in San Francisco on July 15, 1964, Margaret Chase Smith was greeted by a cheering reception of supporters and proclaimed herself "still in the race."[65] At the Cow Palace in San Francisco July 15, 1963, Senator Margaret Chase Smith's name was placed in nomination for the presidency at the Republican National Convention. The only other woman who had given a major speech at the Republican National Convention in 1964 was Elly Peterson, assistant chair of the Republican National Committee who was seeking the Republican nomination for the Senate from Michigan. The female star of the convention was Margaret Chase Smith, who upon hearing herself nominated for president, held a red rose aloft and smiled widely. A New York well-wisher wrote to Senator Smith after her convention appearance and said, "If you had been a man, you would have been elected president long ago."[66] Another admirer noted, "Every woman, Republican and Democrat, owes a debt of gratitude to Margaret Chase Smith because she has opened the door for a woman to serve in the Presidency."[67] She placed second to

Barry Goldwater, who was defeated by President Lyndon Johnson in the November election. Senator Smith arrived in San Francisco with just sixteen votes in her hand, fourteen of which came from the Maine delegation, plus the votes of North Dakota's John Rouzie and Vermont's George Aiken. Aiken, now seventy-five years old and a twenty-five year veteran in the Senate, nominated her.[68] He said:

> Mr. Chairman and Delegates: I intend to nominate for President one of the most capable persons I have ever known and one with whom I have been associated in public service for twenty-four years. I don't like to start a nominating speech with a confession, but the circumstances are compelling. In introducing my candidate, I find myself in a most peculiar position; I am severely restricted in what I can offer for your support. I can't promise you a cabinet job, an ambassador's appointment—or even a shot at a nice government contract. I can't even offer you cigars or chewing gum. For awhile, it looked real promising. I thought I could at least invite you all out for coffee because I knew my candidate was having checks and $10.00 and $1.00 bills and pennies sent her from most every State in the Union. Pennies came from school children—and dollars from low income people who couldn't afford it. Then there were some beautiful checks in three and four figures from real important business people. The outlook was as rosy as a Pacific sunset as portrayed by the Chamber of Commerce. You and I were going to have a wonderful time here in San Francisco. Then do you know what happened? Do you know what my candidate pulled on me? She took every big check—every little check—every $10.00 bill—ever $1.00 bill and sent them straight back to where they came from.

He continued by describing the qualities that made Margaret Chase Smith the best choice for president, and then he concluded: "I am now proud to nominate that candidate—the Senior Senator from the Great Republican State of Maine—Senator Margaret Chase Smith."[69]

Demonstrators and cheerleaders were on the floor of the arena, brought there by Mrs. Donna Wright of San Francisco, and the band was playing "Drink a toast to dear old Maine." By the end of the convention, with Senator Smith hanging tough, she came in second with twenty-seven delegates by the final vote. The editor of *The Mirror*, in New Bern, North Carolina, commented on the presidential candidacy of Margaret Chase Smith: "This distinguished woman never really had a chance to be her party's standard bearer, but the *Mirror* is glad she campaigned for the nation's highest office. It gave millions of Americans a televised glimpse of one of this country's great public servants. As a gathering where true dignity was an oddity . . . she managed to retain the graciousness and charm that has characterized not only her personal life but her career in Congress."[70] Margaret Chase Smith commented that although she had been encouraged to run, Goldwater seemed to have a groundswell of support that couldn't be removed. "If I were to run again," she said in review of her efforts, "I would organize every state and go for the delegates at least two years in advance."

As she had promised going into the convention, the Republican party emerged united when it was over and Margaret Chase Smith campaigned for the Goldwater-Miller ticket. But not all Republicans were as conservative as Goldwater and, therefore, many party leaders were divided. Democratic nominee Lyndon B. Johnson took advantage of Goldwater's mistakes, especially criticizing his nonchalance about nuclear weapons. Following his political hero, Franklin Delano Roosevelt, Johnson proposed a new slogan for America, his "Great Society." In this plan, he proposed an activist approach to ensure a variety of new social programs. On election day, Lyndon B. Johnson's landslide of the popular vote was the largest in United States history. He won 61 percent to Goldwater's 38 percent.

MARGARET CHASE SMITH'S PRESIDENTIAL OBSTACLES

Margaret Chase Smith wasn't willing to neglect her work in the Senate in order to run for president. She was especially interested in the passage of the civil rights bill, and much of the campaign season was spent hurrying back to Washington. Historian Janann Sherman noted: "Her refusal to leave her job or take any money made it very difficult to run a campaign."[71] At the time of her campaign for president, Margaret Chase Smith had piled up an amazing, all-time Senate record of 1,620 consecutive roll call votes.[72]

Funding was also a major obstacle. Margaret Chase Smith refused to accept campaign contributions, and anyone who sent her money soon received their donation back with a kind note that she simply could not accept it. She did, upon her own insistence, receive $2,000 from the Republican National Committee to cover expenses incurred at the national convention, but she refused to accept campaign contributions.

MARGARET CHASE SMITH'S COMMUNICATION STYLE

Margaret Chase Smith described her speaking style: "My speeches in the Senate are blunt and to the point. I do not indulge in political oratory."[73] Her no-nonsense speech style shows the kind of woman she was. Just as she didn't feel right about taking campaign contributions, she didn't feel right about dressing up her communication with excessively descriptive language. She never tried to sound impressive because she felt the magnitude of the issues was impressive enough. In her

"Declaration of Conscience I"[74] speech, Senator Smith expressed a similar dedication to simple speech when she said, "I speak as simply as possible because the issue is too great to be obscured by eloquence, I speak simply and briefly in the hope that my words will be taken to heart."[75] Senator Smith, standing barely five feet four inches tall, and light in weight, would demand to be known as a heavyweight, politically speaking, not by stridently calling attention to herself but by succinctly laying out for her listeners the urgency of the problem as she perceived it and the solution that she proposed. Margaret Chase Smith spoke plainly, but with force. She was not likely to create imagery with her speaking, the way that her husband, Clyde Smith did. She was likely to get to her point without fanfare. For example, Margaret Chase Smith rarely had an introduction of the classic sense in her speeches. The beginning of her speeches rarely grabbed attention with some striking linguistic element. Instead, it was the entire event of Margaret Chase Smith speaking: a feminine, petite woman, with a soft voice, confidently standing and carefully explaining herself that made her audiences want to listen. Elected to Congress only twenty years after women were granted the right to vote, Margaret Chase Smith's femininity gave her power and attention. She was not the usual male standing and speaking, she was the lone female, and that alone caused her audience to prick up its ears, something they would have to do in order to hear her soft voice. But her quiet voice was never to be taken for timidity. Even on the campaign trail for president she enjoyed the "only woman" status that would give her audience a curiosity about her that would guarantee a listen. And once the curiosity was satisfied, audiences continued to listen because her speeches were honest, brave, and simply made sense. When Margaret Chase Smith did extrapolate in her speeches, she did so to educate her audience. Marlene Boyd Vallin wrote: "Margaret Chase Smith's speeches reveal her role as democratic educator. Her orations to women's groups and to the graduates of women's colleges were lectures on the value, power, and responsibility of women, particularly toward the preservation of the democracy and the pursuit of world peace."[76] The campaign speech from her 1964 presidential campaign also showed her penchant for teaching her audience about the democratic process while at the same time persuading them to vote for her: In her 1964 presidential campaign stump speech, she tells how she would handle world events:

> As to my stand on present world problems, I believe the United States has been too long on a "holding operation." I believe it is time to say to Khrushchev—"Prove your good faith—tear down the Berlin Wall." I have had conferences with the leaders of twenty-three countries throughout the

world, and I have been commended for my sincerity and the firmness of my decisions relative to international affairs. In South Vietnam I believe we should either clean it up—or pull out. In Cuba I would have either given the air coverage or not authorized the Bay of Pigs venture. I have said for a long time that Guantanamo should be self-sufficient, and that we should not bolster the Cuban economy by hiring so many Cubans to work there. In Panama I believe we must resume diplomatic relations, and have a more through understanding of exactly what the problems are. I think the Canal is inadequate, and that another one should have been started some years ago.[77]

Her public speaking was without pretense. Notice in the introduction of her only preserved presidential campaign speech, which she used on the stump, how she identified herself:

I am Margaret Chase Smith, Republican Senator from the State of Maine. I grew up in Skowhegan, Maine, the eldest of six children in a humble, honest, hard-working family. My father was the Town barber. My mother waited on tables part-time at the Coburn Hotel, worked in a shoe factory, and clerked at Green Brothers Five and Dime. I am happy to say she lived to see her eldest daughter elected to the United States Senate.[78]

In what several scholars, including Dow and Tonn,[79] Jamieson,[80] and Blankenship and Robson[81] describe as a characteristic of feminine style in public speaking, Margaret Chase Smith based her political judgments on concrete, lived experiences. For example, she explained to her audience her reason for not accepting campaign contributions this way:

At High School age I, too, clerked at Green Brother's Five and Dime. In the evening I operated the switchboard for the Skowhegan Telephone Company at ten cents an hour. I taught school one year for $8.50 a week, then worked for the Telephone Company and later became Office Manager of *The Independent Reporter*, Skowhegan's weekly newspaper. With this background I am extremely conscious of money—particularly the spending of it. I am proud that three campaigns for the Senate have cost something less than $17,000.[82]

When Margaret Chase Smith spoke, she didn't move around the audience, she didn't smile broadly, she didn't use impressive language or call attention to herself with fancy clothing. Instead, she spoke clearly and often urgently about the issues she cared about. Biographer Frank Graham, Jr., noted, "Cool and feminine in this overwhelmingly masculine assembly, Margaret Smith would have been, in any case, an object of admiration. Well-tailored, with a fondness for a fragile rose or a simple necklace . . . poised and contained, with a hint of severity in her dry Yankee voice, she would command respect in any gathering by her physical presence alone.[83]

INVENTION

As a member of Congress, the Senate, as a presidential candidate, and for the rest of her life, Margaret Chase Smith spoke about democratic reform issues that she believed were important to the moral fiber of America. The threat of Communism, Americanism, military affairs, medical care, and women and leadership were topics that dominated her speeches and shaped her identity as a public servant. She spoke of these issues with the utmost seriousness, usually targeting the most dramatic aspect of the issue. Even before she was elected to office, she felt the need to make her speeches matter. An example of this occurred in 1938 when she was invited to give a speech at the Kennebec County Women's Republican Club. Her talk was supposed to be "The Experiences of a Congressman's Wife in Washington." She noted, "I wanted to include something in the speech that would encourage women to work for improvement of their communities. I had often said that the Federal Government is only as strong as the local governments."[84] This shows Margaret's early desire to create change by sharing her ideas about the role of women in democracy. She would have heavier rhetorical burdens as her political activism grew. Margaret Chase Smith's courage to speak out against her fellow Republican senator Joseph McCarthy stands alone as testament to the power of Senator Smith's ability to make meaningful speeches. Another important speech, and one that Senator Smith characterized as "the most critical speech I ever gave,"[85] was given to the Somerset County [Maine] Republican Women's Club in her hometown of Skowhegan on May 21, 1948. It was only one month prior to her Republican Senatorial primary. Senator Smith wanted to be the first woman to win elections to both the House of Representatives and the Senate, and she believed that because of her gender she was the target of a smear campaign to discredit her campaign. Margaret Chase Smith received an anonymous printed sheet alleging analysis of her voting record with the obvious intent to paint her as a traitor to the Republican Party, a tool of the Congress of Industrial Organizations (CIO), and a political companion to Representative Vito Marcantonio. A member of the American Labor Party of New York, Marcantonio was considered to be a radical liberal and was charged by some as being pro-Communist.[86]

In the book, titled "This I Believe," edited by Edward R. Murrow, Margaret outlined her core values by describing her reasons for enduring the sometimes difficult life of a public servant. She also added the statement, "this I believe" to many of her speeches throughout her life, and William C. Lewis, Jr. described it as "her favorite statement."[87] In this statement she used a narrative to describe her feelings:

> Many nights I go home from the office or the Senate Floor tired and discouraged. There's lots of glory and prestige and limelight for a United States Sen-

ator that the public sees. But there's just as much grief and harassment and discouragement that the public doesn't see.[88]

She then went on to describe what her experiences as a public servant had been and asked the pivotal question, "What am I doing this for?" She answered her question: "This I do believe—that life has a real purpose—that God has assigned to each human being a role in life—that each of us has a purposeful task—that our individual roles are all different but that each of us has the same obligation to do the best he can."[89]

DISPOSITION

Margaret Chase Smith organized most of her speeches in an inductive method. She used examples to add support to her arguments. She did not use narrative discourse or emotion to build her case, although many of her topics were emotionally laden issues that could have easily been developed into dramatic pathos, designed to stir her audiences. She stirred her audiences with her serious, pragmatic reasoning, instead of more flowery, emotionally laden rhetoric. Consider her clear attention to the problem in Declaration of Conscience I:

> Mr. President, I would like to speak briefly and simply about a serious national condition. It is a national feeling of fear and frustration that could result in national suicide and the end of everything we Americans hold dear. It is a condition that comes from the lack of effective leadership in either the Legislative Branch or the Executive Branch of our Government.[90]

This straightforward method was not only Margaret Chase Smith's public speaking style, but her conversational style as well. Evidence of her conversational clarity could be found in her interviews, which have been preserved on tape in the Margaret Chase Smith Library, as well as the tone of her 1972 autobiography, *Declaration of Conscience*. Margaret Chase Smith remained the pragmatic, frugal New Englander she was from birth because it was part of her core value system to say what you mean and mean what you say. There was nothing flamboyant or put on about the rhetoric of Margaret Chase Smith. There was no debate club training or college instruction on argumentation. She learned to develop arguments from her life experiences. Furthermore, she organized her statements carefully. A high school graduate, working mostly with law school graduates, Margaret Chase Smith was especially careful in planning her statements because she wanted to be as effective as her well educated colleagues. Often, she was more effective than her colleagues. Similar to a shy student who carefully prepares speeches for public speaking class who is ultimately more successful than loquacious students who do not prepare, Margaret

Chase Smith was more effective than many of the trained debaters with whom she worked. She once reflected on her public speaking training:

> Many people have asked me from time to time what training I have had for public speaking. My answer has been none except following suggestions and advice of those I admired as speakers. When I was with Roland T. Patten at the *Skowhegan Reporter*, his advice was: make notes for an outline of points to make. My husband, Clyde H. Smith, said, "Never rush onto a platform and hastily begin talking. After being introduced, take your place slowly and deliberately, and look the audience over and try to find a person or two you feel you can talk to. Even if you spend two minutes for this, it is time well spent—otherwise you are part way through your speech before you have control over yourself.[91]

MEMORIA

Senator Bob Dole said: "I viewed her [Margaret Chase Smith] as someone with influence. She didn't speak all that much but when she did, people listened."[92] What would cause other politicians to stop and listen intently as the feminine and soft-spoken Gentlewoman from Maine stood to speak? It wasn't her booming voice, because Margaret Chase Smith was always soft-spoken.[93] Her voice was so soft that in a recording of her debate with Eleanor Roosevelt on November 4, 1956, at several points in the debate, it is difficult to hear her.[94] Yet, she considered carefully and planned for a closing statement that would end the debate with drama and make it certain where she stood on issues.

It wasn't her attention-getting introductions, since many times Senator Smith dispensed with introductions and got straight to the thesis of her talk.[95] In more congenial settings, such as her presidential announcement speech or her speech to women's groups to promote leadership in women, she would create immediacy with her audience by identifying something that she had in common with them.[96] Margaret Chase Smith spoke most often with notes in her hand that contained full transcripts of her speeches. She did not leave her messages to memory or chance, most likely because her speeches were historically important and impacted the welfare of the nation. Yet, even with her quiet voice and her fully prepared texts in front of her, she was commanding. It wasn't an exceptional delivery style, but a command of her material that made her an impressive speaker. Her speeches were written by her and often with the help of William C. Lewis, Jr. She did not have any speechwriters. She was a careful writer and thus her material was well known to her when she stood to speak. Her infrequent talks also gave her credibility. When Margaret Chase Smith stood to speak, it became known that she must have "something worthwhile to say."[97] Her combination of straight talk, and the reticence she had for speaking, made Margaret Chase Smith a commanding speaker.

Margaret Chase Smith described her format of speaking from note cards:

> In the 1920s when President of the Maine State Federation of Business and Professional Women's Clubs, I used small index cards for my typed notes and script. Later I followed my husband's system and used 5x8" cards (later paper). I went from small type to all caps to large typewriter type and finally to hand printed, black, two inch marker lettering done by both my secretary, Jackie Potter, and Bill Lewis. I found this most helpful when speaking in a dimly lighted room but especially so when my eyes started dimming.[98]

AFTER HER PRESIDENTIAL BID

For the remainder of her political career, Senator Smith continued to represent Maine. She fiercely guarded her independence and tirelessly worked on behalf of Maine's industries and citizens. Her votes against President Nixon's Supreme Court nominees Clement F. Haynsworth and G. Harrold Carswell illustrated her commitment to principle and independence.

Margaret Chase Smith also played a significant role in Senate deliberations over the Anti-Ballistic Missile Treaty and other arms control efforts during the early 1970s.

Throughout her congressional career, Senator Smith adhered to a two-pronged philosophy that became her political trademark. One of these was her perfect attendance record in Congress. She held an all-time voting record in the United States Senate until 1981 with 2,941 consecutive roll-call votes. The second was the fact that she was scrupulous about spending very little on her campaigns, never accepting campaign contributions. This frugality earned her widespread approval among her constituents and was an important factor in her impressive vote-getting record. Nevertheless, her streak of eight successive terms finally came to an end in 1972, when Senator Smith was narrowly defeated for re-election by Representative William D. Hathaway.

After retiring from political life, Senator Smith commented that her greatest contribution to the country's well-being was her consistent stand against bigotry and injustice. Her opposition to the excesses of "McCarthyism" in the early 1950s demonstrated to the nation her courage and devotion to conscience and justice. She said, "If I am to be remembered in history, it will not be because of legislative accomplishments, but for an act I took as a legislator in the United States Senate when on June 1, I spoke . . . in condemnation of McCarthyism when the junior Senator from

Wisconsin had the Senate paralyzed with fear that he would purge any Senator who disagreed with him. The speech is known as the 'Declaration of Conscience.'"

In 1973 Margaret Chase Smith was one of the first twenty women to be inducted into the National Women's Hall of Fame. Senator Smith launched a second career in education in the mid-1970s. For more than three years she toured the nation's colleges and universities as a Visiting Professor with the Woodrow Wilson National Fellowship Foundation. Accompanying her was Major General William C. Lewis, Jr. Together they planned for the creation of the Northwood University Margaret Chase Smith Library that adjoins her Skowhegan home and stands high above the banks of the Kennebec River. From 1982 until her death, Margaret Chase Smith was instrumental in the library's many programs and she was most enthusiastic about meeting with the visiting school groups.

Senator Smith was the recipient of ninety-five honorary degrees from educational institutions across the country and the culmination of her awards was the Presidential Medal of Freedom, the nation's highest civilian honor, which President George H. W. Bush presented her in July of 1989. Following a brief illness, Margaret Chase Smith passed away on Memorial Day, May 29, 1995, at the age of 97.[99]

NOTES

1. Margaret Chase Smith had gained a reputation from Senate colleagues for being very quiet during her work as a senator. Democratic Senator Fritz Hollings from South Carolina, when he gave his final speech on the Senate floor at the age of 82, noted that there was only one woman, Margaret Chase Smith, R-Maine, in his first years in the Senate, and that she was "outstandingly quiet." "Hollings Gives Final Senate Speech" November 17, 2004, www.cnn.com (accessed March 3, 2005) and in Margaret Chase Smith with William C. Lewis, Jr., *Declaration of Conscience.* (New York: Doubleday, 1972), Editor's Preface, 1.

2. Margaret Chase Smith, speech to announce Presidential Candidacy, January 27, 1964. Margaret Chase Smith with William C. Lewis, Jr., *Declaration of Conscience.* (New York: Doubleday, 1972), 369–370.

3. *The New York Times*, January 28, 1964, 17.

4. Marjorie Hunter. "Margaret Chase Smith Seeks Presidency." *New York Times*, January 28, 1964, 1.

5. Marlene Boyd Vallin. *Margaret Chase Smith: Model Public Servant*. (Westport, Conn.: Greenwood Press, 1998), 207–213.

6. Ibid.

7. Patricia L. Schmidt. *Margaret Chase Smith: Beyond Convention*. (Orono: The University of Maine Press, 1996), 293.

8. *Time*, 7 February 1964, 23.

9. Maria Braden. *Women Politicians and the Media*. (Lexington: University Press of Kentucky, 1996), 186.

10. Vallin, 1998. This was the subtitle of this book on the life of Margaret Chase Smith.

11. Schmidt, 15.

12. Schmidt, 17.

13. Ibid.

14. Patricia Ward Wallace. *Politics of Conscience: A Biography of Margaret Chase Smith.* (Westport, Conn.: Praeger Press, 1995), 8.

15. Ibid., 19.

16. Ward Wallace, 8.

17. Ward Wallace, 9.

18. For example, Ward Wallace, *Politics of Conscience*, begins the first chapter describing the time that Margaret applied for the job at Green's when she was only twelve. Also, in the *New York Times*, "A Chic Lady Who Fights," January 28, 1964, 17, and Patricia L. Schmidt. *Beyond Convention*, 23–24, the author recounts the same story.

19. Ward Wallace, 16.

20. Ibid., 23–25.

21. Schmidt, 26.

22. Ward Wallace, 11.

23. Ward Wallace, 13.

24. Schmidt, 29.

25. *Independent Reporter*, 25 April 1918, 8 and *Independent Reporter*, 24 April 1919, 2.

26. *Independent Reporter*, 5 June 1919, 1–2.

27. Schmidt, 64.

28. Schmidt, 65.

29. Schmidt, 70.

30. Quoted in Schmidt, 80.

31. Frank Graham, Jr. *Margaret Chase Smith: Woman of Courage.* (New York: John Day Company, 1964), 35.

32. Margaret Chase Smith, A Biographical Sketch, compiled by staff of Margaret Chase Smith Library, Skowhegan, Maine. Sent by mail by Angela Stockwell to the author, March 7, 2005.

33. Margaret Chase Smith with William C. Lewis, Jr., 12.

34. Ward Wallace, 148.

35. Margaret Chase Smith with William C. Lewis, Jr., 7.

36. "The Communist Party in the U.S.," *Newsweek*, June 2, 1947, 22–26 and J. Edgar Hoover, "How to Fight Communism," *Newsweek*, June 9, 1947, 30.

37. Vallin, 14.

38. Margaret Chase Smith with William C. Lewis, Jr.

39. Margaret Chase Smith with William C. Lewis, Jr., 27.

40. Vallin, 13.

41. Ward Wallace, 109.

42. *Lewiston Evening Journal*, November 26, 1951, 10.

43. Margaret Chase Smith, A Biographical Sketch, compiled by staff of Margaret Chase Smith Library, Skowhegan, Maine. Sent by mail by Angela Stockwell to the author, March 7, 2005.

44. Margaret Chase Smith with William C. Lewis, Jr., 243.

45. Ibid., 205.

46. Ibid., 210.

47. Ibid.

48. Ibid., 241.

49. Ibid.

50. Hunter, 1.

51. Marie Smith. "Maine Lady Eyes Maine Event." *Washington Post*, August 16, 1963, D1.

52. Ward Wallace, 158.

53. "Face the Nation" as broadcast over the CBS Television Network and the CBS Radio Network. February 2, 1964, 12:30–1:00 P.M. EST. MCS Library and Museum.

54. "From Telephone Operator to President of the U.S.?" *The Ohio Bell News*, March 18, 1964, Number 6, 1.

55. Ibid.

56. Contributed to the Maine Memory Network by the Margaret Chase Smith Library, www.MaineMemory.net (accessed 9 March 2005).

57. Lorin Arnold. "Can She Win?" *Bangor Daily News*, January 28, 1964, 1.

58. Erika Falk and Kathleen Hall Jamieson."Changing the Climate of Expectations," In Robert P. Watson and Ann Gordon, eds., *Anticipating Madam President*, (Boulder: Lynne Reinner Publishing, 2003), 49.

59. Richard Warren, *Evening Star*, February 3, 1964.

60. "Mrs. Smith Says Her Age Is No Bar to Presidency." *New York Times*, February 7, 1964, 14.

61. Ward Wallace, 295.

62. Austin C. Wehrwein. "Mrs. Smith Ran Well in the Suburbs." *New York Times*, April 19, 1964, 81.

63. "Smith Showing in Illinois Almost Overshadows Barry." *Fort Worth Star Telegram*, April 15, 1964.

64. "Coalition Rebuffed by Margaret Smith." *New York Times*, May 21, 1964, 23.

65. "Senator Smith Arrives on Coast, 'Still in Race,'"*New York Times*, July 13, 1964, 16.

66. Josephine Ripley. "Women and the Convention." *Christian Science Monitor*, July 25, 1964, 2.

67. "She Didn't Win, But She Blazed a Political Trail." *Bangor Daily News*, July 17, 1964.

68. Ward Wallace, 296.

69. Margaret Chase Smith with William C. Lewis, Jr., 383, 387.

70. Margaret Chase Smith with William C. Lewis, Jr., 390.

71. Janann Sherman. *No Place for a Woman: The Life of Senator Margaret Chase Smith.* (New Brunswick, N. J.: Rutgers University Press, 2000), 191.

72. Sherman, 188.

73. 1964 presidential campaign speech, the only presidential campaign speech on file, no title, faxed to author 8 March 2005 by Angela Stockwell of the MCS Library.

74. Margaret Chase Smith gave a similar speech twenty years later which became known as "Declaration of Conscience II."

75. Margaret Chase Smith with William C. Lewis, Jr., 13.

76. Vallin, 9.

77. 1964 presidential campaign speech, the only presidential campaign speech on file, no title, faxed to author March 8, 2005 by Angela Stockwell of the MCS Library and Museum.

78. Ibid.

79. Bonnie J. Dow and Marie Boor Tonn. "Feminine Style and Political Judgment in the Rhetoric of Ann Richards." *Quarterly Journal of Speech*, 79: 286–302.

80. Kathleen Hall Jamieson. *Eloquence in an Electronic Age*. (New York: Oxford University Press, 1988), 67–89.

81. Jane Blankenship and Deborah C. Robson. "A 'Feminine Style' in Women's Political Discourse: An Exploratory Essay." *Communication Quarterly*, Summer 1995, Volume 43, Issue 3, 353.

82. Ibid.

83. Graham, 11.

84. Margaret Chase Smith with William C. Lewis, Jr., 13.

85. Ibid., 105.

86. Margaret Chase Smith with William C. Lewis, Jr., 105.

87. Ibid., 446.

88. Ibid.

89. Ibid., 447.

90. "From Telephone Operator to President of the U.S.?" *Ohio Bell News*, March 18, 1964, Number 6, 1.

91. Anecdotes Collection, as told by Margaret Chase Smith, Margaret Chase Smith Library and Museum, in an email from Angie Stockwell to the author, May 11, 2005.

92. Bob Dole's endorsement of Patricia Ward Wallace's book on www.greenwood .com (accessed March 9, 2005).

93. Vallin, 7.

94. Debate between Senator Margaret Chase Smith and Mrs. Eleanor Roosevelt. "Face the Nation." 4 November 1956, videocassette.

95. For example, in Smith's Declaration of Conscience I speech, she got immediately to her thesis, which she also did in "answer to a smear" and her speech on the Senate floor, September 21, 1961 on nuclear credibility. All three speeches appear in Margaret Chase Smith with William C. Lewis, Jr.

96. For example, in Smith's Announcement of Presidential Candidacy speech, and her speech titled "Women and Leadership," which she gave to the National Federation of BPW clubs July 8, 1948, both include an introduction that showed an identification with her audience.

97. Statement from 'Declaration of Conscience I' speech.

98. Anecdotes Collection, as told by Margaret Chase Smith, Margaret Chase Smith Library and Museum, in an email from Angie Stockwell to the author, 11 May 2005.

99. www.mcslibrary.org (accessed 3 March 2005).

This cartoon of Shirley Chisholm appeared in the *New York Times* in 1972. Courtesy of Robert Grossman.

2

Shirley Chisholm "Ms. Chis."[1]

We live in revolutionary times. The shackles that various groups have worn for centuries are being cast off. This is evidenced by the "developing" nations of the world, which we consider, for the most part, underdeveloped. Countries such as India, Ceylon and Israel have women for Prime Ministers and in other decision-making positions. American women must stand and fight—be militant even—for rights which are ours.[2]

On January 25, 1972, poised and determined forty-eight-year-old Shirley Chisholm, Congresswoman from New York's Twelfth District, announced her decision to run for President of the United States in front of a standing-room-only crowd at a press conference in the elementary school auditorium at Brooklyn's largest Baptist church. She was a diminutive woman, who stood barely five feet tall, with a strong, aggressive voice that belied her slight, feminine appearance. With great fortitude and a no-nonsense approach, she faced her chief opponents, Edmond Muskie, Hubert Humphrey, John Lindsay, and George McGovern. The thrust of Congresswoman Chisholm's campaign was her moral character. The announcement was the culmination of years of encouragement from many people. Meticulously dressed in a black and white patterned dress, waving and smiling at the audience and the cameras, Ms. Chisholm, the former nursery school teacher turned congresswoman, began her speech:

I stand before you today as a candidate for the Democratic nomination for the Presidency of the United States of America. I am not the candidate of black America, although I am black and proud. I am not the candidate of the women's movement of this country, although I am a woman, and I am equally proud of that. I am not the candidate of any political bosses or fat cats or special interests. I stand here now without endorsements from any big name politicians or celebrities or any other kind of prop. I do not intend to offer to you the tired and glib clichés, which for too long have been an accepted part of our political life. I am the candidate of the people of America. And my presence before you now symbolizes a new era in American political history. I have always earnestly believed in the great potential of America. Our constitutional democracy will soon celebrate its 200th anniversary, effective testimony, to the longevity to our cherished constitution and its unique bill of rights, which continues to give to the world an inspirational message of freedom and liberty.[3]

Many people, both political insiders and average citizens thought her bid for the presidency was ludicrous. Even Chisholm conceded that "some of these politicians think I'm half crazy."[4] In fact, Shirley Chisholm herself knew that she had no chance to win. But she felt she must "repudiate the ridiculous notion that the American people will not vote for a qualified candidate simply because he is not white or because she is not a male."[5]

She was not demanding her right to *get* in, but she was asserting her right to *be* in.[6] As the campaign took place in the midst of the women's and civil rights movements, many of the candidates attempted to woo women and black voters. Obviously, their efforts were hampered by Chisholm's appeal to these groups. Some of the candidates, including New York City Mayor John Lindsay and George McGovern asked her to drop out of the race, because of the daunting effort of a national campaign, and because they thought she would steal away votes from their campaigns.

Chisholm refused to budge, determined to show that different types of people other than white males could run for president.[7] She responded to their requests for her to end her candidacy succinctly, by stating "My time has come."[8] This was a woman of great persistence and patriotism, who was fluent in Spanish, a skill which gave her an advantage with many inner-city voters. Even more important, Chisholm spoke the language of the oppressed. But what made her into the courageous, peppery, outspoken, hardworking, and tough politician she became? She had the ability to speak her mind when others felt that her silence was golden. She used her words as a political weapon and fired upon her political opponents, as she fought for the rights of the oppressed.[9] To find how this woman, whose fiery use of language and rock solid commitment to her convictions, grew into an advocate and an inspiration for future generations is to explore the early years of Shirley Anita (St. Hill) Chisholm.

BARBADOS AND BROOKLYN SHAPE A FUTURE LEADER

Shirley Chisholm was born Shirley Anita St. Hill on November 30, 1924, in Brooklyn, New York. She was the first of four children born to Charles and Ruby St. Hill. Her father was from British Guiana and her mother was from Barbados. Because her parents had low paying, unskilled jobs and finances were scarce for the young family, in 1927, Shirley was sent to Barbados, with her younger sisters, Odessa and Muriel, to live with their maternal grandmother, Mrs. Emily Seale. Sending the three girls to live with Mrs. Hill's mother would give Charles and Ruby St. Hill a chance to get on their feet financially. When Shirley and her sisters arrived in Barbados, they found a loving, yet demanding grandmother, who saw to it that Shirley and her sisters received a good education from the British school system. This early, provincial educational beginning Shirley later credited with providing her with a strong academic background that started her on the road to success academically and professionally. In Barbados, the school that Shirley and her sisters attended was an austere, one-room building. All the children were together in the building, and the children were separated into smaller groups by age. The teachers were tougher on the students and academics were more rigorous than Shirley found them to be when she returned to America. As a student, she was expected to take her studies very seriously; it was a place to pay attention and learn everything that she could. She writes in her 1970 autobiography, "the Barbadians' drive to achieve and excel is almost an obsession and is a characteristic that other islanders do not share to the same degree. The Barbadians who came to Brooklyn all wanted, and most of them got, the same two things; a brownstone house and a college education for their children."[10] When she arrived at her grandmother's farm in Barbados with her two younger sisters, she noted that the furnishings were sparse. She stated, however, "we found Grandmother's house elaborately furnished with the two necessities: warmth and love."[11]

In 1934, she rejoined her parents and her youngest sister, Selma, in New York. Although the family's four-room apartment was in Brooklyn, their mother was thoroughly British in her ideas, her manners, and her plans for her daughters. Their parents wanted the girls to become young ladies, which meant that they were expected to be poised, modest, accomplished, educated, and graceful. Shirley learned responsibility early in life because as the oldest child, she was put in charge of caring for her younger siblings when her parents worked. Her mother worked as a domestic and a seamstress and her father was a union man. Her father, Charles, was a voracious reader, even though he had only the equivalent of a fifth-grade education. Wishing a better life for his children, he told Shirley and her sisters: "you must make something of yourselves. You've got to go to school, and I'm not sending you to play, either. Study and make something of yourselves. Remember, only the strong people survive in this world. God gave you a brain; use it."[12] Because their parents did not have much formal education, they wanted their children to have the benefits of a better life that schooling would bring.

Mr. and Mrs. St. Hill didn't have to lecture Shirley too much about the merits of working to her potential at school. Shirley excelled in academics at Girls' High School, one of Brooklyn's oldest schools. In high school Shirley distinguished herself by winning a medal for excellence in French, and she was vice president of the Junior Arista Honor Society, which was unusual, since very few African Americans were in honors programs. In 1942 she graduated from high school and received scholarships to Vasaar and Oberlin College. She wanted to attend one of them, but her parents couldn't afford the room and board, and so she enrolled in Brooklyn College, which admitted those students who earned an 89 percent average in high school. She reflected on the difference that attending Brooklyn College, instead of a more prestigious institution may have had on her life: "If I had gone to Vassar, the rest of my life might have been different. Would I have become one of the pseudo-white upper-middle-class black women professionals, or a doctor's wife with furs, limousines, clubs and airs?"[13] She reflects on her decision to have a career in education. "I had already decided to become a teacher. There was no other road open to a young, black woman. I know it would have to be teaching for me; but I took no education courses, for some reason I majored in sociology and minored in Spanish."[14] Her ability to speak fluent Spanish would later enhance her communication with her Spanish-speaking constituents, of whom there were many in the district Shirley would later represent.

When Ms. Chisholm encountered racism at Brooklyn College, she fought against it. After African American students at Brooklyn College were denied admittance to a social club, she formed an alternative one, and named it Ipothia, which stood for "in pursuit of the highest in all."[15] It was this determined spirit and sense of justice that Ms. Chisholm brought to her life's work. Her decision to start her own club when other organizations were closed to her was a precursor to her behavior in the future. "More and more people, white and black, began to tell me things like 'Shirley, you have potential. You should do something with your life.'"[16] One professor, Louis Warsoff, took a special interest in Shirley. A blind political science professor, he was one of the first white men whom Shirley knew and trusted. It was Professor Warsoff who noticed Shirley's impressive debating skills and told her that she should enter politics. To his suggestion, Shirley scoffed and said "you forget two things. I'm black—and I'm a woman."[17] The debating skills that she learned at Brooklyn College later shaped her style of public speaking, since her topics were quintessentially debatable issues, such as the war, education reform, equal rights, and day care initiatives. What Professor Warsoff noticed was Shirley's ability to champion causes in which she believed passionately. This skill came naturally to Shirley and she honed it through her participation on the debate team in college and in her later years as a teacher, administrator, and eventually as a politician.

In 1945 her parents realized their lifelong dream and bought their own home. Shirley was still living at home, a solid three-story on Prospect Place in Brooklyn, when she graduated in 1946, cum laude, from Brooklyn College. Her parents were achieving their dreams of owning their own home and educating their children, and Shirley was getting ready to step out into the world and start her life as an adult. During this time, it was difficult for black college graduates to obtain employment comparable to their education. It was even more difficult for Shirley, since she looked younger than her twenty-one years and employers didn't think she could handle the children that she would be hired to teach. The schools she applied to didn't think the young looking Shirley could even handle the work of a teacher's aide. After being rejected by many employers, she obtained a job at the Mt. Calvary Child Care Center in Harlem, after she emphatically persuaded the director to give her a try. Her response to Mrs. Eula Hodges at Mt. Calvary, who hesitated to hire her because of her youthfulness and slight frame, showcased her debate training. She said "At least you could try me! Put me on as a probationer! Give me a chance to show you! Give me a chance to find out whether I can do the job . . . don't judge me by my size!"[18] She worked there for seven years while attending Columbia University in the evening to obtain her master's degree in early childhood education. At about the same time, she became active in the political clubs, taking the advice of her mentor at Brooklyn College, Professor Warsoff, who saw in Shirley political activism and strong oratory skills that were tailored to meet the needs of her audiences. Political clubs were organizations that existed to help various constituents with needs such as legal services, housing, or welfare, in exchange for the implied pledge of their voting regularity.

On Monday and Thursday nights, the political clubs allowed residents to come and express their concerns or problems. The 17th Assembly District (A.D.), to which Shirley belonged, was a predominantly African American district, but the leadership was mostly made up of white men of Irish ancestry. The organization elected the state senator, assemblyman, city councilman, and other local office holders. Shirley noticed that almost no one asked questions during the question-and-answer period at the meetings. She felt that this was in part due to the way that the administrators, who sat at chairs on a raised platform at the front of the meeting room, intimidated anyone who voiced an opinion. Because most of the constituents were not well educated, they lacked the gumption to speak up. Similar to medical patients who do not feel on equal footing with a doctor who is treating them, they take the medicine he prescribes and don't complain. Shirley did not want to accept what was being handed to her and because of her education and moral character, she was not reticent about speaking up; and she voiced her concerns about several issues that were important to her. She was annoyed with the system at the clubs that discouraged people from speaking out by making those asking questions stand in a line and wait their turn, like, Shirley described, cattle.[19] About this same time she met Wesley McD. Holder, a black man from New Guiana who had been upsetting white politicians since the 1930's. "Mac," as he was called, wanted to elect black politicians to represent black communities. This was an interest that Shirley shared wholeheartedly, but her work in education kept her very busy and she eased into politics gradually. She joined the 17th Assembly District Democratic Club, and got an unlikely start as a cigar box decorator. Shirley had impressive art talent, and she put it to use making the boxes as attractive as possible. The cigar boxes were used to hold raffle tickets and money collected at each table during the meetings. Shirley encouraged the other women at the club to get paid for their work at the meetings and reluctantly the male leaders gave them a small stipend. Shirley was gaining a reputation as an outspoken ringleader who liked to shake up the status quo. It was a reputation that she was starting to relish, because in her heart, she knew that what she was asking for, such as equal rights, was a noble cause.

In 1949, at the age of twenty-five, she married a persistent suitor, Conrad Chisholm, a Jamaican who worked as a private investigator. He was proud of his educated and politically active wife, and he supported her interests. Shirley notes that Conrad was happy to let his wife be the center of attention while he stayed in the background. "Conrad is able to let me have the limelight without a thought; I thrive in it and he doesn't care for it."[20] Shirley and Conrad never had children, a fact that is not discussed in her two autobiographies. In 1977 Shirley and Conrad divorced and later that year she wed Arthur Hardwick, Jr., a Buffalo liquor store owner who had been in the New York State Assembly when Shirley served in the assembly. Mr. Hardwick died in 1986. Her second marriage also produced no children.

In 1953, under the leadership of Mac Holder, Shirley helped to elect Lewis Flagg, Jr., an outstanding African American lawyer for the district's seat on the municipal court's bench. Flagg was the first black judge elected in Brooklyn's history. Even though Shirley was active in the Bedford-Stuyvesant Political League (BSPL), an insurgent political group, whose chief goal was to help elect blacks, she stayed active in the regular Democratic club. While she was made a third vice president, she continued to ask questions that the club leadership didn't like, so they removed her. Shirley didn't back down; ever-confident, and motivated by her convictions, she continued to attend the meetings and said that she learned a political lesson that was important to her for the rest of her life. She says: "Political organizations are formed to keep the powerful in power. Their first rule is 'Don't rock the boat.' If someone makes trouble and you change them, do it. If you can't get him, bring him in. Give him some of the action; let him have a taste of power. Power is all anyone wants, and if he has a promise of it as a reward for being good, he'll be good. Anyone who does not play by those rules is incomprehensible to most politicians."[21] Shirley Chisholm didn't want to conform to whatever "being good" meant to some politicians. She wanted to pursue the issues she felt passionately about. That singlemindedness of purpose made her unpopular with the leaders of the time. Exercising her belief that she should follow her own moral compass, in 1958 she challenged Mac for the presidency of the Bedford-Stuyvesant Political League, and he was so angry he didn't speak with her for almost ten years. Mac felt that he had made Shirley's political career what it was, and she showed her gratitude by challenging him. Shirley lost the election, and the league lasted only a few years after that.

Shirley was content to have a break from politics, since her career was taking off. She was a teacher, not an aide now at the Mt. Calvary Child Care Center, and in 1953 she became director of the Friend in Need nursery school, a private school in Brooklyn. After one year there, she took over the directorship of the large Hamilton-Madison Child Care Center in Manhattan, where she served for five years. In 1959 she became a consultant to the City Division of Day Care. From her position, she had a view of City Hall, which was a landscape that may have whet her appetite for her future political activism.

In 1960, she was drawn back into politics when she and six others started the Unity Democratic Club. The Unity Club was instrumental in mobilizing African American and Hispanic voters, and was implemented to do what the BSPL didn't manage to do: get rid of the white leadership and give blacks and other unrepresented groups leadership that was truly concerned with their needs. In 1962, after hard work, the Unity Club succeeded in getting blacks elected. In 1964 Chisholm ran for a state assembly seat. During the campaign, white opponents tried to attack her gender with statements such as "Women talk too much." "Women are illogical." "Women take everything personally." Betty Friedan's important work, *The Feminine Mystique*,[22] had gained circulation by then, and Shirley knew that the attacks on her were sexism, pure and simple. She often commented over the years that voting for a woman was harder than voting for a black.[23] Nevertheless, she won and served in the New York General Assembly from 1964 to 1968. During her tenure in the legislature, she proposed a bill to provide state aid to day care centers and voted to increase funding for schools on a per-pupil basis. In 1968, after finishing her term in the legislature, Chisholm campaigned to represent New York's Twelfth Congressional District. Her campaign slogan was "Fighting Shirley Chisholm—Unbought and Unbossed." She won the election and became the first African American woman elected to Congress. As Clift and Brazaitis point out, Chisholm's résumé is typical of a woman in Congress, since Chisholm worked her way up by first getting involved in politics at the local level and slowly inching her way toward a run for Congress. They write: "Their résumés tell the story. They ran for PTA, then the city council, then the statehouse, and then the leadership of the statehouse before they dared to attempt a run for Congress."[24] Journalist Susan Brownmiller describes her rise in politics by stating that "Shirley Chisholm is true grit. Her comet like rise from clubhouse worker to Representative in the United States Congress was not an accident in the political heavens. It was accomplished by the wiles of a steely politician with a belief in her own abilities which at times approached almost Messianic fervor." "My rise has been constantly fighting," she likes to say.[25] This fighting was characteristic even before her first speech on the senate floor because during her first term in Congress, Congresswoman Chisholm defied tradition by refusing an assignment to the Agriculture Committee. She forcefully told the powerful leaders that the work of the Agriculture Committee was irrelevant to the needs of her constituency. "The Agriculture Committee seemed like a ridiculous assignment for a black member of Congress from one of the country's most deprived city neighborhoods. . . . "[26] After Shirley bravely lobbied for a change of assignment to the Committee on Committees, she was assigned to the Veteran's Affairs Committee. Even though many of her colleagues were aghast at her unconventional approach, she was applauded in the press for her clarity of purpose. She said her constituents who read about her proposed Agriculture assignment had told her: "Shirley, we don't grow hogs in this district."[27] Shirley agreed with her constituents' concerns, and she was determined to make her work in Congress meaningful to those whom she represented. In support of Ms. Chisholm's advocacy for a committee assignment that made sense geographically, *The New York Daily News* reported that Ms. Chisholm may actually "put an end to the boobery that exiles urban lawmakers to such committees while representatives from the hay-and-hog circuit grapple with city-bred problems of slums, poverty and education beyond their ken."[28] She proceeded to hire an all-female staff and was an outspoken advocate for civil rights, women's rights, and the poor and a fierce opponent of the Vietnam War. In her maiden speech to Congress, she said "We Americans have come to feel that it is our mission to make the world free. We believe that we are the good guys, everywhere, in Vietnam, in Latin America, wherever we go. We believe we are good guys at home, too. When the Kerner Commission told white America what black America has always known, that prejudice and hatred built the nation's slums, maintains them and profits by them, white America could not believe it. But it is true. Unless we start to fight and defeat the enemies in our own country, poverty and racism, and make our talk of equality and opportunity ring true, we are exposed in the eyes of the world as hypocrites when we talk about making people free."[29] In 1970, she was elected to a second term. During her second term, she co-founded the National Organization for Women remarking that, "Women in this country must become revolutionaries. We must refuse to accept the old, the traditional roles and stereotypes."[30]

She went on to serve seven terms in Congress. She introduced fifty pieces of legislation, many of which addressed her concerns about education. As a former school teacher, she was well poised to make the contribution in the education arena. The legislation she introduced also addressed issues such as unemployment, housing, and day care.[31] She was a sought-after public speaker. She reflected about what prompted her to make a presidential bid, after serving so briefly in Congress: "As a black woman active in national politics, these questions have long preoccupied me, and I do not need to say what I believe the answers to them are. But how do we change the way things are? What could I do to change them? This was the real question. It does no good to say, 'Something ought to be done,' or 'Somebody ought to do something.' Until you realize that the important question is "What am I going to do?" you have not begun to be serious about a problem. For this reason—and for a number of others—I began, during 1971, to think more and more about what seemed to very many persons to be a ridiculous idea. Suppose *I* were to run for President?"[32] *The New York Times* reported in August 1971 that she was being encouraged to seek the office [of the presidency] "by quite a number of persons, both black and white."[33] At a news conference at Paunce Hall at Brown University where the fifth annual convention of the National Welfare Rights Organization was taking place, Ms. Chisholm raised her right fist and ended her forty-minute speech by saying "The time has come, brothers and sisters, when we must rise up and assert our rights. Forget conventionalism. Forget whether you are in your place or out of your place. Do that which you have to do. Looking only to your God, whoever your God may be, and to your conscience for approval. Peace and power."[34] A few months later, at a speech she gave at Black Expo, a black and minorities business and cultural exposition held in Chicago, she said "we are tired of tokenism and look-how-far-we-have-comism" and that it was necessary for black women to "turn this country around."[35]

THE TIME HAD COME; CHISHOLM '72, READY OR NOT[36]

Shirley Chisholm was a ringleader and an original thinker from her start in local politics. For those who knew her, it was not a surprise that her political ambitions grew to include a presidential bid. An unlikely candidate because she was a woman and African American was obvious, but because she was a state representative, who had served only three years, she was also novel. Still, it served her sense of urgency, her plea that "government has lost touch with the people." There was a movement afoot to get Shirley to run for president and run she did. Shirley explains that originally, it was not her idea to run for president, it was "the kids."[37] A large number of college students had the privilege to hear Shirley Chisholm speak when she canvassed over one hundred campuses in forty-two states, from the time that she was elected to Congress. Over and over again she heard the question: "Why don't *you* run for President in 1972?"[38] Shirley reflected on her popularity as a speaker on college campuses, especially during her first term in Congress: "Not many members of Congress fill as many college speaking dates as I do; for one thing, not many are asked to. Some of the liberal stars and a handful of ex-professors are exceptions. But most Congressmen go where the votes are, to events in their districts, or, if they speak elsewhere, it is normally as a favor to another politician. No doubt I was originally sought because of my novelty value as the only black woman in Congress. But soon it became more than that, and the invitations flooded in—three times more than I could handle."[39] Shirley Chisholm noted once that, "I have a way of talking that does something to people." One young college student in the audience of a speech that Shirley Chisholm gave at Mills College in California at that time was Barbara

Lee, now a Congresswoman. At the time, Lee, who was president of the Black Student Union, was a mother of two children and she was on public assistance. When she heard Chisholm's words of inspiration, Lee was swept away by the charismatic role model speaking in front of her, and she wanted to get involved in Chisholm's presidential campaign. After Lee approached Chisholm and told her of her interest in volunteering on her presidential campaign, Chisholm told her that the first thing she could do is register to vote. It was the first time Lee thought about registering to vote.[40] Lee was one of countless young people moved to action by Chisholm's stirring oratory. The first action many of them took was to get involved in the political process, something they had never even considered, by registering to vote. Many of these same young people joined the Chisholm Trail[41] and campaigned in 1972 to help Shirley become elected president. She made the connection that running for president and speaking about issues that were ignored by other candidates, could help people who are underrepresented. She said "I could serve to give a voice to the people the major candidates were ignoring as usual. Although I could not win, I still might help all the people who were offering me support, by increasing their influence on the decision about who would be the Democratic nominee. That did not seem an impossible goal; difficult, but not impossible."[42] In a personal interview with Brad Koplinsky, Shirley Chisholm recounts the thinking and organizing both by herself and others that culminated in her presidential run: "Well, my following, the ones that really pushed me to run for leadership positions in government were the women and the minorities. They gathered into little clubs of their own. I didn't even know anything about it. They gathered into little clubs of their own and just constantly told me, 'Shirley you have the leadership ability. You are an articulate person. You speak Spanish and English. You have knowledge of the issues. Why don't you thrust yourself out there?' But I always felt, not always verbalizing it, but I always felt that there's no room for black people in this business. That call got so urgent, that I finally decided bit by bit by bit that I would move out there. Then people began raising money. . . . Then in 1972, I ran for the presidency when the people in Minnesota and Florida raised ten thousand dollars each for me to run for the presidency. I got frightened. I really got frightened. I wanted to know, 'How did this come about? I did not ask you to raise money, I just told you what's involved.' They said 'Well we want you to run so badly that we're going to do what we think we have to do.' That's the time when I really realized that people accepted me as a person, although being black, that had abilities to run for the presidency."[43] Despite her enthusiasm, and the support of many people, including Native Americans, Chicanos, and Spanish-speaking immigrants, and many white and black women, the campaign was a constant uphill battle for credibility, money, and support from fellow politicians. Many African American males argued that her candidacy would divide the black vote as some would choose to ride her star, with others going to one of the more established candidates.[44] The *New York Times* reported that prominent African American political figures, who sought to name a black male for the Democratic Presidential nomination, agreed to back Shirley Chisholm's presidential candidacy, but only after she agreed to the formation of a predominantly black campaign advisory group. The group, which was headed by Manhattan Borough President Percy Sutton, included Reverend Jesse Jackson, Representative Ron Dellums, and Mayor Richard Hatcher.[45] In addition, while Shirley Chisholm's campaign did raise $95,000 for her presidential bid, her campaign spent $300,000.[46] Money problems plagued her candidacy. There wasn't ever enough of it, and there were allegations of mismanagement. Eventually, however, the Justice Department absolved her of any wrongdoing.[47]

Shirley Chisholm enjoyed the support of a large cross section of people in the United States when she traveled the country in 1972 on her "Chisholm for President Bus." But she often expressed that being a woman presidential candidate was a more daunting obstacle than being a black candidate.

Interestingly, however, Shirley Chisholm wasn't the only woman vying to be president in 1972. Patsy Mink, a Democratic Congresswoman from Hawaii, was encouraged to run in 1971 when a group of Oregon citizens were looking for a candidate. The citizens, who were very concerned about the war in Vietnam, didn't think that any of the other candidates were against the war as vehemently as Mink was. Mink's name was placed on the ballot in the Oregon primary, and she finished in eighth place. Congresswoman Mink campaigned from January 1972 until she withdrew her name in May. Mink and Chisholm did not cross paths during the campaign, but by the time Mink withdrew from the race, she had considered her effort worthwhile, since she thought that the issue of the Vietnam War had received more attention.[48]

Conrad Chisholm didn't have a problem with Shirley's goal to become president. He said, "I happily went along with the program because I was used to having a politician in the family. My father was in politics. And Shirley was a brilliant woman who wanted to make a point. The point was that anyone could run for president as long as they were thirty-five years old or older and born in America."[49]

Referring to Shirley Chisholm, journalist Susan Brownmiller notes that when she went out into the country she would speak to everyone she met. She didn't care if you were black or white, old or young, she would speak with anyone. This was a maiden voyage for women and there were many, many white women who campaigned for her, and they were happy to do so."[50] The day after her announcement to run for president, *The New York Times* reported that her prime goal and that of her supporters, was to exert leverage on the choice of the eventual Democratic national ticket, the party's platform and future Cabinet positions if a Democrat was elected president. Former New York Mayor John Lindsay remained silent the day after Shirley's announcement, but his aides expressed unhappiness with the Chisholm presidential candidacy.[51] So while the reaction of politicians and the public was mixed, Shirley Chisholm remained steadfast in her determination to "assert her citizenship," something that Martin Luther King, Jr., told African Americans to do. She also felt that through politics she could create change for black people in the country. She said, "Malcolm [X] defined it succinctly—the ballot or the bullet. Since I believe that human life is uniquely valuable and important, for me the choice had to be the creative use of the ballot. I still believe I was right."[52]

ON THE CAMPAIGN TRAIL

Enthusiasm for Chisholm's campaign resulted in several unique expressions of support. During the Florida primary, Shirley saw a white man wearing a straw hat emblazoned "Chizm for President." When Shirley walked over to him and pointed out that her name was misspelled the man enthusiastically responded "That doesn't matter! I want you for president!"[53] There were even unusual fundraisers, such as the "Blintzes for Chisholm" event. At the 1972 Democratic National Convention, there were more women delegates than in previous years. One delegate waved a sign that read, "Sissy" and an unidentified Florida campaign worker, who was also a songwriter composed a campaign song, the words of which highlighted the main issues of Shirley's Chisholm's campaign.

If looking road to freedom, take the Chisholm Trail . . .
Of peace and equality, take the Chisholm Trail . . .
Proposition coalition
Students, brothers, black and white
Put your efforts in a fight for everyone
If you're looking for brotherhood, take the Chisholm trail
And believe we all are equal, take the Chisholm trail
She will go where we can not

We will nudge her to spot she'll stay come Election Day
She will get us out of Vietnam
She will set our women free
Reach out to the minority
Vote for her on March 14
Make your one vote count
If you're looking for the road to freedom, take the Chisholm Trail
Take the Chisholm Trail[54]

The opening of the campaign was the New Hampshire Primary. Edmund Muskie was victorious. While he won the primary, it was by a smaller margin than was originally thought. He failed to receive 50 percent of the vote, largely because after his tearful speech denouncing a newspaper editorial that attacked his wife, the press portrayed him as emotionally unstable. Florida was the second primary and it was the first state where Chisholm actively campaigned, largely because it had a large population of African-Americans, youth, and a strong women's movement. One campaign stop took her to the Tiger Bay Club, a men's luncheon club that had never had a woman speaker. Chisholm said that the club had 100 percent attendance when she spoke, and the audience was all-white businessmen, whom she perceived to be conservative. In her talk, she brought out the contents of one of her position papers that focused on foreign policy. When she stressed that the plight of the Palestinian refugees was the primary concern Americans should have in the Middle East, some of the audience thought that Shirley was pro-Arab or anti-Israeli. Shirley believed they simply could not see that what she was saying was that the trouble in the situation resulted in large part from the cruel way the refugees were ignored by everyone—including Americans—for more than twenty years.[55] Another Florida speaking event took her to Florida State University where Shirley expected the white students to be cool, even hostile and instead, she found the crowd of two thousand students warm and enthusiastic.[56] Because Shirley Chisholm did not have the funding to hire professional organizers, the volunteers became divisive in their efforts, often competing with each other rather than keeping their efforts focused on the campaign. Shirley commented on her reliance on volunteers: "There was no alternative to depending on volunteers. . . . We never did lack for eager volunteers, but there was no one who could give them clear-cut directions. Some work was duplicated while other chores were left undone."[57] In a southern state, the big issue was busing. Despite large and enthusiastic crowds gathered for Chisholm when she spoke, she received only 4 percent of the Florida vote.[58] Shirley Chisholm continued her campaign wherever she could get on the ballot and had enough volunteers to set up speaking events. She campaigned in New York, New Jersey, California, Massachusetts, Minnesota, Michigan, and North Carolina. There were some states in which Chisholm was on the ballot but never had time to visit, and others in which she won delegates despite a single appearance. Overall, people in fourteen states voted for Shirley Chisholm for president, in some fashion or the other. After six months of campaigning in eleven primaries, she had twenty-eight delegates committed to vote for her at the Democratic Convention.[59] Chisholm received 4.4 percent of the California primary vote, but George McGovern won the primary and California had a "winner take all" primary. After the losers challenged the policy, the credential committee decided to eliminate the "winner take all" policy, giving Chisholm 12 votes. However, when the committee report and recommendations went before the full convention on Monday night in July, the recommendation on California was reversed and all of the McGovern delegates were seated. That decision gave George McGovern a lock on the nomination. All the candidate nominations and speeches after that were just window dressing.[60]

The 1972 Democratic National Convention in July in Miami was the first major convention in which an African American woman was considered for the presidential nomination. Although she did not win the nomination, she received 151 of the delegates' votes. She stuck it out until the end and she did go into the convention with delegates. She wanted to affect political change with the power of her delegates. At a speech of the women's caucus at the 1972 Democratic National Convention, it was clear that Shirley Chisholm felt victorious in her goal to make change within the Democratic party and in the entire political establishment. Smiling widely and speaking even faster than usual, an excited, even exuberant Shirley Chisholm said to the women in the audience of the luncheon meeting held during the week of the convention: "I am just so thankful that in spite of the differences of opinions, the differences of ideology, and even sometimes within the women's movement the differences of approaches, that here we are today at a glorious gathering of women in Miami." At another speech at the Miami convention, this one to the Black caucus, she said in a more serious tone. "My brothers and sisters let me tell it to you this afternoon like it really is. There's only one thing that you my brothers and sisters have going—the only thing you have going is your one vote. DON'T sell that vote out! The black people of America are watching us. Find out what these candidates who need our votes to get across the top are going to do for us concretely." Finally, at the end of the Miami convention, Shirley gave a Unity speech. She remarked, that "In Unity there is strength and that it is the delegates who made history tonight. The delegates that made history tonight. And so, in closing, in closing, God be with all of you and I pledge myself to criss-crossing this country once again in terms of a voter registration campaign to swell those roads to unseat the incumbent, Richard Milhouse Nixon in November.[61]

Shirley Chishom gave George McGovern's campaign for president a lift when she joined him on the campaign trail in October. She had decided to help him campaign for the presidency when he phoned her and asked her to do so. She told a rally at the Bedford-Stuyvesant Restoration Center in her home area that she had found much alienation and confusion among voters and some were wondering whether they should participate in the election. She cautioned that those who did not participate would get "what they deserve if they send Nixon back to the White House."[62] Richard Milhous Nixon won a landslide victory. When his involvement in the break-in at the Democrats' National Committee headquarters at the Watergate building was discovered, he and his administration officials were caught in a cover-up. The cover-up unraveled the Nixon presidency and President Nixon resigned on August 8, 1974. Gerald Ford became the thirty-eighth President of the United State.

SHIRLEY CHISHOLM'S PRESIDENTIAL OBSTACLES

Shirley Chisholm identified the biggest obstacle to her presidential race in a keynote address she gave before the National Women's Political Caucus Convention in Houston in 1973. "One of my biggest problems was that my campaign was viewed as a symbolic gesture. While I realized that my campaign was an important rallying symbol for women and that my presence in the race forced the other candidates to deal with issues relating to women, my primary objective was to force people to accept me as a real, viable candidate."[63] The fact that people thought her campaign was only symbolic was another obstacle that Chisholm noted in the same speech: "Many people, including feminists, thought that since I 'didn't have a chance.'"

The media repeatedly described her as the "first black woman to seek a presidential nomination." The media also reported admirers of Ms. Chisholm conceding privately, that "she had at least two strikes—her sex and her race—against her."[64]

SHIRLEY CHISHOLM'S
COMMUNICATION STYLE

Ms. Chisholm's early training on the debate team at Brooklyn College served her well when she spoke in public as an assemblywoman, a congresswoman, and a presidential candidate. Her experience as a speech writer for other New York assemblymen[65] was evident in the skillful use of language that she used in her own speeches. Chisholm became one of the foremost female orators in the United States. She earned this reputation not because she was African American or a woman during the turbulent period of civil rights advocacy when tokenism to both groups was perceived as a means of appeasement but because she was strong, understood her audience and their needs, and was politically and morally persuasive.[66] Her posture was always ram-rod straight and her earnestness was palpable. Shirley knew she could stir a crowd because she noted: "I have a way of talking that does something to people."[67]

At a luncheon meeting of Delta Sigma Theta sorority—an organization of African American college graduates and professional women, Shirley stated: "Everyone in Washington tells me I'm just a freshman congressman, and you're supposed to keep quiet as a freshman," she told the women. "I listen sweetly to them and then I say, 'Thank you for your advice, gentlemen.' But when I get up there on the floor of Congress, I'm sure you'll understand that I'm speaking with the pent-up emotions of the community!" The audience applauded her warmly and she continued "One thing the people in New York and Washington are afraid of is *her mouth!*"[68] If there is one feature of Shirley Chisholm's oratory that stands out it is her voice. Despite her pronounced lisp, Ms. Chisholm was a forceful speaker who demanded the audience's attention. Her voice was strong and always had a self-righteous tone. She also kept the audience interested with her fast-paced vocal expression and incisive remarks. The audience might have been startled into listening, since her voice was markedly different than the sea of male candidates who were more likely to use euphemisms than Chisholm's to-the-point, street smart, declarative statements. There was no flowery language, no indirect reference. Another characteristic of her public speaking, her clarity, was evident in every speech she gave. When Shirley Chisholm spoke, she made it clear exactly what she meant. Maybe her clarity of purpose stemmed from her early training as a preschool teacher, because she was used to making understandable, to even the youngest mind, what she was trying to explain. More likely, her assertive and no-nonsense tone stemmed from her West Indies roots where she learned early to speak her mind succinctly and directly, so as not to be reprimanded by her teachers and grandmother, who had more to do than wait to figure out what Shirley meant. Her clarity was evident in this statement: "I am a candidate for the Presidency of the United States. I make that statement proudly, in the full knowledge that, as a black person and as a female person, I do not have a chance

of actually gaining that office in this election year. I make that statement seriously, knowing that my candidacy itself can change the face
and future of American politics—that it will be important to the needs
and hopes of every one of you—even though, in the conventional sense,
I will not win."[69] Another example of her clarity of purpose was in her
August 10, 1970, speech delivered to Congress in support of the Equal
Rights Amendment. "This is what it comes down to: artificial distinc-
tions between persons must be wiped out of the law. Legal discrimination between the sexes is, in almost every instance, founded on out-
moded views of society and the pre-scientific beliefs about psychology
and physiology. It is time to sweep away these relics of the past and set
further generations free of them."[70] This tendency of Shirley Chisholm
to state what she meant clearly and matter-of-factly while at the same
time challenging the norms of the time can be found in many of her
speeches.

A characteristic of Shirley Chisholm's public speaking was that she had
the ability to state what seemed far fetched in a tone that made the statement seem an imperative. "Realistic dreaming" is only one of the characteristics of Shirley Chisholm's public speaking. There are others, such as
her genuine message and practical application of her thesis. When Shirley
Chisholm spoke, she did not sound like a political insider. Perhaps her immigrant parents instilled in her the strong idea of helping others, and of
being a citizen of the United States, with all of the rights that privilege
brings that gave her public speaking a personal, genuine characteristic.
Listen to the humanitarian plea and connection to her own life that Ms.
Chisholm makes in this speech on May 21, 1969, on behalf of the Equal
Rights Amendment:

> When a young woman graduates from college and starts looking for a job,
> she is likely to have a frustrating and even demeaning experience ahead of
> her. If she walks into an office for an interview, the first question she will be
> asked is, "Do you type?". . . . A woman who aspires to be the chairman of the
> board or a member of the House does so for exactly the same reason as any
> man: She thinks she can do the job and she wants to try.[71]

She often used heroic language reminiscent of a church hymnal. With her
right fist raised high, she concluded a speech at the National Welfare
Right's Organization's fifth annual convention:

> The time has come, brothers and sisters, when we must rise up and assert our
> rights. Forget conventionalism. Forget whether you are in your place or out of
> your place. DO that which you have to do. Looking only to your God, who-
> ever your God may be, and your conscience for approval. Peace and power.[72]

INVENTION

As a member of Congress, as a presidential candidate and for the rest of her life, Shirley Chisholm spoke on behalf of the marginalized. "She was a mouthpiece for the underdog, the poor, underprivileged people, the people who did not have much of a chance," said her former husband, Conrad Chisholm.[73] While in Congress, she spoke in favor of the Equal Rights Amendment. On August 10, 1970, she said, "Mr. Speaker, House Joint Resolution 264, before us today, which provides for equality under the law for both men and women, represents one of the most clear-cut opportunities we are likely to have to declare our faith in the principles that shaped our constitution. . . . Discrimination against women, solely on the basis of their sex, is so widespread, that it seems, to many persons, normal, neutral, natural and right."[74] When she announced her candidacy for president, the same themes that were a hallmark of her speeches as a congresswoman emerged in her speech at the Baptist church on January 25, 1972: "I have faith in the American people. I believe that we are intelligent enough to recognize the talent, energy and dedication, which all Americans, including women and minorities have to offer."[75] She knew she wouldn't be elected president of the United States and she also knew that in many ways people viewed her as a "side show attraction"[76] but that made her message all the more effective, since she spoke on behalf of those who were outside the margins of acceptability. Because of that her voice is all the more true and the meaning in her message more poignant. As a presidential candidate, she made a speech on May 6, 1972, in the Rose Room of the Palace Hotel at the Commonwealth Club meeting in California. She was warmly introduced with the following words: Shirley Chisholm is a graduate of Brooklyn College and a postgraduate scholar of Columbia University. She serves with inspiring leadership in many educational, charitable, and civic organizations. She represents the district of Brooklyn in the United States Congress. Presently, she is campaigning for the Democratic nomination for president of the United States as a catalyst for change. The Commonwealth Club of California presents the Honorable Shirley A. Chisholm. In her characteristic directness, she began: "Ladies and gentlemen, I am very glad to be here this afternoon. As all of you are well aware of the fact by now, in spite of what has been said about my candidacy, I indeed am a very serious candidate for the presidency of this country. It's recognized that it takes a little bit of time for people to get over a few psychological shocks now and then. But then, if we're going to be able to effect change within the system, even though said system has not given a lot of people hope because of color, sex or other factors, that they have to be people who are just merely Catholics and there have to be people who say, we dare. They have to be people who just say, look we're just as good as the rest of you and even though you may snicker and laugh, you're going to make a try at it. So I'm out here, having lots of fun, giving a message that is sorely needed. . . . " She then states the problems of the country: "The disastrous performance of the economy under the current administration can be largely understood as the result of the big business orientation of this government and its utter disregard for critical problems of the consumer."[77] When the speech was over, Ms. Chisholm fielded several questions from the audience. Most of the questions asked how Ms. Chisholm would handle several issues in her administration, such as "We move now to specific items of legislation. Federal welfare is a mess. As president, what recommendations would you make?"

Shirley agreed with her questioner: "It *is* a mess. It is really a mess, but you can't talk about meaningful welfare in this country unless you understand certain other facts. Over one-third of the public assistance cases in this country fall in the ADC category, the Aid to Dependent Children category. These parents need the childcare centers that were vetoed in the bill. If these parents have the childcare centers, then they'll be able to go to training centers and schools and get the skills necessary for the jobs that are going begging in their specific communities. If we do not talk about nationalization of daycare centers in this country you are not going to have meaningful welfare. You know, you can call any piece of legislation welfare reform, education reform, but you have to look exactly at what is going to be the total and end result of the piece of legislation. Again, you can't have welfare reform by asking people to go out to work for something below the federal minimum, but they should be so glad to go to work. A gentleman said to me the other day, 'These men don't want to work. I had fifty jobs to offer them and Mrs. Chisholm, I only got six of them to take the job.' And I said to him, 'Well, what were you paying and what was the job?' He hesitated. I said, 'No, no, come on, tell me. What were you paying and what were the jobs that you were offering them?' Cleaning out toilet facilities and they were offering them $1.15 an hour! Now, a lot of people in this country think that poor people don't have dignity and don't have pride, they should be so glad to get anything. I think there'd be people in this country that we're willing to give 75 cents an hour and they should salaam!

"Now, I think we have to understand that if we're going to do something about the federal welfare in this country, the whole welfare program which is a mess, we're going to have to restructure it in three basic ways. You're going to have to set up national daycare centers. You're going to have to have training programs to train those who are employable and this is another mistake. There are lots of people on welfare in this country that are not employable. But those who are employable and able to get the kind of training so that they can go out and get one of the jobs that are going begging in their specific communities. You cannot continue to handle welfare in this country in a piecemeal fashion. A lot of programs put together to appease different groups who are yelling about the situation in this country, but the program actually has no meaning or no relevance for the people for whom they're designed. And when I become president, I would be able to fix this mess up." The final question was that of semantics for a title not yet given to anyone in the United States: Do you think a female president should be addressed at Miss, Mrs., Ms., Your Excellency, or Madame? Shirley replied with pragmatism: It really doesn't make that much difference to me. The important thing, the important thing is first of all; get that female president to help straighten out a lot of things in America.[78]

DISPOSITION

Shirley Chisholm frequently organized her ideas by identifying a problem, such as racism or sexism, and then proposing a solution. She didn't ease into her talks; instead she focused immediately on the thesis of the speech. She forcefully brought the problem explained in the speech to the forefront of her talk by calling attention to it in a dramatic way. For example, she began her speech in Congress on March 16, 1969, without mincing words: "Mr. Speaker, on the same day President Nixon announced he had decided the United States will not be safe unless we start to build a defense system against missiles, the Head Start Program in the District of Columbia was cut back for the lack of money."[79] She chose not to ease the listener into the speech; she brought the matter straight to the attention of the listeners in ways that some audience members found confrontational. If she was confrontational, it was because she thought the problem persisted for too long and needed to be solved at once.

Notice in this speech, which Ms. Chisholm delivered several times throughout 1971 and 1972 to various women's groups, how she states upfront the immediate problem and then concludes the speech with the proposed solution:

At one time or another we have all used the phrase "economic justice." This afternoon I would like to turn your attention to economic justice for women.

Of course this is only an illusory phrase, as it is an undeniable fact that economic justice for women in America does not exist. . . . We live in revolutionary times. The shackles that various groups have worn for centuries are being cast off. This is evidenced by the "developing" nations of the world, which we consider, for the most part, underdeveloped. Countries such as India, Ceylon and Israel have women for Prime Ministers and in other decision-making positions. American women must stand and fight—be militant even—for rights which are ours. Not necessarily on soapboxes should we voice our sentiments, but in the community and at the polls. We must demand and get day care centers, better job training, and more opportunities to enter fields and professions of our choosing and stop accepting what is handed to us.[80]

Ms. Chisholm had a heroic use of language. "The time has come in America. We cannot accept things the way they are." Ever-confident, with boldness and bravery, she didn't just "say" her speech and its thesis, she declared it. She demonstrated by her own behavior that you didn't have an excuse for trying harder, doing more, and standing up for what you believed in.

Ms. Chisholm was a prepared public speaker who organized her presentations in a coherent way. She publicly rebuked politicians who she claimed did not prepare for their speeches. She said in a speech to the National Press Club during her presidential bid, "It is pathetic to have to listen to politicians who before they get up, do not know what they are going to say: when they are speaking, do not know what they are saying: and when they have sat down, do not know what they have said."[81]

MEMORIA

Shirley Chisholm's command of her material—rhetorical memoria—is notable. Her precise use of language and her ever-confident delivery make her a speaker who would make a room grow silent in anticipation of her next utterance. "Most of my speeches were ad lib, and if any of them survive, it must be in the form of film or tape."[82]

Her ability to ad lib with eloquence probably stemmed from her utter sincerity and exquisite command of the English language. Because she frequently repeated similar topics, such as equal rights, health care costs, day care, and education, she was able to speak with impact because she had committed the salient features of her arguments to memory.

Ms. Chisholm did have notes inside of a manila folder in front of her when she delivered her speech to announce her presidential bid on January 25, 1972. Speaking behind a bank of many television and radio station microphones, she was able to maintain much eye contact with her audience; she had committed large sections of her announcement speech to memory. Note how she speaks on behalf of all Americans in this statement from her announcement speech:

> Fellow Americans, we have looked in vain to the Nixon administration for the courage, the spirit, the character, and the words to lift us. To bring out the best in us, to rekindle in each of us our faith in the American dream. Yet all we have received in return is just another smooth exercise in political manipulation, deceit and deception, callousness and indifference to our individual problems and a disgusting playing of divisive politics—pitting the young against the old, labor against management, north against south, and black against white. The abiding concern of this administration has been one of political expediency, rather than the needs of man's nature. At the end of her speech, she invited her audience to "go down the Chisholm Trail in 1972."[83]

AFTER HER PRESIDENTIAL BID

She continued to serve in the House of Representatives until 1982. Shirley Chisholm considered a run for mayor of New York City in 1989, but decided not to proceed. She was considered by Independent presidential candidates John Anderson and Ross Perot in 1980 and 1982 as a potential running mate.[84] Shirley Chisholm retired from politics after her last term in office in 1983. She stayed active by teaching politics and women's studies at Mount Holyoke College in Massachusetts. She received nearly forty honorary degrees, and her awards included Alumna of the Year, Brooklyn College; Key Woman of the Year; Outstanding Work in the Field of Child Welfare; and Woman of Achievement. President Bill Clinton nominated her to be ambassador to Jamaica and in August 2004, the White House Project highlighted her career at the Democratic National Convention by showing a biographical film titled "Chisholm '72: Unbought and Unbossed." When Shola Lynch, the producer and director of the documentary, asked Shirley Chisholm how she would like to be remembered, Chisholm replied: "When I die, I want to be remembered as a woman who lived in the twentieth century and who dared to be a catalyst of change. I don't want to be remembered as the first black woman who went to Congress. And I don't even want to be remembered as the first woman who happened to be black to make a bid for the presidency. I want to be remembered as a woman who fought for change in the twentieth century.

That's what I want."[85] Ms. Shirley Chisholm died January 1, 2005, in Ormond, Florida, at the age of eighty. On January 4, 2005, the 109th Congress introduced a bill to posthumously award a Congressional gold medal to Shirley Chisholm, noting that she was an historic figure in American political history. Among other achievements, she inspired and led the march of political achievement by African Americans and women in the three decades since she ran for the presidency of the United States and her election to Congress. Her candidacy for the presidency raised the profile and aspirations of all African Americans and women in the field of politics.

NOTES

1. Slogan from a campaign button pictured at www.jofreeman.com/polhistory/chisholm.htm (accessed February 22, 2005).

2. Shirley Chisholm, speech, Economic Justice for Women, 1971–1972. This speech is printed in the appendix of Shirley Chisholm, *Unbought and Unbossed.* (New York: Harper and Row), 1973.

3. www.chisholm72.net/campaign_an.html (accessed February 22, 2005).

4. Susan Brownmiller. "This Is Fighting Shirley Chisholm." *New York Times*, April 13, 1969, SM32.

5. *New York Times*, January 26, 1972, A1.

6. Statement by former fellow Congressman Ron Dellums in the documentary film "*Chisholm'72: Unbought & Unbossed."* 2003.

7. Brad Koplinski. *Hats in the Ring: Conversations with Presidential Candidates.* Bethesda, Md.: Presidential Publishing, 2000, 100.

8. Shirley Chisholm's quote from "*Chisholm '72: Unbought and Unbossed,"* a documentary film, 2003.

9. Adrienne Yvette Smith. *Trailblazers on the Hill: The First African-American Women in Washington (Shirley Chisholm, New York, Barbara Jordan, Texas, Carol Moseley Braun, Illinois).* Unpublished thesis, Regent University, 1999, 5.

10. Shirley Chisholm. *Unbought and Unbossed.* (Boston, MA: Houghton-Mifflin), 1970), 5.

11. Ibid., 6.

12. Ibid., 15.

13. Ibid., 23.

14. Ibid., 23.

15. Ibid., 26.

16. Ibid., 25

17. Ibid., 26.

18. *Unbought and Unbossed*, 28.

19. Ibid., 31.

20. *Unbought and Unbossed*, 46.

21. Ibid., 37.

22. Betty Friedan. *The Feminine Mystique.* (New York: Dell Publishing), 1963.

23. Myra Marx Ferree. "A Woman for President? Changing Responses 1958–1972." *Public Opinion Quarterly,* Fall 1974, Volume 38, Issue 3, 390–400.

24. Eleanor Clift and Tom Brazaitis. *Madam President: Women Trailblazing the Leadership Trail.* (New York: Routledge, 2003), 267.

25. Brownmiller. SM32.

26. *Unbought and Unbossed,* 81–82.

27. Richard L. Maddens. "Mrs. Chisholm Gets Off House Farm Committee." *New York Times,* January 30, 1969, A16.

28. *Unbought and Unbossed,* 86–87.

29. *Unbought and Unbossed,* 96– 97.

30. www.boxer.senate.gov (accessed 15 March, 2005).

31. Shirley Washington. *Outstanding Women Members of Congress.* (Washington, D.C.: United States Capital Historical Society, 1995), 17.

32. Shirley Chisholm. *The Good Fight.* (New York: Harper and Row, 1973), 12.

33. Thomas A. Johnson. "Rep. Chisholm Declares that She May Run for President." *New York Times,* 1 August 1971, 40.

34. Ibid.

35. "Mrs. Chisholm Says Support Is Growing." *New York Times,* October 4, 1971, 22.

36. Slogan from a campaign button pictured at www.jofreeman.com/polhistory/chisholm.htm (accessed 22 February 2005).

37. Shirley Chisholm. *The Good Fight.* (New York: Harper and Row, 1973), 13.

38. Ibid.

39. Ibid.

40. Statement by Congresswoman Barbara Lee in the documentary film *Chisholm '72: Unbought and Unbossed.* 2003.

41. Slogan from Shirley Chisholm's presidential bid that she used to end her announcement speech January 25, 1972 and which subsequently became the refrain of a campaign speech written for Shirley Chisholm's presidential race.

42. Ibid., 44.

43. Koplinski, 102–103.

44. Koplinski, 99.

45. *New York Times,* 4 February 1972, 10.

46. Koplinski, 98.

47. Maria Braden. *Women Politicians and the Media.* (Lexington: The University Press of Kentucky, 1996), 190.

48. Koplinski. 462–464.

49. Conrad Chisholm, interview with Nichola Gutgold, July 5, 2005.

50. *Chisholm '72: Unbought and Unbossed,* documentary.

51. *New York Times,* January 26, 1972, 1.

52. *Unbought and Unbossed,* 151.

53. *The Good Fight,* 61.

54. www.chisholm72/net/campaign_an.html (accessed March 11, 2005). From the film *Chisholm: Pursuing the Dream* (1972) by Bob Denby and Tom

Werner. Producer/director Shola Lynch in email correspondence with the author noted that the song's author is unknown.

55. The Good Fight, 59.

56. Ibid., 60.

57. Ibid., 64.

58. www.jofreeman.com/polhistory/cisholm.html (accessed February 22, 2005).

59. Ibid.

60. Ibid.

61. These three speech excerpts were transcribed from "*Chisholm '72: Unbought and Unbossed*," documentary film, 2003.

62. Thomas P. Ronan. "Shirley Chisholm Gives McGovern Drive a Push." *New York Times*, October 20, 1972, 20.

63. *Representative American Speeches.* (New York: H. W. Wilson, 1994/1995), Volume 21, 79–81.

64. Frank Lynn. "New Hat in Ring: Mrs. Chisholm's." *New York Times*, January 26, 1972, 1.

65. Bermard K. Duffy and Halford R. Ryan. *American Orators of the Twentieth Century.* (Westport, Conn.: Greenwood Press, 1987), 63.

66. Ibid.

67. Brownmiller. SM32.

68. Susan Brownmiller. *Shirley Chisholm.* (New York: Archway Paperback, 1972), 99–100.

69. Gloria Steinem. "The Ticket That Might Have Been. . . ." *Ms.*, January 13, 1973.

70. Halford Ross Ryan (Ed.). *American Rhetoric from Roosevelt to Reagan*, 2nd edition, (Prospect Heights, Ill.: Waveland Press, 1987), 220–224.

71. Ibid.

72. Thomas A. Johnson. "Representative Chisholm Declares that She May Run for President in 1972." *New York Times*, August 1, 1971, 40.

73. www.commondreams.org/headlines05/0103-01.html (accessed February 28, 2005).

74. Ryan. 220–224.

75. www.chisholm72.net/campaign_an.html (accessed February 22, 2005).

76. This is the term Shirley Chisholm used to describe herself. *Unbought and Unbossed*, xi.

77. www.commonwealthclub.org/archive/20thcentury/72-95chisholm-speech.html (accessed February 24, 2005).

78. Ibid.

79. Ibid.

80. *The Good Fight*, 188 and 192.

81. "Mrs. Chisholm Declares Two Rivals Are Mediocre." *New York Times*, April 21, 1972, 44.

82. Ibid., 187.

83. *The Good Fight*, 88.

84. Brad Koplinski, 98.

85. Transcribed from *Chisholm '72: Unbought and Unbossed.* documentary film, 2003.

Patricia Schroeder. Photo reprinted with permission of Patricia Schroeder.

3

Patricia Scott Schroeder
"Rendezvous with Reality"[1]

I had one idea [running for president] that if I could offer nothing more than honesty and common sense to Americans, they would respond. This country has serious problems that we must face. After seven years of happy talk, we need a rendezvous with reality. And if we address these problems honestly and straightforwardly, we can have a rendezvous with opportunity.[2]

The *New York Times* front page story came before any formal announcement speech that 1988 presidential hopeful Pat Schroeder might have made. "May run for President" appeared under a photo of the forty-six-year-old senior member of the House of Representatives who was urged to run for president after Democratic candidate Gary Hart dropped out of the race.[3] "I was on a plane headed to Denver and when I got off, the world was there. I never had to call a press conference," said Schroeder. She had conceded to an Associated Press reporter that she was thinking about running, and less than an hour later the story appeared on CNN and on the newswires. Her small group of advisors had considered making a public announcement in a couple of weeks, but there was no need after the story broke that made her presidential aspirations known. When she stepped off the plane, she told reporters: "People have asked me to look at it [running for President] seriously, and I feel I have to look at it seriously."[4]

In 1984, when Democrat Geraldine Ferraro made history by being the first female vice presidential candidate of a major party, Schroeder said that "Women have to run like men do. We have to run for president."[5] After years of encouraging other women to run, or as she called it "serving back," Pat Schroeder was encouraged to enter the presidential race. She said she did it because she felt a duty as a woman and a leader. She served as a co-chairperson of Gary Hart's presidential campaign until it collapsed. She was deluged with calls from supporters around the nation asking her to do what she had encouraged so many others to do: run for office. "May your words be tender and juicy because you often have to eat them," she said, with her characteristic glibness.[6]

"Angry" and "frustrated"[7] about Reagan Administration policies, firebrand Congresswoman Schroeder wanted to give the Reagan Administration a "rendezvous with reality." She contemplated entering the race, which included Massachusetts Governor Michael S. Dukakis, Delaware Senator Joseph R. Biden Jr., former Arizona Governor Bruce Babbitt, Missouri Representative Richard A. Gephardt, Illinois Senator Paul Simon, Reverend Jesse Jackson, and Tennessee Senator Albert Gore, Jr. Dukakis would ultimately win the Democratic nomination.

She told an audience at the National Organization for Women Convention during her exploratory bid that "We have got to remind people that America is every bit as progressive as the Philippines, Great Britain, India, Israel, and Norway, which have had female heads of state."[8] She grew up in a time when girls were encouraged to be ladies, marry young, and never utter a word that would offend anyone, and she became a brilliant, energetic, outspoken advocate for children, family life, and matters of national defense. What conditions helped to develop Patricia Scott Schroeder into a leading politician who demonstrated a talent for phrase-turning and outspokenness when most women were content to stay behind the scenes? How did she manage her own young, growing family while championing the cause of improved family conditions for America? To learn what shaped this trailblazer, a look at the early life of Patricia Scott Schroeder is worthwhile.

LEARNING TO FLY AND SOARING
AS A POLITICAL TRAILBLAZER

Patricia Nell Scott was born in Portland, Oregon, in 1940, but she didn't stay there long. By the time Pat graduated from high school she had lived in Missouri, Nebraska, Iowa, Texas, and Ohio. Her father, Lee, who worked in aviation, moved frequently for his job. During World War II her father taught aviation for the Army Air Corps and Pat adjusted by developing a communication strategy to make new friends quickly:

> Starting at three, whenever we moved, I had to find kids to play with in the new neighborhood, so as soon as the moving truck pulled away, I would line up my toys on the sidewalk and sit down next to them. It worked. The toys were like flypaper! I made friends almost at once.[9]

Pat's mother, Bernice, was a public school teacher, who encouraged learning and creativity. Pat said her mother "treated the whole house as a bulletin board," hanging homemade decorations for the holidays. More important, her mother was a strong role model for her daughter. She believed that women should have their own careers, and during the war, she placed Pat and her younger brother Mike in day care so she could work. Pat said that her mother always worked and contributed. "The nice thing was I never had a hang up about having a working mother. She was great and she knew what she was doing."[10] Her parents also taught her to be persistent. When doctors told her parents that she might be blind by the time she was five or six, Lee Schroeder would not accept that. He flew Pat to many doctors around the country until a treatment was discovered that would prevent the loss of her eyesight. Pat was also encouraged early on to take responsibility for her decisions. One way that her parents built a sense of responsibility in her was to give her enough money at the beginning of the month for her school lunch and other small necessities. If she wasn't careful budgeting her money, she would not be able to eat during the school day if her allowance ran out. And even though her parents' friends thought that was too much to ask of a grade school child, she thinks it was that child rearing strategy that made her self-reliant.[11] Later, when she was a teenager, her parents gave her a car, but insisted that she purchase the gas for it and keep from having any accidents. If she couldn't do those things, the car would be taken away. When raising her own children she and her husband Jim followed a similar tack, and found that the "hands off" approach was much better than the "control freak" method that she has noticed so many parents adopting.[12] The family ate dinner together as often as possible, a tradition that Pat brought to her own parenting. During her years as a congresswoman, her family ate at least three dinners a week together, and sometimes they dined in the Congressional Dining Hall when sessions ran late. Growing up, the talk around the table often turned to current events and politics, something that was repeated again as Pat raised her own family.

Her father, who Pat described as "a great Irishman," had a sign over the mantel that proudly stated, "We owe allegiance to no crown." "He was very proud of the great political heritage of this country; of everyone being able to participate."[13] Growing up, she and her brother were encouraged to argue both sides of an argument, and believes that this enabled her to sharpen her verbal skills and hang in to fight [an argument] until the bitter end.[14] She also credited her easygoing flexibility to the "lack of planning" that prevailed in her childhood home. Her parents would take impromptu flying trips in the family plane and her mother's work schedule often called for spontaneous solutions to everyday problems.[15]

When she was just fifteen, she earned her pilot's license, which in 1955 was rare, especially for such a young girl. The ability to fly helped Patricia to pay her own way through college at the University of Minnesota. She worked as an aviator claims adjuster and had even saved enough money for graduate school at Harvard Law School, and a flashy aqua blue Lincoln Continental. She rented planes for $10.00 per hour from the University of Minnesota's ROTC program and she enjoyed the independence that flying gave her. At that time, women were not permitted in ROTC, a rule that has since been rescinded. She described the changes she went through during her college experience:

> A quiet shift away from the conservatism of the postwar Midwest was beginning to take place. The civil rights movement was burgeoning and Senator Hubert Humphrey drew huge crowds when he spoke on campus. He fired our imaginations with talk of racial and economic justice. When, as Senate majority leader, he was able to shepherd through the Congress important civil right legislation, I felt that anything was possible and that I could be a part of it.[16]

Patricia Scott enjoyed her college experience at the University of Minnesota, where women felt they belonged and competed for achievement alongside the male students.[17] Several things really impressed Pat Schroeder and one of the most memorable were the visits by Senator Humphrey. She said "he would really spend a lot of time with the young people there. I got involved in student politics there. He taught people how to be political."[18] She excelled academically, studied Chinese, and finished in three years instead of four. She graduated from the University of Minnesota, magna cum laude and Phi Beta Kappa. She didn't give much thought about what she would do, like most of the women who went to college with her. She noted that most of the women in her sorority, Chi Omega, paid more attention to finding a husband than studying. "I had wanted to go to law school for as long as I could remember,"[19] although her mother lamented that with a law degree from Harvard, no one would ever marry her. In very short time, however, she met her future husband, Jim Schroeder, a fellow classmate at Harvard Law, and married him in 1962. Pat graduated one of only nineteen women in her graduating class in 1964 but had an "absolutely miserable" time at Harvard Law School and described it as the "best preparation for infiltrating the boys' club of Congress."[20] She found herself "submerged in sexism"; on her first day one of her male classmates refused to sit next to her, simply because she was a woman. The bright spot of Harvard Law School was meeting Jim and since they were both students they forged an egalitarian home life from the start. "Part of the key to our successful marriage was that going to law school together taught us how to fight without personalizing or internalizing."[21] While Pat Schroeder became the more famous spouse, Jim Schroeder was an important political figure in his own right, having served as a deputy under secretary of farm and foreign agricultural services at the United States Department of Agriculture during the Clinton administration. Jim Schroeder also made an unsuccessful bid for a Colorado legislature seat in 1970 and previously worked as a Denver district captain, which oversees political workers.[22] When his wife won a congressional seat, Jim moved to Washington, D.C., and practiced international law. Being married to a famous and busy career woman, Jim often was questioned by reporters about his life as "Mr. Mom." Patricia Schroeder often speaks lovingly and proudly about her husband and family, and she makes it clear that while Jim was supportive, he was no "Mr. Mom." Showing his good sense of humor, Jim Schroeder started the "Denis Thatcher Society," (named for the spouse of former Britain Prime Minister, Margaret Thatcher) for "men married to successful women."[23] "Everyone brings expectations to a marriage—I'm sure Jim never expected he'd be sleeping with a congresswoman. But he had always been my biggest booster and never made his support contingent upon his needs being met. Our standard joke was, 'When are we going to get a wife?'"[24] In a speech she gave to college students she said that when reporters asked her what her biggest fear was as a newly elected congresswoman with young children, she would respond, only half joking, "losing my housekeeper."[25] The "Champion of the Great American Family"[26] by all accounts had her own family as a model for the work that she was doing in Washington on behalf of families throughout the country.

When she and Jim moved to Denver she found work in the Denver office of the National Labor Relations Board and when her first child, Scott, was born in 1966, she scaled down her work to include projects of interest to her that she could do at home while she cared for her son. She also did pro bono work for two of her most cherished causes, Rocky Mountain Planned Parenthood and Denver Fair Housing Group. She became a hearing officer for the Colorado State Personnel Board and she taught political science and constitutional law for the University of Colorado and later Regis College. In 1970 their daughter, Jamie, was born. At the time Jim worked for a small law firm and served on an ad hoc committee looking for a candidate to run against the incumbent congressman from Denver's first district. Pat Schroeder's congressional career was not part of a master plan that she and Jim dreamed up while at Harvard Law School together. Instead, it was by chance that she ran and she didn't expect to win. While her explanations that "If I ever thought I was going to win, I never would have run"[27] sometimes get her in trouble with feminists, she notes that her flippant attitude was not formed because of her gender, but rather her political party. "In 1972, no Democrat had a chance. I wasn't trying to act like an unwilling politician, or a little lady; I just didn't think a Democrat could win."[28] Although, when Jim came home and suggested that Pat run she thought he was crazy, but his reasoning made sense after she thought about it. Jim said "There's no way you'll ever win this thing. You probably can't even win the primary. But if you don't get in the race and articulate the issues, they will not be discussed. You think the government's policies about Vietnam and the environment are wrongheaded, and you're always urging your students get involved. It's an opportunity that may not come again."[29] Persuaded to run, she announced her candidacy in a downtown hotel and posed for photos holding her then one-year-old daughter, Jamie. The picture ran in newspapers around the world. Her parents—who had been on a three-week tour of Asia—wanted to have Pat tested for drugs when they returned from their trip. They were shocked to learn that their daughter—a young mother who never wanted to run for anything—was indeed running for Congress.

Pat Schroeder quickly built a willing team of supporters who helped to organize her campaign, mostly from her dining room table. Even though she was sure she couldn't win, she wanted to do as well as she could. Her supporters, which consisted of her college students, and young couples who were friends of the Schroeders, were integral to the campaign. She also had the support of a grass roots team of campaigners that were organized by Craig Barnes, a young lawyer defeated two years earlier by James D. "Mike" McKevitt. The enthusiastic young politicos were ready to roll up their sleeves and do what they could to help her campaign. She said, "Quickly I built a team. My juices were flowing. I figured I couldn't win, but I sure wanted to show."[30] Even Gloria Steinem, who had never met Pat, came to stump for her in Denver. Even with this strong support, Pat was very disappointed when the National Women's Political Caucus, which she helped found in 1970, did not support her. The main reason was that the leaders of the organization felt that it was too early for a woman to run for Congress. Even the National Labor Relations Board, where Pat had worked, sent a mere $50.00 check to support her campaign.

Her campaign was based on direct mail advertising, designed by a friend of the Schroeders' who worked in advertising. It was a thrifty campaign because Pat noted "I didn't want to run up any debt that I'd be stuck with when I lost on Election Day."[31] One of the posters showed gravestones in a military cemetery with a quote from one of Nixon's speeches: "Yes, many of our troops have already been withdrawn."[32] The beginning of the terse one-liners that have shaped the rhetorical message of Pat Schroeder's career may have begun on those campaign posters. As time went on, Pat was known for one-line zingers that despite, or because of their brevity, got tremendous media attention. During her first congressional campaign Pat Schroeder got attention for her brief statement at the Democratic Party convention. While other candidates received several minutes to articulate their views, when Pat stood to speak, party leaders told her that she only had 30 seconds. So, she said succinctly. "I support the lettuce boycott" and the audience roared. During the campaign, she became best known for supporting the lettuce boycott.[33] She described her rhetorical strategy by saying that during her campaigns and congressional career, "I tried to paint word pictures because the media likes colorful, short statements."[34]

On election night both Pat and Jim Schroeder could not believe their eyes and ears when in fact Pat Schroeder had won a congressional seat by 52 percent of the vote. The next day, as they had promised their children, they took a family vacation to Disneyland as they contemplated what the next stage of their lives would involve. Pat noted "What better place to regroup and plan ahead than Tomorrowland?"[35]

When Pat Schroeder arrived in Washington she was "bright, energetic and ready to question everything."[36] The freshman congresswoman was interested in human, quality of life issues, such as better housing, health care, and a better environment. She realized that if she wanted money for her causes, an appointment on the committee where the most discretionary money was spent, which was about 40 percent of the national budget, was the best choice. As she put it, "I can talk all I want about human issues—they've got the dollars."[37] Another reason was her sentiment about the Vietnam War, "I was opposed to the [Vietnam] War and thought some diversity would be good on the committee."[38] With that in mind, she lobbied to get a slot on the Armed Services Committee, which was a male-only committee. The chairman of the committee, F. Edward Hebert, did not consider Pat worthy of a seat. "Women," he claimed, "knew nothing of combat, since historically they have never been a part of it."[39] Through her research of the backgrounds of the members of the committee, Pat discovered that many of the members of the committee had never served in the armed forces themselves. So when Hebert tried to embarrass Pat by asking her "How can you serve on this committee? You have never been in combat," she calmly replied "then you and I have a lot in common."[40] Pat Schroeder got a seat on the committee, the first woman ever to do so, but she was forced to share a chair with Congressman Ron Dellums. She was mistreated and ignored by Chairman Hebert who resented her presence, as well as that of Dellums, the only African American on the committee. She persisted with her goals on the committee and managed to get stockpiles of bombs demilitarized and detoxified, including those in her home state of Colorado where a wildlife sanctuary now exists. Pat Schroeder notes, "From one of America's most contaminated sites to a beautiful wildlife refuge in ten years. Progress is possible."[41] Schroeder thought Hebert was sexist, and she wasn't afraid to stand up to him, although many of her colleagues, both male and female were. In an essay Pat Schroeder wrote in the *Nation* she said that members of Congress "need not and ought not to defer to their more senior peers. There is nothing personal in this at all. It is simply that my constituents elected me to work for sensible changes now, not twenty years from now. I did not keep my views on runaway military budgets secret in Denver. There is no reason why I should keep them secret in Washington."[42] As a sharp critic of excessive defense spending, she advocated defense burden-sharing, which calls upon our allies to share the cost of their military protection by the United States. She also helped to pass the Military Family Acts, defense authorization bills that provide for increased reimbursement for moving expenses. She was the key player in rewriting the country's pension laws so divorced spouses could share in their partners' pensions as part of property settlements. Pension reform efforts began when she proposed changes to benefit spouses of civil service employees. She advocated for Foreign Service wives who had traveled extensively with their husbands, relocating frequently and thus unable to establish careers and pensions of their own while contributing to their husband's careers and their family's welfare. Her initial argument was later extended to secure pension sharing for the spouses of military and CIA personnel who get divorced. These changes in the federal pension rules laid the groundwork for the 1984 revisions in private pension systems so that private pensions would be considered in property settlements.

Through her work in Congress, Pat Schroeder also helped write and pass the 1978 Ethics Act as well as legislation allowing the federal government to start flextime, to hire more part-time workers, and the Civil Reform Act that included protection for whistleblowers. She also introduced legislation later passed by the House to help communities set up child care programs before and after school.[43] Pat also co-sponsored the Equal Rights Amendment. Throughout her congressional career Pat Schroeder had committee assignments that included the House Judiciary Committee and House Select Committee on Children, Youth, and Families, and the Post Office and Civil Service Committee. In addition, she became a Democratic Whip in 1978 and was the co-founder and was co-chair of the Congressional Caucus for Women's Issues. Through her work on the Congressional Caucus for Women's Issues, Pat Schroeder focused on strengthening child support laws, through the Child Support Enforcement Amendment, known more casually as the "Deadbeat Dads' Act." The bill, sponsored by Congresswoman Barbara Kennelly of Connecticut, which calls for mandatory wage withholding if child support payments were thirty days overdue, gained the support of the Reagan Administration, partly because Elizabeth Dole, then Secretary of Transportation and Margaret Heckler, then Secretary of Health and Human Services, persuaded President Reagan that the bill needed to be passed.[44] Because so few women were in positions of power, they bonded together on issues of mutual support, regardless of party affiliation. One of the rhetorical strategies that Pat Schroeder used to help pass the legislation that improves family life, was to take the case to the press. She knew that the concerns of the mostly male, middle-aged Congress were not the same as the younger, financially less well off members of the press.

"We need family leave, they aren't receptive to families, so what do I do?" So I'd think, 'Okay, go to the press. Look at their ages, look at their lifestyles. The press will understand family leave. Can I get them interested and use it as a platform?'"

> When you look at the American public, only ten percent of the American families look like the traditional Norman Rockwell or Ozzie and Harriet. But if you look at Congress, Senate and our elected officials, only ten percent don't look like Ozzie and Harriet. Because they are at an income level where there can be a full time caregiver at home. When you talk about childcare, they hear babysitter for when you play tennis.[45]

RUN, PAT, RUN![46] PATRICIA SCHROEDER FOR PRESIDENT '88

When rumors of his marital infidelity made their way to the press corps, Democratic presidential hopeful Gary Hart had dared the press to "Go ahead and follow me." He could have been talking to Pat, since her decision to explore a run for president was the result of his reputation as a womanizer being verified by *Miami Herald* reporters who took him up on his suggestion. In 1987 Patricia Schroeder was a co-chair of Hart's presidential campaign when it imploded in May shortly after photos of the married Hart, with a woman—not his wife—on a yacht in Florida, appeared in the press. Democrats were devastated that the Hart campaign ended so abruptly and they were in need of a viable replacement. It was late for anyone to start a campaign, but many Hart supporters looked to Pat Schroeder and she felt that she had to respond. She had encouraged others to run for office, she had been outspoken about women getting involved. She commented: "What we have in our society is men going into the huddle, and then coming back to tell us what happened. We as women have to get into the huddle. I want women in the huddle making decisions."[47] Patricia Schroeder had to practice what she preached. She had to go into the huddle.

Although she was going in late, Dan Buck, her administrative assistant, said she would have one advantage over the other Democratic contenders: "She graduated from high school in Iowa, she got married in Iowa and she still has a lot of relatives in Iowa." The Iowa caucuses in February would be the first official voting of the 1988 primary campaign.[48] Another advantage Schroeder had was experience. "She has been in Congress longer than [Richard] Gephardt, has had more legislation enacted than [Joseph] Biden," said Ann Lewis, a political adviser.[49]

"The only reason to go in this is to win. I think America is man enough to back a woman," said Patricia Schroeder as she began an exploratory campaign swing through New Hampshire to get a sense of what financial and grass roots support her bid for the presidency would have.[50] During her exploratory bid, Pat Schroeder had spent nearly four months talking with people, speaking publicly, and determining whether or not her candidacy would be viable. As usual, she had a succinct and memorable way to gauge whether or not she would get in the race with the quip, "No dough, no go."[51] At the end of a three-day swing through Iowa, Minnesota, and New Hampshire, Schroeder said that she believed there were enough uncommitted Democrats to justify her candidacy in 1988, and she promised to make her decision by the end of the summer of 1987. As of June she had raised $235,000–$300,000 and had sent out a mailing asking 27,000 voters for more money. And, although her "no dough, no go" statement meant that she would not continue if she didn't have $2 million by September, her advisers were saying in June that a reasonable promise of money would be enough to make her run anyway.[52] Although she was a member of Congress with fifteen years of experience, she was written about and questioned as a symbol of all women. "Like it or not, my potential candidacy for the highest elective office in our country was going to be a hook for America watchers, political analysts and newspaper columnists to appraise the progress of women in this country."[53] Reporters asked her what sounds like a stupid question, "Are you running as a woman?" (They probably meant: "Are women's issues the main focus of your candidacy?") But, to journalists' poorly worded question, "Are you running as a woman?" the sharp tongued, lightning fast wit of Pat Schroeder simply deadpanned, "Do I have an option?" It had only been three years since Geraldine Ferraro, the only woman in American history to be on a national political ticket, had run for vice president, so there were many comparisons in the press between Schroeder and Ferraro. *New York Times'* Maureen Dowd noted that when Geraldine Ferraro was introduced when she ran for Vice President, the speaker would finish the introduction with "and most of all, a mother."[54] Not much had changed from 1984 to 1987, except that the euphoria that greeted Ms. Ferraro's nomination in 1984 seemed more like ambivalence among Democratic officials and woman activists at the idea of a woman running. One top Democratic woman explained the hesitancy among some politically active women this way: "Partly, it's the pain and danger left over from 1984 and a kind of dread that if Pat's campaign doesn't go well in terms of raising money, it will be one more example of 'you see, women are not ready for prime time.'"[55]

From June through September, Pat traveled to twenty-nine states to "jump start" a presidential campaign and determine if her candidacy for the presidency was viable. She wanted to make her candidacy official by September, if she chose to run, because if she didn't make up her mind her House seat would be in jeopardy.

Toward the end of her exploratory bid, she spoke at the National Press Club in Washington, D.C., and she proposed the following:

> Our presidents would get themselves into considerably less trouble if they were required to read, learn and know the Constitution. Our electoral process could be improved. Many of the candidate forums are nothing more than special interest questionnaires in masquerade. Maybe we should replace the debates with the kinds of interrogations we normally direct at Supreme Court nominees.

She also repeatedly asked the question: "Is America better off?" She said:

> Seven years ago this summer, Ronald Reagan was traveling this land and asking voters if they were individually better off than they were four years previously. In 1988 we need to ask whether the country is better off. Since 1980, stock values have risen by more than two trillion dollars, but the median family income, adjusted for inflation, remains below the 1980 level. Is America better off? Since 1980, prices of homes have escalated beyond the reach of countless young families. Many young people today will never reach the same standard of living their parents did. Is America better off? Since 1980, federal aid to education has been slashed. College students and their parents are daunted by enormous loan payments. Less advantaged students cannot stay in school. Is America better off? Since 1980, the United States has gone from being the world's greatest creditor nation to being the world's greatest debtor. Is America better off? Since 1980, our federal deficit has spurted to record levels, combining all the deficits of our previous presidents from Washington to Carter. Is America better off?[56]

During her travels across the country she met people of all ages who wanted their elected officials to understand what was going on in their lives and that the policies in Washington should reflect that understanding. Because many of her audiences asked her personal questions about how she managed her family life, it became clear to her that most Americans were struggling with the issues of child and family care that she was most compelled to address. Often when Pat spoke during her exploratory bid for the presidency, and addressed the need for government to help America with the concerns of family and child care, she received a standing ovation. By August, Pat Schroeder was third in the *Time* magazine poll. The National Organization of Women had pledged about $400,000, enough for Pat to qualify for federal matching funds in several states.[57] But Pat felt that third place in the poll was as good as she would be able to poll and to make a bid, there would be a need for her to spend a considerable amount of her own money. She also believed she had insufficient time to amass enough delegates to win the nomination.

The 28th of September was a bright, sunny day and 2,000 enthusiastic supporters were gathered outside the Denver Civic Center waiting to hear what their candidate Pat Schroeder would say. They hoped she would tell them what they wanted to hear most: that she would be a candidate for president in 1988. But even though her husband Jim tried to talk her out of quitting the race, Pat Schroeder decided not to go any further. She reflected, "I knew the speech was going to be tricky. My message was a paradox: my summer exploration had been so successful that I was not going to run. I wanted to make it clear that my decision was based on my knowledge that winning would take a lot more preparation, time and money than I had."[58] Pat Schroeder approached the podium, certain the she had made the right choice. As she approached the podium, the crowd started chanting, "Run, Pat, run!" She began her speech thanking the many people that supported her, including her parents and brother Mike, who were in the audience. They had devoted themselves to her exploratory bid all summer. Pat continued her speech by saying: "I learned a lot about America and a lot about Pat Schroeder. And that's why I will not be a candidate for president." The audience began groaning a negative "no" and Pat caught a glimpse of her parents, who had never seen her retreat from a challenge before. The crowd began to earnestly chant again, "Run, Pat, run!" and Pat got emotional and wept for seventeen seconds. She felt so badly about letting her supporters down. She said, "I was probably tired . . . I'd had the whole family together, telling all of them and then all the staff that it was a no go, and everybody was all upset. But it was really having two thousand friends out there, who have given up their vacations, their summers, their weekends, everything. They want you to say, 'By golly, we are going to go on.' You really feel like you are just throwing cold water on their dream."[59]

The press made a big deal of her tears. Some reports indicated that her tears were a sign that women are weak. One New Yorker remarked that she was upset because "people will have this knee-jerk reaction now about women. It's another example that women have to be more perfect than perfect. It's OK for men to show emotion, but not women."[60] "I was frankly stunned when I saw her do it," said Linda DiVall, a Republican pollster. "I certainly sympathize with the fact that it was an incredibly emotional moment, but it seems to me her inability to command her emotions when she was making an announcement about the presidency only served to reinforce some basic stereotypes about women running for office—those stereotypes being lack of composure, inability to make tough decisions."[61] *Washington Post* columnist Judy Mann commented that "people who were dismayed about her tears seemed to feel that she had betrayed womankind by playing into the old stereotypes about women being too emotional and too easily distraught in stressful situations. Heavens, Schroeder might take to tears if arm control negotiations broke down. Does the world need a weepy woman next to the red telephone?"[62] Howard Means, an *Orlando Sentinel* columnist had a positive view of Pat Schroeder's tears, "Schroeder's [speech] at least had a human quality: Tears shed in emotion are one of the great points of differentiation between mankind and the lesser beasts. . . . For presidential stock, I'll take a bona fide human being anytime. Most to the point, if Schroeder was being honest—if she really did get out of the race because she couldn't figure any way to run a campaign 'where you can stay in touch with people'—she should have cried, and people who care about presidential politics should have wept right along with her."[63]

Montague Kern of the *Washington Post* commented, "To the degree that she was expressing the frustration of women candidates, Pat Schroeder's tears were rational ones."[64] During her first speech after her exploratory bid, she acknowledged the media responses to her tears and said, "I will never apologize for my tears. I say, no tears, no heart."[65] She even joked, "The good news is that Kleenex says that if I get back in the race they'll be a corporate sponsor."[66]

Reflecting on her presidential race in a television interview, Pat Schroeder smiled her wide, toothy grin and said, "I learned that I don't look like a president. Everyone said 'you don't look like a president.' And I would say 'you are absolutely right. We've never had a president who looked like me.'" She paused and more seriously, continued, "I learned that as much as you think you know how big this country is, it isn't a country, it is a continent, it really is. And it is magnificent—the diversity between Alaska to the tip of Florida and Maine to way out there in Hawaii which is so wonderful and lovely and all the places in between and you think 'this is an incredible system that keeps us all together because when you look at other countries that are very small and they are all fighting over minor differences. When you see it [America] it is really incredible.'" When asked if she would do anything differently if she ran for president again, she had specific ideas about how presidential races should change:

I think this whole thing where you fly airport to airport and they throw you out on a tarmac like a wind-up doll and you try to play this game that you were "there" and you really care about wherever it is that you happen to be and if it isn't written right on your card, you'll get it wrong. It is really phony and people see through that. I'd like to see a presidential race where you can really talk to real people. I think that the way you do it is you deal with it more through the local media rather than having this whole flying menagerie with you and you are all hermetically sealed together. It is like you are on a safari for thirty-five days. You don't really see America, you see each other in this hermetically sealed metal tube that you all live in. There's got to be a better way to break it out [a presidential race] and regionalize it more. And I think all Americans would learn from it too because you would have more of a regional impact. And we'd learn more about the different regions. Maybe we'd be more understanding why one region feels one issue is more important than another. Instead of the same old canned spiel for everybody and basically because you are so terrorized that you will offend someone the canned spiel is nothing. It's how to sound profound and say nothing.[67]

After Pat Schroeder's exploratory bid ended she viewed it as "a positive thing—we answered a lot of questions, learned a tremendous amount. . . . We just have to keep working on it. Women must not wait to be asked [to run]. They're never going to be asked, especially for a seat where somebody thinks they can win. We have to keep building networks of financial support, political support, issue support. It isn't easy. It's very tough."[68]

PATRICIA SCHROEDER'S PRESIDENTIAL OBSTACLES

She got in late. When Patricia Schroeder began to test the waters in 1987 as the Democratic replacement candidate for Gary Hart, "She did publicly this summer what most politicians like [Bill] Bradley and [Sam] Nunn, did privately: they made some calls, met with the money people, tested the waters quietly."[69] Her lateness was said to be the reason the PBS political show *Firing Line* refused to allow her in the first debate, and the AFL-CIO refused to include her videotape in the candidate tapes sent to all local union meetings for potential convention delegates.[70]

The first double bind for women in leadership noted by Kathleen Hall Jamieson, "women can exercise their wombs or their brains, but not both"[71] was one that Patricia Schroeder faced. Her first day on Capitol Hill, she responded to male colleagues who questioned her ability to lead with: "I have a brain and a uterus and I use them both."[72] She was barraged with the usual gender questions and comments: "Are you running as a woman?" and "You don't look like the President." Schroeder said, "I didn't want to deny my gender, but I didn't want my gender to block my message. Many could not get beyond the fact that I looked so different from the others."[73] On her swing through some southern states during her exploratory bid, a Democratic state chairman introduced her in glowing terms, admiring her style, that she know more about national defense than all the other candidates combined, and then ended the introduction by saying, "Of course I won't vote for her, because I have a problem with a man for First Lady."[74] Another similar reference to the problem of a woman candidate's image, Schroeder said, "Nobody knows what to do with a woman . . . wear earrings; don't wear earrings. Wear jewelry; don't wear jewelry. Wear bright colors; don't wear bright colors. We know what a male candidate looks like who's hard working: You loosen the shirt collar, you loosen the tie, you throw the coat over the shoulder, you're running down steps and there's a dome over your shoulder. But there just is not a model for women."[75] An article in the *Boston Globe* summed up the sentiment in the feminist community of the Schroeder near candidacy: "Far from being a unifying force, Schroeder's brief candidacy rent the women's community, splitting it into camps. There were those who rallied to Schroeder because of her pioneer status, her scimitar wit, and her own unfailing support for issues of concern to women during her fifteen years in Congress; and others who said Schroeder's bid, despite her best efforts, was merely symbolic, and who choose instead to work on electing a progressive man."[76]

While Shirley Chisholm stated, "As a black person and as a female person, I do not have a chance of actually gaining that office [President of the United States] in this election year," Schroeder refused to speak in the same way, that is, acknowledging that her presidential bid was only a symbolic one. Schroeder made it clear that she did not want her race to be a "suicide mission" or a symbolic campaign.

PATRICIA SCHROEDER'S COMMUNICATION STYLE

Patricia Schroeder is a prolific public speaker, who receives offers weekly to speak at educational institutions, business gatherings and political fundraisers. She is registered as a speaker at the Harry Walker Agency, New York, an agency that schedules speaking events for celebrities and earns a percentage of the fees paid to the speaker. She is aware of the power of effective speech and understands the importance of her role as a speaker.

Her style is self-confident, and informal, yet articulate. Her strong patriotism and her love of country come through even when she strikes her often cynical tone. In a speech she gave toward the end of her almost four-month presidential exploratory bid, Patricia Schroeder said:

> The Washington I left behind was not only humid, but stale. Here, we are always fighting yesterday's battles. The horse is always out of the barn. The water is always over the dam. The bridge is always crossed—or if it is not crossed, it's burned. But out in America, all is still tomorrow. The American spirit is still alive and braced to soar into the 21st century. And although there is also turbulence in America, we have one calming influence. One document, several pieces of paper, whose 200th anniversary we celebrated last Thursday. The United States Constitution.[77]

Pat Schroeder's speeches are more like conversations where she tells stories about her experiences, often with self-deprecating humor. In some respects her speeches, while always dealing with important interests of global concern, sound like stand-up comedy routines. For example, in a speech she gave at the University of Denver in December 2002 as part of the Joint Lecture Series, "Bridges to the Future," she sarcastically said,

> Now, I never want to be controversial, so I, of course, will be very professor-like tonight. Let me say I am so surprised the Vice President isn't here. I phoned his office, and told him I was going to be here and I really thought he'd come by but he hasn't made it yet. So if he comes in, we'll point him out. I'll interrupt my speech at that point. I'm sure he'll want to hear this."[78]

For all of her jokes and humor, other, more admirable traits of Pat Schroeder come through when she speaks in public. Foremost, Patricia Schroeder's brilliance is apparent when she speaks in public. Her wealth of knowledge of politics and specifically her understanding of the issues she has heralded over the span of her career is obvious to anyone who listens to her for more than a few minutes. While she may frame her stances in terms that average citizens could easily understand, her own understanding is far more comprehensive. She speaks in a method that is reminiscent of a favorite college professor who, while brilliant beyond measure, weaves a simple story for the class so that students will understand the concept. For example, when she addressed the House of Representatives after she retired, to urge them to take the Comstock Act off the records, her research for her topic and adaptation for her audience, was evident. She began,

> There was in the past century a man named Mr. Comstock, and Mr. Comstock was one of these people who decided only he knew what was virtuous and right, and somehow he managed to convince all sorts of people that this was correct. He even in 1873 was able to get on the floor of this House, if you can imagine such a thing, and he stayed here all day long while the Congress was in session. He ran around with a satchel full of books and pictures, and he buttonholed every Member he could find saying, 'look at this, look at this.' He wanted a bill passed, which the Congress then passed unanimously, and they named it the Comstock Act after him because he had pushed so very hard for it.[79]

Another characteristic of Pat Schroeder's public speaking is her ability to take issues that others are not talking about and make people listen by relating the issues to the lives of the audience.

Finally, Pat Schroeder, for all of her deprecating humor, is a stunning and commanding woman. Tall and slim, with a youthful energy, she carries herself with poise and grace and is always fashionably attired. Her brown hair from youth, now a becoming silvery-white, her smile lights up her face and adds to her appeal as an authoritative and attractive rhetor. When she speaks her fast paced, yet low pitched and melodious tone, along with attention to her audience through relevant storytelling and direct eye contact are captivating.

INVENTION

Gadfly Pat Schroeder has consistently spoken out about issues which she is passionate about. Throughout her entire career she has articulated views about women and family, the ERA, the deficit, national defense, and health care issues. She often refers to her own experiences or those of people that she has met as reference points for the issues that are important to her, then she offers statistical proof for her claim. For example:

> I don't know how young couples manage to get their feet off the ground. Today, a car costs what a house did when I was first married. And college tuition is so expensive that universities have begun to arrange advance payment: new parents can now pay the going rate for four years of college for their child that will begin school seventeen or eighteen years later! Families are borrowing more money today than ever before to make ends meet. Sixty-five percent of the United States households are in debt and 55 percent owe more than they own in financial assets.[80]

She includes herself in the issues that she addresses:

> The American family is no longer a Norman Rockwell painting. We have become a nation of two income families, of single parent families—a nation of families under stress. We juggle jobs, schedules, parenting, family obligations and household budgets so that we can give our children the best life possible.[81]

In her speech to college students she compared the child care systems in America and Germany:

> You look at all developed countries. About once a year in the *Washington Post*, there is an article that says "If a lawyer working for the German government and spouse have a baby, what do they get, and if a lawyer and spouse working for the Federal government in the United States, what do they get?" Here, they get bills, stress and in Germany they get childcare, paid leave for both parents. In our society we tend to think that if we did this people would start having many, many babies for these benefits (Laughter).[82]

DISPOSITION

Patricia Schroeder is known for her memorable phrases. The most famous, perhaps is referring to Ronald Reagan as the "Teflon" president, because nothing sticks to him. The phrase literally popped into her head as she was frying eggs for her family for breakfast one morning. She said, "I was frying eggs and they slid off the pan, and I said 'that's it!' Reagan has Teflon coat, because nothing ever sticks to him."[83] Pat Schroeder explains her reasoning for use of these memorable phrases. "I think the hardest thing for me, even when I announced [my candidacy for Congress] in 1972 was that one of the problems I had with politics is that I couldn't really understand what people were talking about. It seems to me that the game is to say what you mean in all these words so that by the time you are finished everyone's eyes are glazed over . . . so I think the thing is to figure out how you take it and grab [and say what you mean] so that people understand it at the kitchen table. So people say 'that's right, that's what it is,' and people will get much more involved in the process."[84]

Pat Schroeder is also a direct public speaker; she gets to her point as succinctly as possible. She notes that it is more difficult to be direct than long winded, "I always got criticism that this was flip, shooting at the hip, but I always thought it was hard work. Like the old adage; 'I'm writing a long letter because I don't have time for a short one.'"[85]

MEMORIA

Patricia Schroeder's delivery is usually extemporaneous, with reliance only on a few words written down to jog her memory about points that she wants to address. "I basically just write down four to five key words."[86] She objects to prepared speeches, because she feels that it is pandering to an audience. She notes that because she has had so many experiences, "you could press a button [on her] and a speech comes out."[87] She also doesn't have time to re-write speeches that a speechwriter would write for her, and she thinks that she would have trouble sticking to the script of a prepared text:

> Folks are always asking for my text. The office always laughs and says [to me],"why would we give you a text? You are a text deviate if we do give you one." They just don't have time to do it. And I've never found anyone who wrote the way that I spoke. So anything they did write, I've never been able to deliver smoothly if I read it. I'd have to rewrite it and I just don't have that kind of time. I literally put in eighteen-hour days so there's no extra time to sit around and rewrite speeches.[88]

As a member of Congress, Patricia Schroeder did her own reading, research, and cataloging of material that she used to make arguments on the House floor. Her staff was always impressed with her ability to retain the material, particularly statistics and to bring it out extemporaneously in speeches.[89]

She doesn't have any concern about forgetting her speech, because she retells many of the stories that are contained in both of her autobiographies. Even though she is retelling these stories, they do not sound retold since she often changes them slightly to fit the occasion, without sacrificing the integrity of the story. She tries to create a conversational atmosphere by speaking in a way that is less formal than many public speakers do. For example, she uses many colloquial words, such as "folks," "sort of," "of course," "a bit."

Before she speaks, Pat Schroeder considers the people in her audience, what they are going through, and tries to relate their experiences with the main points of her speech. As she spoke she casually sipped a drink from a paper Pepsi cup, adding the casual, approachable style for which she has become known. During the forty-five-minute speech at Penn State, Patricia Schroeder stood at a podium and appeared to speak from memory, using no visible notes. Her style was casual and stream of consciousness, as she moved from one point to another, as if reminded by the previous point of another interesting story from her years in Congress. She often elicited laughter from the audience. Her persona was warm and intelligent; her voice low and melodious.

AFTER HER PRESIDENTIAL BID

In January 1988, Patricia Schroeder organized the *Great American Family Tour*, a traveling road show that focused on family issues. The tour coincided with the presidential primary races. Pat Schroeder felt that even though she wasn't a presidential candidate, she could impact the race by continuing to make the issues important to her in the news. Accompanying her on the tour were Dr. T. Berry Brazelton, the Harvard professor and authority on child development and Gary David Goldberg, executive producer of the enormously popular television show at the time, *Family Ties*.[90] Their mission was to bring to the forefront issues the she didn't think the presidential candidates were talking about enough, such as child care, family medical leave, flexibility in the workplace and pay equity. They visited hospitals, day cares, and community centers. Brazelton said that their goal was to show "how people are being hurt by the failure to support positive family policies."[91] Her tour even made some members of the press and other political campaigns skeptical that it signaled Pat Schroeder wasn't really out of the presidential race, or that she was angling for the job of vice president. Schroeder insisted that her objective wasn't to promote her own political career, but instead it was to try to solve the problems surrounding child care and other family needs.

As a result of the *Great American Family Tour*, Pat Schroeder noted that all the candidates ran off to day care centers. Pat told an interviewer, "It was very funny. They [the candidates] had no idea why they were there or what the issues were, but they were going, and we all tried to keep a straight face. We even had George Bush coming out for family medical leave, though he later vetoed it."[92]

After her exploratory bid for the presidency Pat Schroeder returned to her work in Congress and served until she retired in 1996. Soon after her exploratory bid she was asked if she might become a candidate for president in the future and she responded, "Oh sure. It's not like I've retired and gone into a spa."[93] But when 1992 got closer, and Democratic hopefuls wished she would consider a presidential race Pat Schroeder said that it was unlikely that she would run in 1992 because of the mood [in the country] created by the [Gulf] war. "You know what their [presidential candidates] campaign commercials are going to look like right now. They're not going to be about child care centers."[94] In the late 1990's when asked if she would run for President, she replied, "No, to be perfectly honest."[95]

She continues to be a strong and forceful advocate of the causes that she had championed since the beginning of her congressional career. She also spends a lot of time on college campuses, speaking with young people. She says: "I really think that if we don't keep working with our young people, we are in trouble. You meet these young people who their heroes are rock stars or athletes and they don't want anything to do with politics. We are the leaders of the free world and we have a generation growing up that doesn't care about politics and they don't want to be in politics . . . this country isn't going to make it if we don't excite the best and the brightest to get involved."[96]

Throughout her congressional career, Pat Schroeder, who was a co-sponsor of the Equal Rights Amendment, remained a strong supporter of the ERA and spoke about it whenever she could. From the start until the end of her congressional career she championed equal rights. In a televised debate on the ABC television program "Issues and Answers" opposite Phyllis Schafley, Schroeder noted that rhetorical strategy of her opponent frustrating: "she sounded like a lawyer, yet her fluffy, feminine attire and artificially sweet voice kept him [the moderator] from treating her like one."[97] She also formed a group that would police hiring practices within the Congress, since to her dismay, she noticed that there were no female pages or Capitol police. She felt that since "governments tax men and women equally, men and women [should] be treated equally at all levels of government."[98] Currently, Pat Schroeder still speaks out on issues about gender equality.

Throughout her congressional career, Pat Schroeder was a voice for many who were underrepresented. In 1991 she was one of six congresswomen who defiantly walked over to the Senate office building to ask Senate Majority Leader George Mitchell why a woman who alleges sexual harassment by Supreme Court Justice nominee Clarence Thomas, was told that she could not testify. After Anita Hill testified, and became a symbol of women's status in American life and, in particular, their exclusion from the halls of power,[99] the percentage of women elected to Congress in 1992 went from 5 percent to 10 percent[100] and 1992 became known as "the year of the woman."[101] Perhaps Pat Schroeder's outspokenness sprang from her constant realization that there were so many fewer women than men in Congress, and to be heard they would have to speak forcefully and persistently about the issues they cared about most. About Anita Hill's testimony, Schroeder said, "What shocked millions of viewers was the fact that the committee originally had decided not to investigate the charges brought against Thomas." The reason this happened, says Schroeder, is because of the imbalance of the committee's membership. All fourteen members of the Senate Judiciary Committee were men. "What upset me about the Thomas affair," Schroeder says, "was that they [the senators] didn't understand Ms. Hill's charges or how she felt." Schroeder says that what is true of the Judiciary Committee is true of Congress as a whole, it is not representative of the nation. "This is not to say that a man cannot understand women's concerns," Schroeder says. "But there is such a strong majority of men in Congress that it becomes like a locker room. As a result, women are like parsley flakes on a potato; they stand out because they are very few and far between."[102] Pat Schroeder echoed the same sentiment regarding the gender imbalance among elected officials when she appeared on the WNET and WTTW television program "Women in Politics" hosted by Bill Moyers. She said, "Imagine a picture of the House Floor of 406 women and 28 men or the Senate floor with 98 women and two men."[103]

A frequent speaker on college campuses around the country, on April 14, 1999, she spoke at Pennsylvania State University's Behrend College in Erie, Pennsylvania, as part of the college's distinguished speaker series. During her speech she said:

> Picture this: it is 1972 and a thirty-two-year-old woman is elected from "Marlboro Country." One of my favorite phone calls I got was from Bella Abzug and she said [Schroeder mimicked her voice] "I hear you got elected and I hear you have young kids. I don't think you can do it." And she was a progressive—our feminist at the time. Growing up my children felt like science experiments, because everyone kept asking them if they are alright. I was living and working family issues every single day.

In 1993, Pat Schroeder became the chairperson of the Subcommittee of Science Technology of the Armed Services Committee. The young Denver lawyer who had said "I never thought I would run for anything," had served twelve terms in Congress and made an historic exploration for the presidency. When she left Congress in 1996 after 24 years, she said that she did so because she "wanted to be on the top of my game." She also retorted, "The other [reason to leave Congress] was Newt [Gingrich, then GOP House Speaker]. I wondered if the body was big enough for both of us."[104] Her first six months out of office were spent teaching at Princeton University.

In 1997, Patricia Schroeder became president and CEO of the Association of American Publishers, Washington, D.C. She travels the country giving speeches about her role as AAP president and about issues she championed during her twenty-four-year congressional career. Pat especially enjoys speaking to college students. Like the public servant who inspired her, Senator Hubert Humphrey, she wants to fire up the young people in America and get them involved in the electoral process. In her 1999 speech to college students at Penn State University's Behrend College, she looked directly at her audience and said, "We are going to hand the torch off to you and you are going to keep the progress going."[105] She also enjoys spending time with her family, husband Jim, her two grown children, and her new baby granddaughter.

NOTES

1. This was the slogan from Pat Schroeder's presidential race.
2. Patricia Schroeder, speech, National Press Club, September 23, 1987. Obtained from the National Press Club Archives.
3. Phil Gailey. "Schroeder Considers Running for President." *New York Times*, June 6, 1987, 1, 33.
4. Pat Schroeder. *24 years of Housework and the Place is Still a Mess: My Life in Politics.* (Kansas City: Andrew McMeel Publishing, 1998), 178.
5. Judy Mann. "Schroeder for President." *Washington Post*, June 10, 1987, D–3.
6. John Aloysius Farrell. "Schroeder Tests Waters in New Hampshire for a Presidential Bid." *Boston Globe*, June 16, 1987, 1.
7. Elizabeth Mehren. "Representative Schroeder Tests Presidential Waters; Congresswoman in Iowa to Study Entry into Democratic Race." *Los Angeles Times*, June 13, 1987, 22.
8. "Schroeder Says United States Is Ready for Woman President; Eyes Bid." *Houston Chronicle*, July 19, 1987, 12. (HoustonChronicle.com accessed March 23, 2005).
9. Pat Schroeder. *Champion of the Great American Family.* (New York: Random House, 1989), 14.
10. American Profile Interview. "Life and Career of Patricia Schroeder," December 23, 1988. Obtained from www.cspan.org.
11. Pat Schroeder, interview with Nichola Gutgold, March 24, 2005.
12. Ibid.
13. American Profile Interview.
14. Ibid.
15. *Champion of the Great American Family*, 17.
16. Ibid., 88.
17. Ibid.
18. American Profile Interview.
19. Ibid., 89.
20. *24 Years*, 93, 94.

21. *24 Years*, 132.

22. Marie Lazzara. "Mr. Schroeder goes to Washington." *Elmhurst Press*, January 20, 1999.

23. Bryna J. Fireside. *Is There a Woman in the House . . . or Senate?* (Morton Grove, Ill.: Albert Whitman & Co. 1994), 83.

24. *24 years*, 131.

25. Speech obtained from Penn State University library system. Recorded speech from Penn State Behrend Speaker's Series, April 14, 1999.

26. Name of Schroeder's first autobiography, previously noted.

27. E. Claire Jerry and Michael Spangle. "Patricia Scott Scroeder." Chapter in *Women Public Speakers in the United States: A Bio-Critical Sourcebook*. Karlyn Kohrs Campbell, ed. (Wesport, Conn.: Greenwood Press, 1994), 396.

28. Pat Schroeder, interview with Nichola Gutgold, March 24, 2005.

29. *24 years*, 6.

30. Ibid., 10.

31. Ibid., 14.

32. Ibid., 11.

33. Ibid., 13.

34. Pat Schroeder, interview with Nichola Gutgold, July 30, 1998.

35. *24 years*, 17.

36. "People on the Cover." *Newsweek*. November, 1973, 4.

37. Judith Virst. "Congresswoman Pat Schroeder: The Woman Who Has a Bear by the Tail." *Newsweek*. November 1973, 7.

38. Bill McAllister. "Schroeder's Political Humor Leaves National Archives Crowd in Stitches." *Denver Post*, March 19, 2000, A10.

39. *Champion of the Great American Family*, 25.

40. Ibid., 25.

41. *24 years*, 48.

42. Claudia Smith Brinson. "Woman of the Year: Pat Schroeder." *Ms. Arlington*, January/February 1997, 56.

43. Mary S. Hartman. *Talking Leadership: Conversations with Powerful Women*. (New Brunswick, N.J.: Rutgers University Press, 1999), 226.

44. *Champion of the Great American Family*, 126–127.

45. Ibid., 17.

46. Run, Pat, run! was the chant of the crowd on September 28, 1987 when Pat Schroeder approached the microphone to explain to the crowd why she would not seek the presidency. *Champion of the Great American Family*, 7.

47. Patricia Schroeder, interview with Nichola Gutgold, July 30, 1998.

48. Gailey, 33.

49. "Schroeder Toe in Water." *Washington Post*, June 7, 1987, A6.

50. Farrell, 1.

51. Mehren, 22.

52. Maureen Dowd. "Schroeder at Ease with Femininity and Issues." *New York Times*, 23 August 1987.

53. Maria Braden. *Women Politicians and the Media*. (Lexington: University Press of Kentucky, 1996), 192.

54. Maureen Dowd. "Schroeder at Ease with Femininity and Issues." *New York Times*, August 23, 1987.

55. Ibid.

56. Patricia Schroeder, speech, National Press Club, September 23, 1987. Obtained from National Press Club Archives.

57. *24 years*, 181, 184.

58. *24 years*, 184–185.

59. Jane O'Reilly and Gloria Jacobs. "Watch Pat Run." *Ms.*, February 16, 1988, 44–51.

60. "I Did Not Plan to Be Emotional." *San Francisco Chronicle*, September 30, 1987, A 21.

61. Ibid.

62. Judy Mann. "Tears, Idle Tears." *Washington Post*. October 2, 1987, B3.

63. Howard Means. "At Least Pat Schroeder's Teary Adieu Has a Human Quality." *Orlando Sentinel*. October 4, 1987. www.infoweb.newsbank.com (accessed March 21, 2005).

64. Montague Kern. "Pat Schroeder's Real Tears." *Washington Post*. November 7, 1987. www.infoweb.newsback.com (accessed March 21, 2005).

65. "Schroeder: Female Candidates Trivialized." *Orlando Sentinel*, November 23, 1987. www.infoweb.newsbank.com (accessed March 21, 2005).

66. John Aloysius Farrell. "The Once and Future Candidate Pat Schroeder Still Has Her Eye on a White House Run." *Boston Globe*, 28 November 1987. www.infoweb.newsbank.com (accessed March 21, 2005).

67. American Profile Interview. "Life and Career of Patricia Schroeder." December 23, 1988. Obtained from www.cspan.org.

68. Marilyn Gardner. "Schroeder Sees Void in Campaign of Family Issues." *Christian Science Monitor*, November 30, 1987. www.infoweb.newsbank.com (accessed March 21, 2005).

69. Jane O'Reilly and Gloria Jacobs. "Watch Pat Run." *Ms.*, February 16, 1988, 44–51.

70. Ibid.

71. Kathleen Hall Jamieson. *Beyond the Double Bind*. (New York: Oxford University Press, 1995), 16.

72. Maureen Dowd. "Schroeder at Ease with Femininity and Issues." *New York Times*, August 23, 1987, Section 1, 24.

73. *24 years*, 180.

74. Ibid., 183.

75. John Aloysius Farrell. "The Once and Future Candidate Pat Schroeder Still Has Her Eye on a White House Run." *Boston Globe*, November 28, 1987. www.infoweb.newsbank.com (accessed March 21, 2005).

76. Renee Loth. "The Immigrants of the Political System. Patricia Schroeder's Exploratory Campaign Crystallized the Deep Conflicts Among Women." *Boston Globe*, November 1, 1987. www.infoweb.newsbank.com (accessed March 21, 2005).

77. Patricia Schroeder, speech, National Press Club, September 23, 1987. Obtained from the National Press Club archives.

78. *Vital Speeches of the Day*, January 1, 2003, 162–167.

79. Patricia Schroeder, speech, "Comstock Act Still on the Books," September 24, 1996. www.gos.sbc.edu (accessed April 4, 2005).

80. Patricia Schroeder, speech. National Press Club, September 23, 1987. Obtained from the National Press Club archives.

81. Patricia Schroeder, speech. April 14, 1999. Obtained from Penn State University's Behrend Speaker's Series.

82. Ibid.

83. Patricia Schroeder, speech. National Press Club, September 23, 1987. Obtained from National Press Club archives.

84. Ibid.

85. Patricia Schroeder, interview with Nichola Gutgold, July 30, 1998.

86. Ibid.

87. Ibid.

88. E. Claire Jerry and Michael Spangle. "Patricia Scott Scroeder." In *Women Public Speakers in the United States: A Bio-Critical Sourcebook.* Karlyn Kohrs Campbell, ed. (Wesport, Conn.: Greenwood Press, 1994), 397.

89. E. Claire Jerry and Michael Spangle, 399.

90. Jane O'Reilly and Gloria Jacobs. "Watch Pat Run." *Ms.*, February 16, 1988, 44–51.

91. Ibid.

92. Ruth B. Mandel and Mary S. Hartman. "Patricia Schroeder." In: *Conversations with Powerful Women.* Mary S. Hartman, ed. (New Brunswick, N. J.: Rutgers University Press, 1999), 232.

93. Marilyn Gardner. "Schroeder Sees Void in Campaign of Family Issues." *Christian Science Monitor*, November 30, 1987. www.infoweb.newsbank.com (accessed March 21, 2005).

94. Kirsten Lee Swartz. "Women's Conference Knows No Limits: Cal Lutheran Keynote Speaker Representative Patricia Schroeder Sees the Military as 'King of the Hill' not in Washington." *The Los Angeles Times*, March 3, 1991, B–3.

95. Mandel and Hartman, 232.

96. American Profile Interview. "Life and Career of Patricia Schroeder." December 23, 1988. Obtained from www.cspan.org.

97. Ibid., 94.

98. Ibid., 92.

99. Linda Witt, Karen M. Paget, and Glenna Matthews. *Running as a Woman: Gender and Power in American Politics.* (New York: The Free Press, 1994), 1.

100. *24 years*, 24.

101. Previously, 1974 and 1990 were called the "year of the woman" when women sought political office.

102. http://teacher.scholastic.com/researchtools/articlearchives/civics/usgovt/legis/timchcon.htm (accessed April 1, 2005).

103. *Women in Politics*, WNET and WTTW. August 15, 1991.

104. Bill McAllister. "Schroeder's Political Humor Leaves National Archives Crowd in Stitches." *Denver Post*, March 19, 2000, A10.

105. Speech obtained from Penn State University library system. Recorded speech from Penn State Behrend Speaker's Series, April 14, 1999.

Elizabeth Hanford Dole campaigns for the presidency. Courtesy of Elizabeth Hanford Dole.

4

Elizabeth Hanford Dole
"It's Her Turn"

I'm throwing down the gauntlet—to Members of Congress, both parties—Republicans and Democrats—and to the Members of this Administration. My challenge is this—by the time America's students begin their summer vacation next year, legislation that truly reforms education should be passed and signed into law. Let's not allow American students and teachers to begin another school year under the status quo. I can assure you this: If the President and the 106th Congress cannot reinvent public education, then President Dole and the 107th Congress will.[1]

"If I run, this will be why—I believe our people are looking for leaders who will call America to her better nature," said Elizabeth Dole. "Yes, we've been let down, and by people we should have been able to look up to."[2] With this swipe at the Clinton Administration, Elizabeth Dole began her exploratory bid for the presidency in Iowa on March 10, 1999. Earlier that year in January, when Elizabeth Dole stepped down as president of the American Red Cross, speculation in the press abounded that her next big move would be a run for the White House. Her attention-getting speech, to 500 cheering, sometimes teary-eyed employees, that she was leaving the Red Cross was highly publicized on television and in newspapers and magazines around the country. On January 18th, *Newsweek* said, "Elizabeth Dole may soon establish a campaign committee." CNN's popular political show, *Inside Politics* with Judy Woodruff, even named Dole's announcement the "Political Play of the Week," a testament to the public relations savvy of Elizabeth Dole. *Business Week* described her speech as a "media event" that was "vintage Elizabeth Dole."[3]

Even the choice of a slow news day, Monday, to make the announcement ensured that the press would pick up the story. In her Red Cross resignation speech, the ever polished and poised Elizabeth Dole told her audience: "I have not made definite plans about what I will do next. I didn't feel it was right to spend the time I owed to you thinking about anything but our work together. Soon, I will begin to consider new paths and there are exciting possibilities."[4] In an interview after her resignation speech, Elizabeth Dole said that she planned to decide by March whether to run. She said, "I'm going to give it serious consideration."[5] Elizabeth Dole did explore the viability of a presidential campaign in an exploratory campaign that lasted from March 1999 to October 1999 and during that time she consistently ran second in the polls to George W. Bush and well ahead of John McCain, Steve Forbes, Gary Bauer, and Alan Keyes. She also had high favorability ratings and consistently beat Al Gore in hypothetical head-to-head match-ups.[6] While she was a newcomer as a candidate, she was hardly a Washington outsider. Her career started in the Johnson Administration, giving her thirty-plus years of political experience. To discover where and when and how this notable public servant got her beginnings, a look at the early life and career of Elizabeth Hanford Dole is important.

SOUTHERN BELLE TURNED BELTWAY MAINSTAY

Mary Elizabeth Alexander Hanford came into the world on July 29, 1939, a welcomed only daughter for John and Mary Hanford, who thirteen years earlier had a son, John, Jr.[7] A beautiful baby grew into a precocious and curious toddler, who, by the age of two had nicknamed herself "Liddy." The name stuck and friends, family, and colleagues knew her as Liddy for many years in both Salisbury and Washington, D.C., until she made known that she preferred the more elegant "Elizabeth."

Young Elizabeth grew up in Salisbury, North Carolina, a genteel yet bustling Southern town located in the heartland of North Carolina, halfway between Charlotte and Greensboro. Elizabeth noted, "local residents nurtured a distinctively Southern ambience."[8] Her father was a local floral wholesaler, who built his company into a well-known entity, especially noted for its beautiful "Hanford" roses. The comfortable lifestyle protected the Hanford family from the hardship of the Depression. In addition to his floral company, John Hanford also owned real estate, including apartment buildings and rented apartments to area residents. Her mother, an accomplished musician, happily sacrificed the opportunity to study music at Juilliard for marriage and a family. Elizabeth said, "having abandoned her own career pursuit early on, she poured all the more love and energy into the lives of her children."⁹ Mrs. Hanford was a civic leader in Salisbury and a volunteer in her church. Until Mary Hanford's death in 2004, at the age of 102, Elizabeth described her as her "best friend," whom she called daily and visited often.

Both Hanford children excelled in school and tried their best to make the most of the opportunities afforded them. Elizabeth had a competitive streak from an early age, evidenced by her campaign, at age three, to become the mascot of her brother's high school graduation class. She won and by third grade, her political career was off the ground when she also won president of her third grade bird club. Both Elizabeth and her brother John were encouraged to make the most of every spare moment, and her goal-oriented parents often encouraged her to enter contests or get involved in community causes. After the attacks on Pearl Harbor, little Liddy Hanford worked with the Girl Scouts to collect stamps, tinfoil, and wastepaper. She excelled academically, by studying and often memorizing her work for spelling, mathematics, and reading, which was her favorite. One summer, she read forty books and in the fall, she established a book club at school and felt entitled to name herself president.¹⁰

The Hanford's comfortable lifestyle afforded Elizabeth the opportunity to travel and her family took train trips across country. These trips fostered Elizabeth's love of learning and encouraged her to aim high in her education and career goals. In high school, she was active in student government and made an unsuccessful bid for its presidency when she was a senior. Elizabeth ran for senior class president at Boyden High School and although she didn't win, her effort gave her a "lesson in how to lose," a lesson that she says is something "no one likes but from which most of us can benefit."¹¹ Elizabeth's potential as a leader was noticed by her classmates and she was voted "Most likely to succeed."

After Elizabeth graduated from high school, she followed in her brother's footsteps and enrolled at prestigious Duke University. At the time, the campus was split into male (West Campus) and female (East Campus). The segregation of males and females was extended to classrooms, where screens divided the room; in the girls' dormitory, windows were painted over so that neither sex could look in or out at the other. A freshman handbook stated the anticipated conduct for women: "A Duchess should have the tact and good judgment to know when the occasion requires her to be serious and when to be gay, when to dress up and when to be casual. Everything she does is in good taste and up to the highest standards."¹² Other rules at Duke that were distributed to freshmen upon admission included, Eat breakfast every day, Wear hats and hosiery to church, and write thank-you notes to your date and your hostess. With such a strong focus on conduct and demeanor, Duke University was as much a finishing school as it was a college. Elizabeth notes, "There might have been a moat surrounding the Duke Forrest, so insulated was our world."[13]

Although social opportunities abounded at Duke, and Elizabeth enjoyed some, her focus was more on her studies; she majored in political science, which was also unusual at the time. Upon graduation she won the Political Science Department's highest honors. As a freshman, she ran unsuccessfully for class representative, but in 1957 she was elected president of the Women's Student Government Association. Her campaign skills and leadership ability were so apparent, that even her opponent voted for her. "She was so well spoken, so thoughtful, so poised—I had to support her," recalled Karen Black Miller who remembers the Duke election.[14] In her campaign speech, Elizabeth forecasted, "With our changing world, it was and is necessary for us to change in order to adapt, even in our university life. We must remember that our influence is far reaching."[15] She developed her public speaking skills by taking a course in speech, which was unusual for women at the time, and she also learned parliamentary procedure. In her senior year, 1958, she was named "Leader of the Year" by both the men's and women's campuses. At the same time she was elected May Queen and a debutante in Raleigh. Duke University was a wonderfully positive experience for Dole, who "found the deans to be strong mentors, like her mother and grandmother."[16]

Most of her female classmates at Duke were preparing for marriage, but Elizabeth didn't feel ready. She graduated Phi Beta Kappa from Duke University and then moved to Boston, Massachusetts, where she became secretary to the head librarian at the Harvard Law School Library. She also enrolled in the Master of Arts degree program in Harvard University's School of Education, with a dual major in government. She was an engaging student teacher, but she decided that teaching wasn't the career path she wanted to pursue. She completed the master's program in 1960, and then moved to Washington, D.C., where she found a position as a secretary, working in the office of North Carolina Democratic Senator B. Everett Jordan. Elizabeth's mother said that her daughter was drawn "like a magnet" to Washington, D.C., and while Elizabeth was there she consulted Maine Senator Margaret Chase Smith for professional guidance. Senator Smith encouraged Elizabeth Hanford to earn a law degree if she wanted to contribute more to a job in public policy. The meeting with Senator Smith made such an impression on Elizabeth that to this day Dole notes, "whenever a young woman calls my office . . . I make time to see her. It's my way of paying a debt to the lady from Skowhegan."[17]

Elizabeth returned to Cambridge in September 1960 and began her studies at Harvard Law School. Despite her academic excellence and her considerable experience in the library of the law school and in Washington, D.C., Elizabeth notes, "I was less prepared for my first year of law school than I thought. There was nothing at Duke or the School of Education that compared with the impossible hours or beady eyed competition of Harvard Law."[18] Her experience at Harvard was "thoroughly unpleasant," mostly because of the sexism that Elizabeth Hanford faced as one of only twenty-four women in a class of 550 students.

Upon her graduation from Harvard Law School, twenty-nine-year-old Elizabeth moved to Washington, D.C., where she found a temporary position with the Department of Health, Education and Welfare (HEW), organizing a conference on deaf education. After passing the D.C. Bar Exam, she spent a year as a defender in night court. Her next position was with the Johnson Administration, working for the White House Office of Consumer Affairs under the direction of commercial spokeswoman Betty Furness. After Nixon became president, Elizabeth kept her position, under a new supervisor, Virginia Knauer, who had been head of the Pennsylvania Consumer Protection Bureau. The office was renamed the President's Committee on Consumer Interests, and Elizabeth was promoted to deputy. The committee was responsible for ensuring proper labeling on food items and enforcing expiration dates. Elizabeth excelled in the position and more and more her boss relied on her to make speeches on behalf of the organization. In 1972, Virginia Knauer introduced Elizabeth to Republican Senator Robert Dole from Kansas, who was also serving as the national chairman of the Republican Party. Several months after they met they began dating and three years later on December 5, 1975, they married; he was fifty-two and she was thirty-nine.

The newlyweds didn't have much time to grow accustomed to a prosaic routine as a couple, since just eight months later, Gerald Ford, who had replaced Nixon after his resignation, won the Republican nomination for president and asked Bob Dole to be his vice presidential candidate. Elizabeth was surprised by the turn her life took: "I wasn't too prepared for campaigning in general, since Bob and I were married in December and then we started campaigning barely eight months after the wedding. I was dropped into the middle of a national campaign."[19] While the new couple reveled in the thrill of the campaign, Elizabeth wondered what her husband's political aspirations meant to her career at the FTC. Elizabeth resolved the dilemma of a possible conflict of interest by taking a leave of absence from her position, but not before she received criticism from reporters who wondered why she would interrupt her career for her husband. Elizabeth Dole discovered she loved campaigning. She spent only one week on the campaign trail with her husband and then proposed going on the road alone, putting to use the public speaking skills she had fostered over the years. The Ford-Dole ticket lost to the Democratic ticket of Jimmy Carter and Walter Mondale.

In 1979, Bob Dole announced that he would be a candidate for the presidency in the 1980 election. Elizabeth's role in his campaign again became a matter of debate among her friends and colleagues and the press. Begging her not to send the wrong message to professional women, her feminist friends told Elizabeth that she shouldn't step down from her post at the FTC to campaign. But in March 1979, Elizabeth resigned from the FTC to devote her full attention to Bob's campaign.[20] She campaigned so much for Bob, that some confused voters thought that she was running. He dropped out of the race in the spring of 1980, saying with humor, "at about the time Elizabeth passed me in the polls."[21] Elizabeth Dole, now known as a viable campaigner in the Republican Party, campaigned vigorously for Ronald Reagan and George H. W. Bush. When Ronald Reagan won the presidency, he appointed Elizabeth head of the Office of Public Liaison. In that position, it was Elizabeth's job to marshal grass roots and organization support for the president's policies. In 1983, President Reagan invited Elizabeth to serve as secretary of transportation, a cabinet position responsible for 100,000 employees nationwide with a budget of $27 billion. As secretary of transportation, Dole made safety her priority and she instituted the third brake light, which came to be known as the "Dole light." She served in that position for almost five years, until she stepped down to campaign for her husband for the presidency in the 1988 election. Again there were complaints from those who thought Elizabeth Dole gave up her career to help her husband's. One article called, "Transportation Secretary Elizabeth H. Dole's resignation last week an important social story that illustrated the dilemma facing thousands of career women in the United States."[22] Elizabeth explained that it was her choice to campaign for her husband and that it was simply "giving up one cause and taking up another."[23] Once George H. W. Bush won the nomination, both Elizabeth and Bob were rumored to be on the short list of vice presidential candidates, but the choice was young Indiana Senator Dan Quayle. Once Bush was elected, Elizabeth was asked to be Secretary of Labor and she began to serve in that position in early 1989. During her tenure she targeted at-risk youth, women, and minorities. She left her work at the Labor Department to become President of the American Red Cross in 1991 to devote her energies to dire human needs on a full-time basis. She described her work at the American Red Cross as a "glorious mission field." In 1995, however, she took a one-year leave of absence to assist her husband in his bid for the presidency when Bob Dole won the Republican nomination. Elizabeth Dole was a tireless campaigner. Her years of campaigning seemed to culminate with this election. The presidency was handily won, however, by incumbent President Bill Clinton.

In 1999 Elizabeth Dole resigned from the American Red Cross to "consider new paths." In March 1999 she announced her exploratory bid for the presidency and withdrew from the race in October, citing a lack of funds. In her withdrawal speech, Elizabeth Dole promised that she was a "long way from the Twilight," which proved true when, in 2002 she won a U. S. Senate seat from her home state of North Carolina.

"LET'S MAKE HISTORY,"[24] ELIZABETH DOLE PRESIDENTIAL BID

Suggestions that Elizabeth Dole should run for president have been in the press since the 1980s. At the 1984 Republican National Convention, "Dole in '88" over cameo pictures of Bob and Elizabeth Dole were everywhere. During campaign 1984, Bob Dole said "There are a lot of people around here talking about 1988 . . . they're not talking to me, they're talking to Elizabeth." In 1988, one article speculated that, "One wonders, if her husband doesn't win this time, have they made an agreement that she gets the next crack at it?"[25] When Bob Dole withdrew from the 1988 race, the press focused on which one of them would be tapped for vice president. Columnist Ellen Goodman opined that one of Elizabeth's assets as vice president in 1988 was her appeal to both liberals and conservatives, and the kind of "ladylike women's rights advocate that passes muster in Republican circles."[26] And the *Washington Post* reported, "Elizabeth Dole is the very picture of a candidate's spouse, despite the fact that she continues to be on the short list of candidates herself."[27] Press buzz about the presidential potential of Elizabeth Dole hit an all-time high after her rousing speech at the 1996 GOP convention. At the conclusion of her speech, CBS anchor Dan Rather announced, "What you have witnessed here tonight is the birth of a new form of campaigning and a new standard for convention speeches by which others will likely be judged for a long time." Tom Brokaw, NBC anchor said, "You can almost hear, if you listen carefully now, across the country, in living rooms and bars and wherever people watch this, folks turning to each other and saying "Wow, why isn't she on the ticket?"[28]

Less than a year after her husband's 1996 presidential quest ended, and Elizabeth's star turn at the GOP Convention, she told reporters that "I don't have any plans to run for president." Then she added: "I said when Bob was running that, win or lose, I was coming back to the Red Cross." She even joked and said, "Besides, I'm already president," referring to her work as the Red Cross's chief.[29]

Then, in 1998, Washington, D.C.-based Public Affairs Council polled thirty-meisters on their guesses for the major parties' vice presidential nominees, and their answer was women. Elizabeth Dole and then New Jersey Governor Christine Todd Whitman were named as likely running mates of George W. Bush.[30] An article in the *Philadelphia Inquirer* at the same time predicted that there would be a woman on the next ticket, in either the Democratic or Republican party. Even further, the article predicted that there could be an "all female face off for the vice president's job. Elizabeth Dole for the GOP and Dianne Feinstein for the Democrats."[31] Even though Elizabeth consistently denied that she had any plans to run, one article described that "all the demurring in the world will not slow supporters and star-starved Republicans from dreaming up 'other Dole' scenarios for 2000."[32] One of those was Republican activist Earl Cox, who in 1996 tried to draft retired General Colin Powell for a White House run. As soon as Elizabeth stepped down as Red Cross president, Cox and other Dole supporters had begun a national movement to "Draft Dole" and held a kickoff rally in Elizabeth's hometown in late January.[33]

After Elizabeth Dole stepped down from the Red Cross, she visited Iowa and New Hampshire, which increased speculation in the press that her announcement of an exploratory bid would be imminent. "I think she is going to run, unless she finds some compelling reason not to,"[34] said Tom Daffron, a political adviser who had been tapped to coordinate Dole's campaign.

ON THE CAMPAIGN TRAIL

My presidency would make the kind of history that would reverberate around the world.[35]

On March 10 in Des Moines, Elizabeth Dole launched her exploratory bid and told her audience, "I'm not a politician, and today, that may be a plus."[36] During her exploratory bid, she outlined her abortion stance, which can be a tricky subject, especially for conservative candidates. She wrote, in a letter to a supporter, that she is anti-abortion, however, like Governor George W. Bush, she said she believes abortion should be allowed in cases of rape or incest, or when pregnancy may endanger the life of the mother.[37] In April, she made a trip to Macedonia, during the conflict in Bosnia, where she spent time in a refugee camp, lending a hand and listening to the needs of the people. She told Cokie Roberts of ABC News, "As I have talked with so many of the refugees, the deportees, I'm even more convinced that there's absolutely no alternative but an all-out win. That means driving Milosevic and his forces out of Kosovo." She also said, "I think Milosevic should be labeled a war criminal. From what I've seen and heard, he is not fighting a war. He is—and his forces certainly are committing crimes against humanity."[38] While the Dole campaign had hoped that Elizabeth's trip would invigorate her exploratory bid, a *Newsweek* survey showed that half of Republicans questioned said they would support Texas Governor George W. Bush as the GOP presidential nominee, with Dole running a distant second with 16 percent.

Elizabeth Dole's fundraising got a boost in April when her first fundraiser picked up more than $500,000 and the endorsement of United Nations Ambassador Jeanne Kirkpatrick. Although the amount seemed impressive, George W. Bush was averaging about $300,000 per day in the first 28 days of his campaign.[39] Criticism came from columnist Robert Novak, who reported that Elizabeth Dole was still making speeches for profit on a lecture circuit that had been booked before her exploratory campaign began. In one instance, Dole's aides informed the National Petrochemical and Refiners Association that their paid speaker—Elizabeth Dole—would supply the questions and the answers for the Q&A after her speech.[40] A similar criticism came from the *Christian Science Monitor,* which claimed one of the challenges facing Dole's campaign was her "unwillingness to deal with the press." "Her campaign appearances so far have been limited to talk-show style canned presentations."[41]

In May, Elizabeth Dole gave one of the most substantive speeches of her exploratory presidential race to Yale Medical School graduates when she held a bottle of children's aspirin in her right hand and a handgun trigger lock in her left. She said "This will protect our children," holding up the black trigger lock. "It will also help you as future physicians, so you don't have to treat accidentally wounded children in hospital emergency rooms."[42] In the speech, Elizabeth wanted to distance herself from the other Republican candidates on the issue of gun control. She told the audience of her belief that guns should come with safety locks and that no civilian needs an assault rifle. Response to her stand on gun control was mixed, depending on the crowd. At Yale, she was warmly applauded, but in New Hampshire, where the state's motto is "live free or die" there were boos from the crowd when she made a similar speech. One audience member remarked after her speech, "I don't know what she was thinking. Half the guys [in the audience] were packing."[43] At another campaign stop in New Hampshire, Elizabeth made a stance on education. She said, "We can't run public schools by remote control from Washington." She advocated universities strengthening the requirements for those studying to be teachers and more parent involvement in the schools.[44]

Bob Dole had been keeping a low profile in the campaign. When asked why Bob wasn't more visible, Elizabeth told the *New York Times* that "It's important that I go solo here for a while. Bob will certainly be willing to do his share of campaigning, but I'll be making the decisions."[45] Not much about her husband appeared in the press during Elizabeth's bid, until the interview Bob gave to a reporter in mid-May hit the newsstand. The headline on the front page of the *New York Times* said it all: "As Political Spouse, Bob Dole Strays From Campaign Script." In the article, Bob Dole said that he wanted to give money to John McCain's campaign, especially since McCain needed the money and had been a loyal supporter to Bob when he ran against Bill Clinton in 1996. Even worse, he was not very confident about Elizabeth's exploratory bid. He said, "I'm sort of leaning that she'll do it," [run for president]. "But she hasn't told me point blank. If there's no response out there, or if it looks impossible, this is not her whole life. If she can't raise the money, obviously it's pretty hard to be a candidate."[46]

The press reaction to Bob Dole's *New York Times* interview focused on how badly his comments may have hurt Elizabeth's chances to have a successful bid for the presidency. Journalist Gail Collins was one of the most critical of Bob Dole. She said, "If Elizabeth Dole seriously wants to be a presidential candidate, the first thing she is going to have to do is lock up her husband." She even went as far as to say that the timing of Bob Dole's television commercials for Viagra, the medicine for erectile dysfunction, was planned to steal the limelight away from Elizabeth. Collins concluded that, "With spouses like this, who needs opponents?"[47] But Elizabeth laughed off the issue publicly and noted that Bob was "in the woodshed" while she continued to make her exploratory bid.

Both Elizabeth Dole and George W. Bush marched in the Amherst, New Hampshire Fourth of July parade and photographers snapped photos of them, with Bush's arm around Dole, causing some to speculate that Elizabeth Dole could be a vice presidential pick for George W. Bush who was consistently running in first place in the polls. Still, Elizabeth stressed that it was the presidency—not the vice presidency that she was seeking. *Mirabella* magazine reported, "Elizabeth Dole is campaigning hard, but it seems her best chance of making it to the White House is to bring out the woman's vote . . . for that sonofaBush."[48] She reiterated her presidential—not vice presidential goals by saying, "I'm running to win; you don't make this kind of arduous undertaking if you don't intend to win."[49] And she told the *Ladies Home Journal* that her top goals as president would be to "Restore public education. Also to lead a crusade with the vision of ridding this country of drugs." She added, "We know that many crimes are drug related, and if we're talking about being tough on crime, this is an integral part."[50] She also told the editor of *Ladies Home Journal* what she told the reporter of *Mirabella*, that she wasn't making the effort to be vice president, she wanted to win the presidency.

In August, Elizabeth Dole's exploratory bid got a major boost when she finished third in the Iowa Straw Poll. Two-thirds of Dole's vote in the Iowa straw poll came from women, many of whom had never been involved in politics.[51]

In September, Elizabeth Dole accepted an open invitation made by school administrators to "come back anytime" as an opportunity to present a potent campaign speech that outlined her philosophy for education reform in America. The speech was given to 200 select students, parents, and teachers at Melrose High School, where young Elizabeth Hanford had spent the 1959–1960 school year working as a student teacher. She said that the "true heroes of our society are not to be found on a movie screen or a football field. They are to be found in our classrooms."

She drew upon her experience as a teacher to gain ethos for her proposed education initiatives as president.

> A lot has changed since I taught here, but some things are still the same. The key to a great school is still committed, creative teachers . . . involved parents . . . and an energetic, supportive principal and staff. Let me say that I am especially pleased to share this day with your new principal, Dr. Burke. Talk about energy! He and so many other dedicated educators are living proof that education is not just a profession, it is a passion. It is a calling. There is nothing more fundamental to the success of our democracy than the education of our children in a robust public education system.[52]

Similar to her speech on gun control, where Dole held a bottle of children's aspirin in one hand and a trigger lock in the other, she used a prop in her education speech. She asked her audience to "Take a look at this unwieldy stack of paper," she said, pointing to a more than 600-page copy of the "Clinton-Gore" Elementary and Secondary Education reauthorization bill.[53] Her thoughtful remarks about education reform were not missed by officials in her home state of North Carolina. Proud of their native daughter, an elementary school was renamed for Elizabeth in her home town of Salisbury and it is known today as Elizabeth Hanford Dole Elementary School. During her campaign, Elizabeth visited the school, and a $250 per plate fundraising dinner was held in her honor.[54]

As fall came, Elizabeth Dole gave a campaign speech in Charleston, South Carolina, where she planned to rebuild the United States' military might. Speaking to a standing-room-only crowd of about 800 people at the College of Charleston, Elizabeth said, "We will be strong because peace and security can only endure through strength." She continued: "In the Dole administration, this era of wishful thinking, vacillation, and equivocation will end. I will lead the United States firmly and resolutely. I will advance and defend our military issues."[55]

While Elizabeth Dole's campaign speeches were substantive and the numbers of people in her audience were large, her campaign manager, Tom Daffron, admitted in early October that Elizabeth's inability to raise enough money was a concern. He said, "It's been a hard go for us," to a reporter who claimed that the "curiosity in Dole exceeds [financial] support." In other words, there were large crowds that came to see Elizabeth Dole campaign, but not everyone in the audience was contributing to her campaign.[56] Columnist Ellen Goodman echoed this thinking, saying, "more voters seemed interested in her as a celebrity than as a candidate."[57] Frequently women brought their daughters to her speeches, so that young girls could see that a woman could vie for the presidency.

On October 20, with Bob Dole by her side, Elizabeth Dole abandoned her bid to be America's first woman president, saying that, "The odds are overwhelming. It would be futile to continue." While her campaign raised $4.7 million, compared with then-Texas Governor George W. Bush's $57 million, she was at a tremendous financial disadvantage.[58] At her New Hampshire headquarters, a hand-lettered poster board went up that changed *"Let's make history"* to *"We made history."* When she announced her withdrawal, Elizabeth Dole talked about "seeing some women sit up a little straighter because you are trying to empower them. In fact, parents would bring their daughters to see 'a woman.'"

ELIZABETH DOLE'S PRESIDENTIAL OBSTACLES

Elizabeth Dole was repeatedly described as the "first" woman to wage a serious campaign for president. One article went so far as to say that Dole was "the first viable female presidential candidate in American history." *Boston Globe* columnist Ellen Goodman summed up this concentration on Dole's gender and pioneering status:

> Her opponents delivered eulogies to her gender. George W. Bush praised her as a "trailblazer" and "an inspiration to a lot of women." John McCain said "Someday a woman will be president of the United States and Elizabeth Dole will have led the way". . . . The broadcasts and newspaper stories all described her as "the only woman in the race." Even the sign in her own headquarters went from "Let's Make History" to "She Made History."[59]

A study was commissioned by the White House Project to determine if the newspaper coverage of five Republican candidates for the presidency was balanced. The report found that "newspaper coverage of female political candidates tends to focus more on their personal qualities than where they stand on the issues, a trend that gives their male competitors an edge in crafting an image of authority and readiness to lead. . . ."[60]

About half the money she raised was from women, but it wasn't enough for her to get into the really big fund-raising that a person needs to make it. According to Marie Wilson of the White House Project, the "big payers 'didn't gather around this woman and say, you're the person we want to win with.'"[61] According to New Jersey governor, Christine Todd Whitman: "It's been one of the biggest barriers to women achieving success in public office." Pat Schroeder says that is why she had to drop out of the race in 1988, but she thinks that women are now making enough money to make donations. And that people will start donating more when they see women running credible campaigns—campaigns that have a chance of winning.[62]

A "Generation Gap" may have also been a culprit in Elizabeth Dole's failed presidential bid. Elizabeth's message may not have resonated with younger women. She may be able to bridge the "gender gap," but she doesn't seem able to bridge the "generation gap." She spoke to an audience of young career women in Manhattan who were only lukewarm about her stories of what she went through to get where she is. She is quoted as saying: "Although I predate the [women's revolution], I was deeply involved in living it." She talked about her mother's reaction to her decision to go to law school and the story was received "tepidly." They want to hear less of her history-of-feminism and more of what she will do to make things better for them. Her campaign message was also muddled. Elizabeth equivocated somewhat when she was asked whether a woman would be able to win the presidency. On the one hand she said, "yes" absolutely and that "People are not thinking male/female or African American/Hispanic American—it's who's the best qualified." Yet she was not entirely comfortable with that, since she told a group of New York women that the women's movement doesn't exactly fit her. Quoting her: "For most women of my generation" "we struggled individually to find the answer to our own identities. Although I predate the revolution, I was deeply involved in living it, sometimes consciously, more often unconsciously. When we women knocked on the doors of America's law schools and medical schools and business schools in the '50s and '60s, we were simply following our dreams, which seemed as natural to us as staying home and getting married was to others."[63] R. Sean Wilentz, history professor at Princeton University has said: "That she is a woman is *a* reason, not *the* reason to vote for her. . . . Nor is it the reason she's running. She's running because she thinks she can run the country better than the other guys can.[64] There is something to learn from her campaign, said columnist Ellen Goodman: "As long as there is only one woman in the pack, one skirt among the suits, she is always and forever going to be running 'as a woman.'"[65] The *New York Times* chose Elizabeth Dole's words as the "quotation of the day" when she exited the presidential stage with, "I've learned that the current political calendar and election laws favor those who get an early start and can tap into huge private fortunes or who have a pre-existing network of political supporters."[66]

ELIZABETH DOLE'S COMMUNICATION STYLE

Elizabeth Dole has become an important contemporary American politician and her well prepared and engagingly delivered public speaking has contributed to her success. There are specific traits of Elizabeth Dole's public speaking that are worth noting. The most compelling is Elizabeth's ability to address more than one purpose in the same speech, known as "rhetorical multi-tasking."[67] Senator Dole is able to meet the specific exigencies of her speech, as well as cast a wider net and pave the way for a new initiative. For example, in 1988 at the GOP Convention, she was designated as the speaker who was to explain the "gender gap" to the audience and try to decrease the number of female voters who were likely to vote for the Democratic opponent. The phenomenon known as the "gender gap" emerged during the Reagan administration when support for Reagan's policies was waning. In 1980, Ronald Reagan had received almost as many votes from women as he had from men; the difference was only eight percentage points, with fewer votes being cast for him by women. Two years later, however, public opinion polls and other sources revealed that the gap between male and female supporters was widening. Elizabeth Dole addressed this problem in 1984 and again in 1988.[68] Her speech also highlighted her knowledge of workforce issues and once George H. W. Bush won, Elizabeth was tapped for the labor secretary position. In 1998, Elizabeth Dole toured the country, giving a speech titled "An America We Can Be." The speech was replete with stories of her early D.C. days and described for the audience the progress that has been made with respect to women's issues. At the same time, she was disclosing her résumé to the audience, which would help her if she decided that she wanted to run for political office. When she resigned from the American Red Cross in 1999, the speech got more attention for what she only hinted at in the speech—a possible political future—instead of the explicit purpose of the speech, which was for Elizabeth to step down as president of the humanitarian organization. This ability for Elizabeth to make the most of her speeches relates to a quote attributed to her at an exhibit on American women at the Hoover Library in Stanford: "Women have had to be over achievers to succeed. We worked twice as hard as men to be considered as good."

Another notable trait of Elizabeth Dole's public speaking is the novel approach that she takes when planning her presentation. Elizabeth Dole knows that in order to capture her audience's attention, in an increasingly fast paced and media saturated society, she must do something unusual that will ensure her speech looks interesting to the audience. From descending the steps at the GOP Convention in 1996, to holding up props as she speaks, she has capitalized on catching the audience by surprise, and thus, holding its attention better than if she stayed still and didn't incorporate these strategies into her speeches. Elizabeth Dole commented on some of the thinking and planning that made her 1996 GOP convention speech so attention-getting speech, and she acknowledged that her unorthodox introduction created curiosity in her audience:

> But I think when the audience saw me come down, they all got quiet. They hadn't seen this before. They all wondered 'what is she doing? And because of that, they were more attentive and cooperative as I walked around the audience. And the Secret Service did a wonderful job of keeping the aisles clear. That walking around really works well for me in other speeches as well. I like doing that and I frequently use that style when I speak for the American Red Cross and I speak to victims and their families. I think that it is a very effective way for me to reach the audience. The audience seems to respond so much better when I move around and I am not behind the podium with bright lights glaring at me. I now feel that the podium is a barrier between the audience and me. Her animated delivery, brightly colored suits all serve the purpose of entertaining the audience, so that they stay tuned for her presentation.[69]

Elizabeth Dole is a speaker who has been able to effectively present herself in this media-oriented age. Elizabeth Dole's speeches show a high degree of media savvy, which media scholar Thomas Hollihan observes is imperative for the successful modern politician:

> Candidates who have an attractive image, who can create memorable sound bites, and who demonstrate that they possess media savvy are likely to make the best impression on voters.[70]

For example, in her 1996 GOP convention speech, she was widely compared to talk show host Oprah Winfrey. Elizabeth Dole moved around the audience like a hostess making eye contact with guests at her party. Like Winfrey, Dole's speech focused on the impact that Bob Dole made in the lives of people, and she had those people in the audience, ready to stand and provide proof in the form of their presence, that Bob Dole made a difference in their lives. Viewers of talk shows, such as the Oprah Winfrey Show, would have recognized this formula, (of the host and admiring audience) because it makes for good television. Dole's 1996 GOP convention speech was truly a "made for TV" speech. The engaging way that Elizabeth Dole, attractive and agile, moved about the audience was far more entertaining and visual than it would have been had she stood behind the podium and delivered her speech like the other speakers at the convention. The different method she chose called attention to herself and the purpose of her speech, which was to trumpet the benefits of a Bob Dole presidency. After the success of her 1996 speech, she repeated the style in her speeches for the American Red Cross and she would frequently stand next to a child who was affected by a natural disaster and describe the benefits that the Red Cross was able to administer. Her step down from the American Red Cross was another speech that drew positive media attention. Elizabeth knows well that it is important to get favorable media coverage to propel a political career forward.

Another hallmark of Elizabeth Dole's public speaking is her penchant for preparation. Elizabeth Dole doesn't like to be caught unprepared for anything, and her public speaking is no exception. Her husband, by comparison, has a public speaking style that has been described as "shooting from the hip" and by his own admission, he doesn't give public speaking nearly the attention that Elizabeth does:

> She is much more disciplined [than I am.] I hear a voice coming out of the bedroom and it is Elizabeth rehearsing her speech. She probably gave it twenty-eight times already, but she is giving it the next day and she just wants to rehearse it twice. Now, if I've given it once, [a speech] well the old story in the Congress is that you only give a speech once, and that is when you read it for the first time. (Laughter) That's why we're not any good. You don't hear any good speeches in the senate any more, and that is because we're reading them.[71]

Elizabeth Dole's preparation has served her well. She has given speeches throughout her career, and it has been her anticipation of the event that has made her successful. For example, her speechwriter, Kerry Tymchuk, described a time when Elizabeth was in Poland as secretary of labor and she knew that she would be attending dinners with dignitaries. Just in case she would be asked to give a toast, she had worked with Kerry to prepare appropriate toasts. He noted that "the male secretaries were over there stumbling through their remarks, and she has these beautiful toasts memorized. People were crying when she was finished."[72] Her preparation was ridiculed when Elizabeth Dole was a presidential candidate. The *New York Times* described Elizabeth as a "controlled performer and well-known perfectionist."[73] Another article noted, "she displayed a caution with the public and the press, limited her time for casual schmoozing with both."[74] Another columnist went further; he said, "Dole was positively awful as a candidate . . . she rarely ever gave a hint of what we expect of leaders, instead following the down-to-the-second script developed by her aides. Combined with her saccharine delivery, the script failed, if only because all who heard her could tell how exactly scripted she was."[75] Cartoonist Garry Trudeau lampooned Elizabeth Dole in his "Doonesbury" strip as a Stepford-like personality who spouts sound bites on command, never varying so much as a semicolon. Ari Fleisher, Dole's communications director, wondered why men are called "disciplined" and women are "scripted."[76]

INVENTION

Many of the topics of Elizabeth Dole's speeches are based on the foundation of her Methodist religion. Growing up in the Piedmont region of North Carolina, in what she described as "the buckle of the Bible Belt,[77]" she is a devout Christian, who crafts her speeches and their message in light of her own core belief system. As a presidential candidate, her religious background was evident. Similar to Abraham Lincoln, who in his inaugural address in 1861, ended his speech with "when again touched, as surely as they will be, by the better angels of our nature," when Elizabeth Dole began her exploratory bid on March 10th, she pledged to "call America to her better nature." The theme of religion was focused on in the 2000 race by several front-running candidates. Vice President Al Gore wanted to reclaim God for the Democrats and he talked of involving faith-based groups in government and social programs. George W. Bush coined the term "compassionate conservatism" and said that Americans needed to talk again about the "values" that made them great.[78] During her exploratory bid, Elizabeth Dole reprised a speech that she gave in 1987 at the National Prayer Breakfast and spoke at the 15th Annual Philadelphia Prayer Breakfast. In the speech, Elizabeth shared with her audience her spiritual journey and described a time in her life when she had to find a way out of the "spiritual starvation" that was caused by her hectic career. She told her audience that her "spiritual journey began many years ago in a Carolina home where Sunday was the Lord's Day, reserved for acts of mercy and necessity."[79] She drew parallels between Queen Esther's experiences and her own. She told her audience that "dependence" is the true meaning of the story of Esther. She said that she had to learn that dependence is a good thing, that "when I've used up my own resources, when I can't control things and make them come out my way, when I'm willing to trust God with the outcome, when I'm weak, then I am strong."[80] *Newsweek* reported that she portrayed her possible candidacy as a witness for Christian decency. "There's yearning to make us a better nation," she said. "We need to get back to basic values: personal responsibility, honesty, integrity . . . cooperation over conflict." Leading the Red Cross, she said, she'd enabled people to share their blessings. "Aren't we blessed?" she asked.[81]

Through Elizabeth Dole's long career, humanitarian interests have been the underpinning of all of her work. Her speeches reflect the ways that she plans to apply her faith to practical matters. Her faith has been lived through the choices she has made to serve others and spearhead causes. If she won the presidency, there is evidence to suggest that she would have continued to communicate her faith through her speeches and in her initiatives.

DISPOSITION

Elizabeth Dole likes to warm up her audiences with humorous stories or even a conversational, "how are you doing?" when the situation is more casual. She does this to create rapport and goodwill with her audience. A warm and engaging person interpersonally, she attempts to create the same reciprocity of a conversation at the beginning of her speeches. She often retells stories of her Washington, D.C., career and particularly likes to stress the progress that women have made in the mostly male corridors of politics. It is also common for Elizabeth Dole to remind the audience of her experience and education. This was especially true during her exploratory bid for the presidency, when she was frequently described as a candidate who "never held elected office." For example, in the speech she gave at the United States Naval Academy in April 1999, she reminded her audience of her tenure as Red Cross president when she said, "And for eight years I was honored to join thousands of Red Cross workers and volunteers who share these values, who're making a positive difference at home and abroad. I know that many other people from humanitarian organizations—a number of you—here tonight—share that passion for service."[82] Later in the same speech she mentioned her role as secretary of labor, as it pertained to the topic of the speech. She said, "As United States Secretary of Labor, I found myself in Poland in the summer of 1989, meeting with Solidarity labor leaders. It was August and the Soviet bloc was crumbling."[83] Once she gets to the thesis of her talk, she is likely to organize her speech in a problem-solution format. The stories that she often tells in her speeches perform an important function, since they link the ideals that she believes America must return to, or the progress upon which America should continue to build in order to create a strong country. The storytelling device that Elizabeth Dole so often employs in her speaking is an important part of her organization, and one that deserves note. Quite often, Elizabeth Dole tells a series of stories as her entire speech. This narrative style serves to create a warm and engaging environment for the audience, since narrative style is one of the most enjoyable for an audience. Speech scholar W. Lance Bennett, states, "Narratives help us impose order on the flow of experience so that we can make sense of events and actions in our lives."[84] Elizabeth said that telling stories, instead of using a lot of data in speeches is "one thing I've learned." She explained: "You start out thinking that they [the audience] really wants to know the statistics and the policy, and a lot of times audiences are much more interested in the vignettes and the little stories that illustrate it than the hard data."[85] An example of storytelling from one of Elizabeth Dole's presidential campaign speeches is evident in this speech she gave at Melrose High School in Massachusetts. She said, "For a brief period— when I was working toward a master's degree in education and government, I had the opportunity to serve as an 11th grade history teacher. Back then in the public schools, the classroom was really a showroom—a showroom of American excellence and achievement. Needless to say, we've lost a lot of ground in the last few decades, for a variety of reasons. I spent an afternoon combing through forty years of dusty files. Lo and behold, I found the name of a surviving member of the force. Well I tracked him down in West Roxbury and recorded his memories on tape. He was such a hit with my class that they insisted he come in and tell his story in person!" She also interacted with her audience when she asked: "Would the teachers in the audience please raise your hands? I won't call on you! Now let me ask you to please stand up, so we can show our appreciation for you. Thank you. Teaching is not just a job, it is a calling, a noble endeavor. Thank you for all you do for our children." Later in the same speech she told a story about her experience at Ground Zero: "One of the most emotional experiences of my life was a visit to Ground Zero. As I walked on that now hallowed ground, through the wreckage of the World Trade Center, three of my life's most important experiences came together."[86] She then went on to tell of how the transportation and labor departments, as well as the Red Cross were all organizations affected by the World Trade Center terrorist attacks of 2001. She was able to relate more closely to the tragedy because of her experience in those organizations. By telling those stories, she connected with the audience and established her credibility as a leader.

MEMORIA

Dole's ability to master her material—her rhetorical memoria—is impressive. President Bill Clinton's "photographic memory" was greatly discussed when he was in office. His ability to read something once and know it was one of the hallmarks of his communication ability. Elizabeth Dole's retention ability is similar to that of Bill Clinton's. Her ability to memorize huge passages, without forgetting anything, is one of the best speaking assets she has. Kerry Tymchuk, a speechwriter for Elizabeth Dole, commented on her talent with respect to the work he did on Elizabeth Dole's 1996 GOP convention speech. He said, "I was on the convention floor, with a script of the speech in my hand, and Mrs. Dole did not miss a word."[87] Granted, Elizabeth Dole gave a very similar version of this speech on the stump for her husband throughout the campaign year. But only those who follow her around, such as reporters, would know that she wasn't giving that speech for the first time. Elizabeth Dole's ability to deliver her speeches over and over again, while still captivating her audience, as she did in 1996, I have dubbed "well rehearsed spontaneity." This is clearly a gift for any politician. In an interview with Geraldine Ferraro, she described Elizabeth Dole's repeat performances in a negative way. She said, "She does something that I won't do, she has a shtick that she repeats so often, you could almost hear her GOP convention speech when she spoke to the Chamber [an event they both attended]. That reminds me of something that happened on this campaign [New York senate race against Charles Schumer]. Chuck [Schumer] has a "sub speech" and the first time you hear it, you think 'this guy is terrific,' and then when you hear it for the twenty-fifth time, you say, "God is he able to move off that at all?" but of course, people are listening to the candidates, and most of them are not listening for the twenty-fifth time."[88] Ms. Ferraro described an important aspect of speech delivery for politicians. If they repeat a speech often, like Elizabeth Dole does, they will master the delivery and wow the crowd. If they create a new speech each time, they may not seem as dynamic to the audience.

AFTER HER PRESIDENTIAL BID

In her withdrawal speech, Elizabeth Dole promised her audience that she wasn't going to disappear from the political landscape. She said, "So while I may not be a candidate for president in 2000, I'm a long way from the twilight."[89] When CNN reporter Daryn Kagan asked her colleague, Candy Crowley, if this would be the last of Elizabeth Dole in public life, Crowley, a long-time political correspondent, responded: "I can't imagine it will be the last that we see of her. This has been a woman who'd been very active in public life. She—you can see her back in the Cabinet, if there were a Republican president. You can see her going back to a Red-Cross-kind-of-place. This is a woman who thrives in the—in public life, not necessarily the public spotlight. So, I expect we'll hear from her again."[90]

No sooner had Elizabeth withdrawn her name from the presidential race, when petition coordinators from around the country started a grass roots effort to get Elizabeth Dole named as George W. Bush's running mate. Elizabeth had made strong objections against such an initiative, but the organizers went ahead anyway, saying that they believed so strongly in Dole and that they thought, "it is the right thing for America."[91]

After George W. Bush won the presidency, Elizabeth Dole was reported to be considered for the position of UN Ambassador. The *Boston Globe* reported that Elizabeth wanted the position but only if the UN Ambassador post held cabinet rank as it did in the Clinton administration. Another issue about the position for Elizabeth Dole was that whoever got that position might have to push for the repeal of a law that Senator Bob Dole pushed through the Congress in 1994. The legislation caps at 25 percent what the United States pays toward United Nations peacekeeping.[92] Elizabeth Dole did not received the position and continued to contemplate her future.

USING HER OWN "SOUTHERN STRATEGY" FOR HER NORTH CAROLINA SENATE RACE

On September 11, 2001, Mrs. Dole planned to announce her bid to run for the United States Senate in North Carolina, her home state. After the terrorist attacks, she postponed her official announcement and instead set down to the task of running for the senate.

Instead, she announced her candidacy on February 27, 2002, in her hometown of Salisbury. Even though Elizabeth had lived in Washington, D.C., more than thirty years, and Democrats branded her a carpetbagger, her roots to North Carolina were never severed. If anything, her connection to her native North Carolina was strengthened over the years through her speeches and many visits home. She consistently exalted her southern heritage and when she returned home to North Carolina to announce her senate candidacy, with her husband and mother by her side, she was the favorite candidate. Ted Arrington, a political science professor at the University of North Carolina at Charlotte said, "She has three advantages—name recognition, name recognition, name recognition."[93] In her campaign announcement speech, Elizabeth described her southern beginnings and how her core values relate to her work as a public servant. She said, "I am Mary and John Hanford's daughter, raised to believe that there are no limits to individual achievement and no excuses to justify indifference. From an early age I was taught that success is measured, not in material accumulations, but in service to others. I was encouraged to join causes larger than myself, to pursue positive change through a sense of mission and to stand up for what I believe."[94] In her announcement speech, she also told the audience where she stood on issues of special importance to the constituents. She discussed veteran's rights, security, the economy, education, and health care and abortion. As she had done throughout her career, through an engaging story, she related her experiences in her work at the American Red Cross, labor and transportation departments, and with the White House Office of Public Liaison, to establish her ethos for the work that she wanted to do on behalf of North Carolinians. She said:

> Since September 11th, we have experienced a sense of universal fraternity— love of country, love of community, love of neighbor. Ultimately, what is the source of that love? When I was serving in the White House as Assistant to the President, Ronald Reagan and I found ourselves alone in a holding room as he waited to give a major speech. I was always amazed at his inner peace and sense of direction, so I asked him how he handled the challenges of the nation's highest office. He told me, "When I was governor of California, Elizabeth, it seemed like every day yet another disaster was put on my desk. And I felt an urge to look behind me for someone to hand it off to. One day, I realized I was looking in the wrong direction. I looked up instead of back. I'm still looking up, Elizabeth. I couldn't do another day in this office," President Reagan said, "if I didn't know I could ask God's help and it would be given."[95]

Elizabeth Dole was an ambitious candidate who visited one hundred counties in North Carolina and she stressed her "Dole Plan" which described the specific goals she had for the residents of the state. She was an agile campaigner, who spoke extemporaneously and impromptu. She stressed that because of the fast pace, and the many different venues, "you have to be ready for any sort of set up," and "you want to have it set up so that it is the proper lighting, but you can't control that." She focused heavily on the loss of jobs and tried to assure voters that their job security would be a major concern of hers as senator. She said, "A lot of people have lost their jobs, or they're worried about losing their jobs. Textile workers have really suffered during the last recession. We've got to open up foreign markets."[96] In one campaign speech, Elizabeth used a prop, as she had done on the campaign trail for president. This time she held up a blank sheet of paper and described it as the "Bowles Social Security Plan."

The primary was delayed from May 7th because of a drawn-out court fight over legislative districts. Nonetheless, on September 10, 2002, Elizabeth Dole handily won the primary race in North Carolina, making her the Republican candidate for the senate seat left vacant by retiring conservative stalwart, Jesse Helms. Her best-known opponent in the race, lawyer Jim Snyder, described himself as the true conservative by raising questions about Dole's positions on gun rights and abortion. Snyder even poured $100,000 of his own money into his campaign in an effort to shake Dole's lead. Elizabeth Dole's ardent campaigning, wealth of political experience, name recognition, and fundraising were formidable over the field of six other Republicans. Elizabeth even won the endorsement of Senator Helms, who broke his long tradition of staying out of GOP primaries when he encouraged voters to support Elizabeth's candidacy at the Conservative Political Action Conference in late January in Arlington, Virginia.[97]

Elizabeth Dole won endorsements from President Bush, who visited North Carolina five times to campaign for her. Also visiting the state on behalf of Elizabeth Dole's senate race was First Lady Laura Bush, who came the day before election day. Vice President Dick Cheney visited the state twice and Senator Kay Bailey Hutchinson and former New York Mayor Rudy Giuliani all visited North Carolina to show support for Elizabeth's bid.

In mid-October she participated in a televised debate with her opponent, Democrat Erskine Bowles, who had served in the Clinton Administration as chief of staff. In the debate, Dole showed a tough side, telling her opponent, the moderator, and the audience that she is "results oriented" and that she is interested in "working across the aisle." During the debate, Elizabeth said, "At every opportunity my opponent is for higher taxes, bigger government, and more regulation." The debate, held on the campus of Meredith College in Raleigh, demonstrated that Elizabeth Dole is capable of stating her positions pointedly, yet remaining civil—even warm. She referred to her opponent by his first name, Erskine, while he continued to call her "Mrs. Dole." At one point Elizabeth told Erskine, "you can call me Elizabeth," but Mr. Bowles continued to call her "Mrs. Dole."

Election night, November 5, 2002, was a jubilant evening for Elizabeth Dole and her family. Her husband, mother, brother, and sister-in-law present, among hundreds of cheering supporters, she made her victory speech.

Oh, wow! What a night! I'm so proud to be a North Carolinian! I'm just as thrilled as you are! We'll never forget this night, will we? A few moments ago, I got a call from Erskine Bowles. He congratulated me on my victory, and he was very gracious. He obviously cares very much about the people of

North Carolina, and I want to say to those who voted for Erskine Bowles, give me a chance. I intend to be a senator for all of North Carolina![98]

With the theme song from the movie "Rocky III" playing in the background, she continued her speech by thanking those in her campaign who made it possible for her to run her campaign. She concluded her speech with "Thank you so much and God bless you." At age sixty-six, Elizabeth Dole's Washington career was very much alive, and she reflected on how she felt more comfortable sharing her religious convictions in her speeches to fellow North Carolinians. She noted:

> I mention it [a book] in my speeches, it is called *The Greatest Thing in the World*. And I found myself using that in speeches, because it gave me a chance to share a little bit of my faith. And if you want to know who a person is, that is kind of central. A lot of your humanitarian yearnings flow from that and some people might think, 'oh, you should never say a word about faith.' Maybe in the South, and especially North Carolina, that isn't hard to do, because your audience is agreeing with you."

Her humanitarian convictions were evident in her maiden Senate speech, when she spoke on world hunger. She eloquently petitioned her fellow senators to make a commitment to feeding the hungry of North Carolina and other regions of the United States and the world. She used several poignant stories to drive home her message. For example, she said,

> My office was blessed recently to meet a young veteran, Michael Williams, and his family. Michael served his country for eight years in the United States Army, before leaving to work in private industry to use the computer skills he gained in the military. He was earning a good living, but after the September 11th terrorist attacks, he and his wife Gloria felt it was time to move their two children closer to family, back to North Carolina. But Michael found a shortage of jobs since his return. He worked with a temp agency . . . but that job ended. It has been so hard to make ends meet that the family goes to a food bank near their Clayton, North Carolina, home twice a month . . . because with rent, utilities and other bills, there is little left to buy food.[99]

On November 17, 2004, Elizabeth Dole was elected by her senate Republican colleagues to chair the National Republican Senatorial Committee for the 2006 election cycle. From this leadership position, Dole will work to protect the seats of Republican incumbents, recruit outstanding candidates, and raise the necessary funds to increase the majority. Of her new position, Elizabeth said, "It truly is an honor to have this trust and responsibility bestowed upon me by my colleagues. It will be a privilege to work to not only grow the Republican Party, but to give back to the Republican Party. And as a member of leadership, I look forward to promoting issues important to North Carolina."[100] Elizabeth Dole continues her work as a public servant, on a mission to make a difference—a mission rooted in the motto of her North Carolina roots—"to *be* rather than to seem."

NOTES

1. Elizabeth Dole, speech, Melrose High School, September 22, 1999. Obtained from Molly Meijer Wertheimer and Nichola D. Gutgold, *Elizabeth Hanford Dole, Speaking from the Heart*. (Westport, Conn.: Praeger Press: 2004), 217–223.

2. Mike Glover, Associated Press, March 10, 1999. www.lexis.nexis.com (accessed April 10, 2005).

3. "Red Cross Wonder Woman?" *Business Week*, January 25, 1999, 81.

4. Molly Meijer Wertheimer and Nichola D. Gutgold. *Elizabeth Hanford Dole: Speaking from the Heart*. (Westport, Conn.: Praeger Press, 2004), 208.

5. Ron Fournier. "Dole Leaving Red Cross, Eyeing White House." *The Morning Call*, January 5, 1999, A3.

6. Susan J. Carroll, Carol Heldman, and Stephanie Olson. "'She Brought Only a Skirt: Gender Bias in Newspaper Coverage of Elizabeth Dole's Campaign for the Republican Nomination." Unpublished paper, White House Project Conference, Washington, D.C., February 20, 2000.

7. This biographical section was culled from several sources including: Robert Dole, Elizabeth Dole, Richard Norton Smith, and Kerry Tymchuk. *Unlimited Partners, Our American Story*. (New York: Simon and Schuster, 1996), Richard Kozar. *Elizabeth Dole*. (Philadelphia: Chelsea House Publishers, 2000), and Molly Meijer Wertheimer and Nichola D. Gutgold. *Elizabeth Hanford Dole: Speaking from the Heart*. (Westport, Conn.: Praeger Press, 2004).

8. Robert Dole, Elizabeth Dole, Richard Norton Smith, and Kerry Tymchuk. *Unlimited Partners: Our American Story*. (New York: Simon and Schuster, 1996), 42.

9. Ibid., 47.

10. Richard Kozar. *Elizabeth Dole*. (Philadelphia: Chelsea House Publishers, 2000), 21.

11. *Unlimited Partners*, 52.

12. Ibid., 77.

13. Ibid., 78.

14. Mary Leonard. "A Life in Politics, Liddy's Way; In Elizabeth Dole's Formative Years, Hints of Her Drive to Challenge, Compete." *Boston Globe*, May 9, 1999, A1.

15. Ibid.

16. Ibid.

17. Ibid., 87.

18. Ibid., 90.

19. Elizabeth Dole, interview with Nichola Gutgold, April 7, 1998.

20. Kozar, 38

21. *Unlimited Partners*, 10.

22. Stephen C. Fehr. "Dole Resignation Revives 'Stand by your Man' Debate. *Kansas City Times*, September 20, 1987, B1.

23. Betty Cuniberti. "Dole's Decision: Why She's Quitting to Hit the Campaign Trail." *Los Angeles Times*, September 18, 1987, D10.

24. This was the slogan of Elizabeth Dole's presidential campaign. It was included in a campaign brochure, "Elizabeth Dole for President." Brochure produced by the Elizabeth Dole for President Exploratory Committee, P.O. Box 98132, Washington, D.C. 20077.

25. Katie Leishman. "A Very Private Person." *McCalls*, April 1988, 135.

26. Ellen Goodman. "A Dole on the National Ticket?" *Boston Globe*, April 5, 1988, 10A.

27. Marjorie Williams. "Bob & Liddy Dole, Doing the Town; On the Run with a Well-Oiled Political Act." *Washington Post*, August 16, 1988, E1.

28. Henry Louis Gates, Jr. "The Next President Dole 2000." *New Yorker*, October 20 & 27, 1997, 228.

29. Ed Hayward. "Elizabeth Dole Denies Presidential Goal." *Boston Herald*, May 9, 1997, 14.

30. "That's Madam Vice President." *Morning Call* (Allentown, PA), November 1, 1998, A2.

31. Dick Polman. "Female Faces in the 2000 Race?" *Philadelphia Inquirer*, April 12, 1998, E4.

32. Ron Fournier. "President Dole? Some see Elizabeth as a Hot Prospect." *Morning Cal* (Allentown, PA), May 20, 1998, A14.

33. Elizabeth Dole Resigns Red Cross Post, May Test Presidential Waters." www.cnn.com/allpolitics/stories/1999/01/04/president.2000/dole/ (accessed April 14, 2005).

34. Steve Campbell. "Daffron to run Elizabeth Dole's Exploratory Campaign." *Portland Press Herald* (Maine) March 7, 1999, 2C.

35. Elizabeth Dole, speech, Melrose High School, September 22, 1999, in Molly Meijer Wertheimer and Nichola D. Gutgold, *Elizabeth Hanford Dole: Speaking from the Heart*. (Westport, Conn.: Praeger Press, 2004), 217–222.

36. Mike Glover. "Dole Joins Exploratory Offering 'Better Nature.'" Associated Press, March 10, 1999. www.lexis.nexis.com (accessed April 10, 2005).

37. "Elizabeth Dole outlines abortion stance." *Patriot Ledger* (Quincy, MA), April 10, 1999, 8.

38. "ABC News This Week." *ABC News*, April 18, 1999, 11:30 A.M., transcript #99041803-j12.

39. "Dole Pushes Fundraising and Garners Endorsement." *Boston Globe*, April 28, 1999, A13.

40. Robert Novak. "Strategists Need to Decontrol Elizabeth Dole." *Standard Speaker* (Hazleton, PA), April 27, 1999, 16.

41. "The Monitor's View." *Christian Science Monitor*, 19 April 1999, 8.

42. Bridgette Greenberg. "Dole Pushes Gun Control in Commencement Speech," *Standard-Speaker* (Hazleton, PA), May 25, 1999, 2.

43. John F. Dickerson and Nancy Gibbs. "Elizabeth Unplugged." *Time*, May 10, 1999. www.time.com (accessed February 22, 2004).

44. Amy Diaz. "Dole: Milosevic Must Be Defeated 'Absolutely." *Union Leader* (Manchester, N.H.), May 25, 1999, A13.

45. Richard L. Berke. "As Political Spouse, Bob Dole Strays from Campaign Script." *New York Times*, May 17, 1999, A1.

46. Ibid.

47. Gail Collins. "Politics: Taking the 'Help' Out of 'Helpmate.'" *New York Times*, May 18, 1999, A22.

48. Paul Alexander. "Vice Can Be Nice." *Mirabella*, September 2000, 66–69.

49. Ibid.

50. Myrna Blyth. "One Smart Lady." *Ladies Home Journal*, August 1999, 44.

51. "A Softer Look, A Strong Appeal." *Newsweek*, August 30, 1999, 4.

52. Molly Meijer Wertheimer and Nichola D. Gutgold. *Elizabeth Hanford Dole: Speaking from the Heart*. (Westport, Conn.: Praeger Press, 2004), 217–222.

53. Tom Kirchofer. "Dole's Education Platform Urges Locker, Backpack Searches." *Daily Collegian*, (Penn State), September 23, 1999, 10.

54. Mark Wineka. "Dole Returns to Salisbury." *Salisbury Post*, October 3, 1999, 1.

55. Bruce Smith. "Elizabeth Dole Pledges to Rebuilt U.S. Military Might." *Morning Call*, (Allentown, PA), September 28, 1999, A4.

56. Diana Jean Schemo. "Curiosity in Dole Exceeds Support." *New York Times*, October 6, 1999, A28.

57. Ellen Goodman. "Gender Spotlight Cuts Both Ways," The Boston Globe, 24 October 1999, E7.

58. "Dole drop out; her poor showing wasn't just a money problem." *Pittsburgh Post Gazette.*" 22 October 1999, A22.

59. Ellen Goodman. "Gender Spotlight."

60. Mieke H. Bomann. "Newspaper Reporting on Women Candidates Differs from That on Men." *Times Union* (Albany, NY), A5.

61. Ellen Goodman. "Gender Spotlight."

62. Paul Alexander. "Vice Can be Nice."

63. "Gender Isn't the Only Gap." *Newsweek*, May 17, 1999, 6.

64. Paul Alexander. "Nice Can be Nice."

65. Ellen Goodman. "Gender Spotlight."

66. *New York Times.* "Quotation of the Day." October 21, 1999, A2.

67. The term "rhetorical multi-tasking" was coined in my co-authored book (with Molly Meijer Wertheimer). *Elizabeth Hanford Dole: Speaking from the Heart* (Westport, Conn.: Praeger, 2004). It was first presented in a paper "Rhetorical Multi-tasking of Elizabeth Dole," presented by Nichola Gutgold, Pennsylvania Speech Communication Annual Conference, Bloomsburg, PA, 1999.

68. Eileen Putnam. "Mrs. Dole Acknowledges Gender Gap, Asks Women to have an Open Mind." Associated Press, August 16, 1988.

69. Elizabeth Dole, interview with Nichola Gutgold, April 7, 1998.

70. Thomas A. Hollihan. *Uncivil Wars: Political Campaigns in a Media Age.* (New York: Bedford/St. Martin's, 2001), 39.

71. Bob Dole, interview with Nichola Gutgold and Molly Meijer Wertheimer, December 17, 2001.

72. Kerry Tymchuk, interview with Nichola Gutgold, 11 September 2000.

73. Katherine Q. Seelye. "The Dole Candidacy: The Overview." *New York Times*, October 21, 1999, A1.

74. Linda Feldmann. "Dole's Candidacy Had Historic Impact." *Christian Science Monitor*, October 21, 1999, 1.

75. Michael Kramer. "Liddy Without Tears." *Daily News* (New York) October 24, 1999, 47.

76. Eleanor Clift and Tom Brazaitis. *Madam President: Women Blazing the Leadership Trail.* (New York: Routledge, 2003), 99.

77. Elizabeth Dole, interview with Molly Meijer Wertheimer and Nichola Gutgold, July 8, 2003.

78. Ann McFeatters. "Presidential Candidates Saying Something of Values: Religious References Fill Slates of GOP, Democratic Hopefuls." *Pittsburgh Post-Gazette*, May 30, 1999, A–11.

79. Molly Meijer Wertheimer and Nichola D. Gutgold. *Elizabeth Hanford Dole: Speaking from the Heart.* (Westport, Conn.: Praeger, 2004), 134.

80. Ibid., 137.

81. Howard Fineman and Matthew Cooper. "Back in the Amen Corner." *Newsweek*, March 22, 1999, 33.

82. Wertheimer and Gutgold. *Elizabeth Hanford Dole: Speaking from the Heart*, 210.

83. Ibid., 213.

84. W. Lance Bennett. "Storytelling in Criminal Trials: A Model of Social Judgment." *Quarterly Journal of Speech*, *64* (February 1978), 1–22.

85. Elizabeth Dole, interview with Wertheimer and Gutgold, July 8, 2003.

86. Wertheimer and Gutgold. *Elizabeth Hanford Dole: Speaking from the Heart*, 239 and 241.

87. Kerry Tymchuk, 1996 GOP convention speech, email to Nichola Gutgold, November 11, 2000.

88. Geraldine Ferraro, interview with Nichola Gutgold, October 20, 1998.

89. Ibid., 225.

90. *CNN Morning News.* "Elizabeth Dole Bows Out of the Presidential Race: What Was Behind the Decision Not to Run?" October 20, 1999, 11:00 A.M. ET, Transcript # 99102010V09.

91. Rose Post. "Effort to Have Dole on Bush's Ticket Getting Under Way." *Salisbury Post*, March 19, 2000. www.salisburypost.com/2000march/031900c.htm (accessed April 4, 2005).

92. Elizabeth Neuffer. "Elizabeth Dole Said to Be Interested in Envoy, Decision Hangs on Whether Position is in the Cabinet." *Boston Globe*, January 17, 2001, A8.

93. Scott Mooneyham. "Dole's Celebrity is Risky Campaign Asset." *Morning Call* (Allentown, PA) February 10, 2002, A21.

94. Wertheimer and Gutgold. *Elizabeth Hanford Dole: Speaking From the Heart*, 236.

95. Wertheimer and Gutgold. *Elizabeth Hanford Dole: Speaking from the Heart*, 241–242.

96. Amy Frazier. "Dole Welcomed with Down-home Dinner." *Winston Salem Journal*, April 3, 2002. www.elizabethdole.org (accessed March 5, 2004).

97. Mooneyham. "Dole's celebrity."

98. Wertheimer and Gutgold. *Elizabeth Hanford Dole: Speaking from the Heart*, 242.

99. Ibid., 245.

100. dole.senate.gov (accessed April 20, 2005) quoted in Wertheimer and Gutgold. *Elizabeth Hanford Dole: Speaking from the Heart*, 242.

Ambassador Carol Moseley Braun. Photo reprinted with permission of Ambassador Carol Moseley Braun.

5

Carol Moseley Braun
"A Fiscal Hawk and
a Peace Dove"[1]

As President, I will give you an America as good as its promise. I will reach out to bring us together to create an American renaissance, revival and renewal . . . America is at a tipping point; if we stay the course we are on, we won't recognize this country five years from now. But if we shift gears, try another way, tap some of the talent that have been relegated to the sidelines of leadership, we can heal and renew and save our country.[2]

Carol Moseley Braun's announcement at Howard University in Washington, D.C., on September 22, 2003, gave Claire, Braun's nine-year-old niece, and countless other girls and women from around the country the inspiration of seeing a woman vie for the ultimate political prize: The White House. In her speech, fifty-six-year-old Carol Moseley Braun recounted her niece declaring, somewhat indignantly, with a copy of her social studies book in hand, "But Auntie Carol, all the presidents are boys!" When she ran for president, it was Carol Moseley Braun's goal to take the "men only" sign off the White House. Those who knew or worked with Moseley Braun, and many who have followed her political career, were not surprised that she made a bid for the presidency. She was an articulate addition to the group of Democratic hopefuls that included retired General Wesley Clark, Massachusetts Senator John Kerry, former Vermont Governor Howard Dean, Reverend Al Sharpton, Connecticut Senator Joe Lieberman, Florida Senator Bob Graham, Ohio Representative Dennis Kucinich, Missouri Representative Richard Gephardt, and North Carolina Senator John Edwards.

In an interview with National Public Radio, Carol Moseley Braun voiced her opposition to the Iraq war and her desire to rebuild America, both physically and spiritually. She told radio host Bob Edwards,

> I want to rebuild America. If we can rebuild Iraq, we can rebuild Illinois and Indiana and if we can do Baghdad, we can do Baltimore. I want to rebuild this country and I want to start with, on the one hand, a rebuilding of the physical America, the infrastructure. We can use the traditional stimulus for the economy, to get the economy going, to create jobs, to allow for wealth creation. We can explore new technologies that will allow us to lessen our dependence on foreign fuel, on foreign oil. There are a number of steps that we can take to reinvigorate and rebuild the economic and the physical infrastructure of our country and then to rebuild us, frankly, on a spiritual level. To me, that means getting back to the point where our Constitution means that you don't tap people's phones and poke into their e-mail and you don't arrest people and keep them hidden for a year and a half without charging them. Those are the kind of fundamentals that I think the American people have every right to expect. I just think that the American people want to believe again. I'm here to take a message of hope.[3]

Carol told NPR that she was opposed to the war from the beginning and that "If you pick a fight with somebody that's smaller than you and you beat them, where's the honor in that?"[4] She also admitted that her presidential bid was a "long shot," but that didn't mean that she didn't think she could win. "Long shots" are Carol Moseley Braun's specialty, so to speak, since her entrance and meteoric rise in politics could best be described as an outside chance. How this working class urban girl rose to make history in the United States Senate requires a look at the early life and career path of Carol Moseley Braun.

A TOUGH CHICAGO UPBRINGING STEELS CAROL MOSELEY BRAUN'S RESOLVE

Carol Moseley, born August 16, 1947, was the first of four children born to Edna Davie and Joseph John Moseley.[5] Growing up on the Southside of Chicago, her family owned an apartment building and occupied the first floor. Carol and her three younger siblings, Marsha, Joseph, and Johnny, all attended public schools on the Southside of Chicago, and they were all encouraged to go to college. Her father, a police officer, was an accomplished musician and spoke several languages. His brothers were also police officers and together they were among the first

African Americans on the police force. In the 1960s Joseph left the police force and worked as a real estate salesman on the Southside. His violent temper became a growing concern for the family and Carol, the oldest child, would often take her younger siblings and flee the difficult situation by going to grandmother's house. Her mother was a medical technician who worked full time. There were very few black medical technicians at that time and Edna worked hard to help support her family. Dealing with her husband's mood swings was often difficult and she relied on Carol to be a peacemaker for the family. Even though family life was often rocky for the Moseleys, together they encouraged their children to work hard in school and make the most of opportunities. In *Ebony* magazine, Carol noted that her parents were "the perfect counterpoints to one another." She added, "He, the confrontational idealist and she, the accommodating realist."[6] When Carol was fifteen, her parents divorced, and she went to live with her grandmother in a part of Chicago that was high in crime and so dangerous, it was known as the "Bucket of Blood."

THE CIVIL RIGHTS MOVEMENT: A LIVING HISTORY LESSON

Carol experienced the sting of racism at a young age. She made friends with a white girl who lived next door and learned that her new friend was spanked for playing with her. A family vacation down south introduced young Carol to Jim Crow laws that required her family to use different bathrooms and drinking fountains than white travelers. In Montgomery, Alabama, young Carol simply refused to drink from the "colored" drinking fountain because she felt that the segregation laws were wrong. At her elementary school, white children, angry that blacks had been admitted, threw rocks at the windows of the school, and Carol and her black classmates were forced to duck under the desks to avoid being hit. Although this type of racism was common when Carol was growing up, her parents taught her to have ethnic pride. She said, "They raised us in a world that did not acknowledge or legitimize racism."[7]

Historic civil rights legislation was passed that immediately affected young Carol's life. In 1954, when she was only seven years old, the United States Supreme Court ruled on *Brown, et al. vs. the Board of Education of Topeka*. The decision was handed down that segregation of children in public schools solely on the basis of race, even though the physical facilities and other tangible factors may be equal, deprives children of the minority groups equal educational opportunities. The court stated: "We conclude, unanimously, that in the field of public education the doctrine of 'separate but equal' has no place. Separate educational facilities are inherently un-equal."[8] A year later, a fourteen-year-old neighborhood boy, Emmitt Till was lynched by whites for merely speaking with a white person when he was in Mississippi visiting relatives. Blacks and women were banned from serving on the jury and the white men charged in the crime were quickly found "not guilty." The Till case brought to Carol's attention that her own aunt, her mother's oldest sister, died when struck by a truck driven by a white man who never even faced charges in the death. These harsh realities made a lasting impression on Carol that would later shape her activism and outspokenness on behalf of her race.

The Till case reverberated throughout the country and prompted Rosa Parks to refuse to give up her seat on a bus in Montgomery, Alabama, just four months after Emmitt Till was murdered. When Rosa Parks was removed from the bus, blacks, in response to Dr. Martin Luther King, Jr.'s urging, refused to ride the buses, starting a bus boycott that lasted almost a year.

Carol, although still a young school girl, was passionately involved in the civil rights movement and mesmerized by the inspiration of Dr. Martin Luther King, Jr. Once, she staged a one-person sit-in at a restaurant that refused to serve her, and she had rocks thrown at her when she refused to leave a whites-only beach, known as Rainbow Beach. Despite the rock throwing, Carol, like the civil rights leader she followed, did not throw the rocks back. She wanted to promote peace, and so she, like her hero, King, behaved nonviolently. A feisty sixteen-year-old Carol marched with Dr. Martin Luther King, Jr. in an all-white Chicago neighborhood to protest segregation.

Since her parents were divorced, Carol lived in Oakwood during her high school years, an area of Chicago where mostly very poor blacks lived. Carol wanted to get away from Oakwood, and her mother wanted that, too, but money was tight, so Carol worked part time as a checker in a grocery store to help her mother make ends meet. Her determination to exert herself and be recognized showed in her high school days when she wanted to make the very competitive and clique-controlled cheerleading squad. "I wanted to be a cheerleader, but I wasn't popular; I wasn't in the 'in crowd.' And I wanted it [to be a cheerleader] so badly that I practiced harder than anyone. I was a tumbler and I wound up being better than anyone else. Well, when the tryouts were over the other cheerleaders weren't going to let me in, Coach Bonner said, 'you can't possibly cut the most talented tumbler we have.' So, I became a cheerleader."[9] By the time Carol graduated from Parker High School, she was committed to Dr. King's philosophy of nonviolence. While some of her friends joined militant black groups, such as the Black Panthers, Carol did not want to engage in violence to end segregation. She continued her passionate crusade against segregation by marching with Dr. King again in 1966 near her Oakwood neighborhood. This time, the marchers were attacked by the crowd who threw rocks. Carol fell to her knees and shielded her head from the rocks. Dr. King was only a few feet away and Carol could see him being hit. Without skipping a beat, Dr. King continued to march. Even though Carol wished that she could throw a rock back at the angry crowd, she knew that Dr. King stood for peacefulness, and she wanted her career to follow a similar path.

After high school, Carol majored in political science at the University of Illinois in Chicago, and then pursued a law degree at the University of Chicago Law School. Carol Moseley Braun went to law school "Largely because of my father. I wanted to be an art historian, but my father was a frustrated lawyer himself. He had gone to law school, but never finished. My sister Marsha is a lawyer, and she has better credentials than me and my brother is about to start law school."[10] At the law school, Carol organized the Black Law Students Association and she was the organization's first president. Her reputation as an articulate leader was growing. In law school, Carol began dating a fellow law student named Michael Braun, and in 1973, a year after Carol completed law school, she and Michael were married. In 1977 they had a son, Matthew. Carol worked as an assistant attorney for three years in the United States Attorney's office. She quickly gained a reputation as a rising star and earned the U.S. Attorney General Special Achievement Award. The ambitious young attorney also worked for the Davis, Niner, and Barnhill law firm. Always interested in politics, Carol volunteered to help Harold Washington's campaign for the Illinois state legislature. Washington won the campaign, and Carol discovered that she enjoyed the excitement of a political campaign and the political process. Harold Washington served for twelve years in the state House of Representatives, four years in the state Senate, and four years in the U.S. House of Representatives. He also served as Chicago's first black mayor, but died shortly after he won re-election to a second term. In 1978, when her friends and neighbors started to urge her to run for office, Carol, a thirty-one-year-old mother, ran for state representative. She ran for the seat that Robert Mann, a noted liberal, was leaving. Moseley Braun defeated eleven other candidates for the seat. In a short time, Carol distinguished herself as an effective debater and as a passionate advocate for education. In 1985, Carol was the chief sponsor of the Illinois Urban Schools Improvement Act, a law that helped create parents' councils at every city school. The idea was modeled after a similar program in California. The purpose of the councils was to identify the problems that impede students' progress and to devise solutions. Moseley Braun's proposal of this act was so popular, that politicians from opposing political camps supported it. Republican Chicago Aldermen Joseph Kotlarz and Danny Davis said they supported the act because the councils "provide parents and the community with meaningful control of their schools."[11] Moved by her own difficult public school experience, and the label that Chicago schools were the "Worst in America,"[12] Carol also sponsored every school-funding bill for eight consecutive years, 1980–1987. During her ten years in the Illinois General Assembly, Carol was lauded as a qualified legislator and a notable debater. She was voted "Best Legislator" every year of her term. For eight years she served as assistant majority leader in the Illinois House of Representatives, and likely would have won re-election to the House if she had run again.

Instead, in 1988 Moseley Braun sought a new challenge, and a job closer to home to help her care for her son and her sick mother. Carol emphasized her experience in her campaign for Cook County Recorder of Deeds. She told voters: "Look at my years in the legislature; I've been productive and that's what makes me qualified for this office."[13] Her Republican opponent, Alderman Bernard Stone, published a campaign brochure that included a photo of Moseley Braun. The press ran a story that quoted Stone telling a newspaper's editorial board: "I don't expect your newspaper to endorse me. Just run a picture of Braun. That's all I ask."[14] Since most Cook County voters are white and Moseley Braun is black, the use of Carol's picture in her opponent's campaign brochure was thought by some press reports and Carol's political advisers to be a racial tactic. Al Raby, campaign manager for Moseley Braun said that the brochure "smacks of desperation, the politics of division."[15] The *Chicago Sun Time*s endorsed her candidacy, calling her an "articulate lawyer" with "leadership ability."[16] Despite the rough campaign, Carol easily won the position of Cook County Recorder of Deeds. The Recorder of Deeds office was hardly an exciting prospect for Carol, who was seen as a rising star in Illinois politics, yet she made the most of the position.

The record keeping system in the Recorder of Deeds office was antiquated and the office was losing money. It was in need of a physical renovation as well as an upgraded computer system. In less than a year, Moseley Braun turned the office, which employed three hundred people and had a budget of $8 million, around. The poem that Carol had grown up hearing her mother repeat: "When a job is once begun, never stop until it's done. Be the job large or small, do it right or not at all,"[17] characterized Carol's work at the Recorder of Deeds office, and Moseley Braun was noticed for her efforts. Her commununication skills helped persuade more than fifty business executives to volunteer their time to serve on a "Blue Ribbon Committee" that would study the needs of the recorder's office. An editorial in the *Chicago Tribune* noted that "When Carol Moseley Braun campaigned for Cook County recorder of deeds, her sales pitch stressed competence, integrity, accomplishment and leadership. Half a year in office, Braun has demonstrated all four."[18] Moseley Braun wanted the recorder's office to run like a business, and she was able, in short order, to make the office an income-producing one for the county.

TIMING IS EVERYTHING: THE YEAR OF THE WOMAN

After three successful years at the helm of the Recorder of Deeds office, Carol was deciding whether or not she should run for re-election. At the same time, President George H. W. Bush nominated Republican Judge Clarence Thomas for the United States Supreme Court. The choice of staunchly conservative Thomas to replace liberal Thurgood Marshall, was unsettling to many civil rights and women's groups. Thomas's nomination process lasted more than three months, and at the end of the questioning, his nomination was passed on to the full Senate without a recommendation. It was then that thirty-five-year-old law professor Anita Hill charged to the Judiciary Committee, that Clarence Thomas had sexually harassed her when she was a subordinate of Thomas's at the Department of Education and later at the Equal Employment Opportunity Commission. When the public learned of Hill's charges, Thomas's efforts to join the Supreme Court became a televised drama starring Thomas and Hill that pitted the all-male establishment against a young black female. The country was spellbound in front of television sets when Hill testified. She had to "go public" with the charges that she had made to the Judiciary Committee, even though testifying about such personal information was humiliating and embarrassing. She described Thomas's lewd behavior, which included details about pornographic films and the use of sexually explicit language. In the end, Thomas won Senate confirmation by a 52–48 margin. Still, many people, especially women were outraged. Immediately after the confirmation, 100 women, including women legislators, marched up the steps of Capital Hill chanting, "We'll remember in November." Many women were angry that the Senate operated like an old boy's club, instead of the democratic institution it was meant to be. In particular, National Organization for Women President, Patricia Ireland, said, that "the all male Senate Judiciary Committee's cavalier treatment of Anita Hill galvanized NOW to "the feminization of power."[19] Carol Moseley Braun reacted to the hearings by feeling outraged about how the Senate looked and operated. She told CNN's Catherine Crier: "We saw the Senate in action on television and it just did not look like democracy, it didn't look like representative democracy and people, I think, had a sense that somehow the institution had gotten out of kilter, and I started getting phone calls to run [for Senate]."[20]

One of the senators who voted for Thomas's confirmation was Illinois Senator Alan Dixon. Without money or political backing, Carol decided to launch a grass roots campaign on November 19, 1991, to run against Dixon for Senate. A wealthy Chicago lawyer, Al Hofeld also entered the race and he and Senator Dixon engaged in a vicious attack against each other through expensive ads and during a pivotal debate that included Carol Moseley Braun. During a debate, Hofeld and Dixon hurled insults at each other and Carol started to look like the most reasonable, professional choice for the nomination. Carol, as she had done as a young supporter of the civil rights movement, refused to resort to a negative campaign. Instead, she carried out a positive campaign, promising voters that she would create jobs by shifting money from the Pentagon budget to domestic public works projects and taxing the wealthy. She was opposed to congressional term limits, the death penalty, and the ban on using federal funds for abortions. During the primary, women's activist Gloria Steinem endorsed her candidacy by visiting Illinois and speaking on Carol's behalf. Carol reflected that "Gloria Steinem was the single most important source of support for my candidacy bar none."[21]

During the primary campaign, Hofeld and Dixon were favored to win, and they outspent Carol Moseley Braun 10–1. Alan Dixon had not lost a race in forty-two years. To many people's surprise, Carol went on to win the primary race, receiving 38 percent of the vote. The press described her primary victory as "stunning" and "startling." One journalist said her win "exemplified the 1991 World Series expression 'from last to first.' She was last in funding, last in organization and last in on-air commercials."[22] When she made her primary victory speech at the McCormick Center Hotel on election night, she said, "We have had to fight big money, deep pockets, entrenched power." We had a sound message, and people chose substance over sound bites in this election."[23] Savoring her upset victory, she joyously danced to the song "Ain't No Stopping Us Now."

In the general election, Carol faced Republican Richard Williamson, a well-connected Kenilworth, Chicago, lawyer. He, was a former diplomat and in the early 1980s worked in the White House as an assistant to President Reagan for intergovernmental affairs. His stern business style was in sharp contrast to the energetic, warm, and vivacious Moseley Braun's, who often garnered "wild whoops and cheers" from her audiences. Often, she made blunt statements directed at women in the audience:

"The Government has no more role in telling a woman what to do with her body than it would a man."[24]

When Carol won the primary, she caught the attention and gained support from prominent politicians. President Bill Clinton and Vice President Al Gore campaigned with Carol, on what was dubbed a "Victory Tour." Even Republican James S. Brady, who served as White House Press Secretary for President Reagan endorsed Carol's Senate bid, even though he worked with her Republican opponent Williamson. Brady, who was injured by a gunshot wound that was meant for President Reagan said, "Voters have a very clear choice in Illinois. I'm supporting Carol Braun because she's the candidate to be counted on to support strong gun laws." He added that, "Braun made it clear that she would be a strong ally in the Senate, and that's why I'm supporting her."[25] Other support came from *Crain's Chicago Business*. Her communication style, described as "inclusive" was thought to be more likely to bring people together in the diverse city of Chicago. The business publication expressed concern that Braun had "much to learn about industries" but noted that, "As a state legislator, she became a key player in the Democratic caucus, rising to the post of assistant majority leader, where she was a strong, independent voice for Illinois."[26] A *Sun Times* article described her as "warm, telegenic and charismatic."[27] The *Sun Times* endorsed Moseley Braun's candidacy, with some misgivings about "the emphasis placed by Braun's supporters on the fact, as if it were all that mattered, that she will be, if she wins, the first black woman elected to the U.S. Senate." While the paper acknowledged the importance of that, it commented, that "the purpose of this election is to choose a senator, not commit an historic act." The endorsement for Moseley Braun, however, was because of her emphasis on "early childhood programs, universal literacy, [and] increased federal support for higher education."[28]

During the campaign Moseley Braun made bus trips throughout the state. One trip, to an area downstate, was nicknamed "Forgotonia" because it lacks a major highway or urban center. At a campaign rally, Moseley Braun drew the biggest cheer when she bluntly declared, "They said they wanted to give you freedom to make choices in your life and yet they want to get into your bedroom and tell you whether or not you have to be pregnant."[29]

Support and endorsements were the high point of Carol's senate race, but accusations of financial mishandling and campaign staff turnover followed Carol wherever she went. Carol tried to minimize the damage that such bad press levied on her campaign by saying "the buck stops here," and that she was just carrying out the wishes of her seventy-one-year-old mother, Edna Moseley, when she disbursed her mother's $28,750 windfall without applying it to her nursing home bill.[30] She blamed the story on her opponent: "The same people who attempted to peddle racism in this campaign found that it wasn't being bought by the people of Illinois, and now they are trying to manufacture scandal," she said.[31] In reference to Williamson's negative campaign, Moseley Braun said that he is "trying to frighten people with the image of a bomb-throwing welfare mother running for the Senate."[32] Williamson campaigned vigorously against Moseley Braun, painting her as a candidate with a "pattern of deception"[33] and questioning whether or not she could be trusted. Williamson ran radio commercials that linked Moseley Braun with Mayor Washington and tried to raise questions in voters' minds about Moseley Braun's financial handlings. One spot asked, "What is there in Carol Moseley Braun's 1988 tax returns that she doesn't want the *Chicago Tribune* or the people of Illinois to see?" In response, Carol ran radio commercials that took the high road. In the commercials, she said, "My campaign will be positive. It will be about issues and who is the best qualified candidate to represent Illinois in the U.S. Senate . . . this election is too important to waste time being negative."[34] With a healthy lead in the polls, Carol tried to keep her promise to remain positive during two televised debates with Williamson. The first debate was called "acrimonious," because it focused mostly on Moseley Braun's ethics, in particular the $28,750 inheritance that wasn't reported to Medicaid. Williamson tried to convince voters that it was part of a "pattern of deceit." In the second debate, candidates discussed their positions on healthcare, education, crime, and the economy, and after just a few minutes, as in the first debate, they began to criticize each other. Williamson described Moseley Braun's positions as "goofy," "reckless," "silly," and "liberal." He said that she was "out of the mainstream."[35] He even chided Moseley Braun for touting education reform but sending her child to a private school. Carol felt that Williamson "crossed the line" by discussing her child and she retorted, "You've distorted my record one too many times." "The fact is I've been under constant attack for the past six months because he wants to scare people about who Carol Moseley Braun is and doesn't want to talk about his own record."[36] Carol told voters that "It's time for a change" and she would be a "fighter for the working class."[37] In the end, Williamson's negative attacks would prove unsuccessful and Carol's promise of a change is what voters got.

CAROL MOSELEY BRAUN GOES TO WASHINGTON

On November 3, Election Day, 1992, Carol Moseley Braun, who just six months earlier was an obscure recorder of deeds, became the United

States senator from Illinois by an impressive 10 percent of the vote. In her acceptance speech, Carol said,

> It's a new day in America. We have won a great victory tonight. You have made history. You are showing the way to the future for the entire country. You have shown what we can do when we come together, when we stop them from dividing us along race lines, along gender lines.[38]

The Illinois senate race was the "most watched" senate race in the nation,[39] and the *New York Times* attributed her win to "the symbolism of her campaign combined with an army of angry women voters."[40] That army of angry voters gave Moseley Braun the company of other women who were going to the Senate for the first time. Dianne Feinstein and Barbara Boxer, both Democrats from California, and Patty Murray, Democrat from Washington, who described herself as a "mom in tennis shoes." The new women senators joined the incumbent Senator Barbara Mikulski, a Maryland Democrat, and Nancy Kassebaum, a Kansas Republican, to make up the greatest number of women ever in the Senate. When Senate Majority Leader George Mitchell welcomed the new senators he said that the freshmen class would make the Senate "more representative" of the country. He added that because of their presence "There will be new and different perspectives."[41] At one of several ceremonies celebrating her victory, she and a crowd of about 1,000 onlookers, most of whom were black, stood in somewhat bemused silence as ninety-year-old Senator Strom Thurmond, a Republican from South Carolina, a onetime symbol of segregation, stated "We're proud of this country" and that he wanted to "cooperate with the ladies."[42] Democratic Senator Joseph Biden of Delaware noted the significance of the moment. He said, "If there's anyone in this room over forty then you would certainly be surprised at what you saw today. Who would ever have thought they would see Strom Thurmond welcome to the Senate the first African-American female Senator."[43] Less than one year later, Republican Kay Bailey Hutchinson of Texas won a special election to fill the term of Lloyd Bentsen, Jr., bringing the total number of women senators to seven.

An editorial in *Ebony* magazine described 1992 as the "Year of the Black Woman" because two African American women made history. Enthusiastically, the author wrote: "Carol Moseley Braun is going to the U.S. Senate and Dr. Mae Jemison went to outer space."[44] Senator Paul Simon, an Illinois Democrat who like most other Democrats supported Dixon in the primary, welcomed his new colleague by saying, "We have a Senator-elect who's going to appeal to the best in us."[45]

Wasting no time when she got to the Senate, the freshman senator, who was appointed to the Judiciary Committee, the same committee that held the Thomas hearings, Moseley Braun took on one of the senate's oldest members—Senator Jesse Helms of North Carolina. Helms had been in the Senate more than twenty years, and Moseley Braun was only six months into her tenure. Helms had added an amendment to a bill on national service that would extend a patent to the symbol of the United Daughters of the Confederacy. The symbol's design included the Confederate flag. Even though Helms was a formidable figure in the Senate, many senators agreed with the junior senator, Braun, and persuaded colleagues to let her speak on behalf of African Americans. Senator Joseph Biden of Delaware described Carol as "the one single voice speaking for millions and millions of voices in this country who feel disenfranchised." Moseley Braun made an impassioned speech against the patent extension. She argued, "The fact of the matter is the emblems of the Confederacy have meaning to Americans even 100 years after the end of the Civil War."

The Senate vote to table the measure was defeated 52–48. Braun was visibly shaken, but she composed herself and began to speak impromptu about the issue. She first reiterated some of the topics she had covered in her first utterance, before the vote. Then, in an exasperated and dramatic plea, she said:

> What I did not talk about and what I am constrained now to talk about with no small degree of emotion is the symbolism of what this vote really means. I have to tell you, this vote is about race. It is about racial symbolism. It is about racial symbols, the racial past, and the single most painful episode in American history. I have to, on many occasions, as the only African American here, constrain myself to be calm, to be laid back, to talk about these issues in very intellectual, non-emotional terms.
>
> There are those who would keep us slipping back into the darkness of division, into the snake pit of racial hatred, of racial antagonism and of support for symbols—symbols to struggle to keep African Americans, American of African descent, in bondage.
>
> On this issue, there can be no consensus. It is an outrage. It is an insult. It is absolutely unacceptable to me and to millions of Americans, black and white, that would put an imprimatur of the United States Senate on a symbol of this kind of idea.[16]

Senator Dianne Feinstein, seeing an emotional Moseley Braun, moved toward Carol and held her hand as she spoke. When Carol finished her impassioned plea and the vote was taken again, the amendment was tabled 75–25. Carol's persuasive skills gained considerable attention among her Senate colleagues and the press, including the *New York Times*, which reported, that "Carol Moseley Braun made the senate listen today as freshmen seldom do."[47] Exasperated, she shouted, "You are the party of Lincoln!" "The party of Lincoln defeated that flag and abolished slavery," Sen. Bill Bradley, Democrat of New Jersey, said to Republicans supporting the amendment. But the most moving comment came from Sen. Howell Heflin, Democrat of Alabama, who told the chamber that one of his great-grandfathers signed the order declaring Alabama's secession from the Union, and that one of his grandfathers was a surgeon in the Confederate army. "I come from a family background that is deeply rooted in the Confederacy. . . . What they did at the time they thought was right," he said, but then added: "We must get racism behind, and we must move forward."[48] The *New York Times* reported, that "she matched reason to passion with splendid results."[49] Celeste M. Walls explained Moseley Braun's ability to persuade more effectively the second time she spoke. She wrote: "Because she [Carol Moseley Braun] recognized the ineffectiveness of her initial arguments—arguments that were more clearly rooted in logic and rationality—Moseley Braun chose to change her rhetorical status in ways that both promoted and cast as positive her identity as a double minority [both black and female] in the Senate. She accomplished this by empowering herself via enactment and the use of inspirational appeals. Both of these rhetorical tools elevated her rhetorical status."[50] In an essay in *Argumentation and Advocacy*, John Butler explained that Moseley Braun either had to shift her argument or give up. Moseley Braun's shift was so dramatic the only thing that remained was the outcome she desired.[51] Carol Moseley Braun's speech was not prepared in advance. She explained that she switched her method of appeal the second time she spoke because "My first inclination is to be reasonable, but it doesn't captivate. You have to turn on the juice and touch people."[52] Senator Helms, upon meeting Moseley Braun in the elevator later that day, began to sing "Dixie." Helms said "I'm going to sing Dixie until she cries."[53]

In addition to her work on the Judiciary Committee, Carol also served on the Finance and Banking Committees. The issue most passionately pursued by Carol during her Senate term was education. She authored a complicated, wide-reaching education bill that sought to gain support from the federal government for its share of the costs of school renovations and building. One of her arguments was, "Study after study has demonstrated a direct correlation between the conditions of school facilities and student achievement. A disturbing number of our schools are literally crumbling around our students." She wanted support for new buildings because she argued "it is useless to have a computer in the classroom without a socket to plug it into."[54] But her efforts were futile, since a lack of support for this bill, including none from President Clinton, caused the bill to die. Not one to give up easily, Moseley Braun reworked the bill and called for $22 billion in interest-free bonds from the federal government to the school districts over two years. President Clinton reconsidered and backed Moseley

Braun's efforts. So strongly did the president support Moseley Braun's idea, that he mentioned the school facilities problem in his 1998 State of the Union address. President Clinton said,

> My balanced budget will help to hire 100,000 new teachers who pass the state competency test. Now, with these teachers—listen, with these teachers, we will actually be able to reduce class size in the first, second and third grades to an average of eighteen students a class all across America. If I got the math right, more teachers, teaching smaller classes requires more classrooms. So I also propose a school construction tax cut to help communities modernize or build 5,000 schools.

President Clinton included the money needed for the program in one of his budget requests to Congress. When Carol ran for re-election to the Senate, President Clinton campaigned for her and told supporters about her work on behalf of education. At a dinner for Senator Carol Moseley-Braun in Chicago in July 1997, President Clinton told the audience:

> Carol Moseley Braun is the first person who came to me and said, "Mr. President, I know the National Government has never done this before, but we ought to try to do something about the crumbling buildings in our country's school system." "I was in Philadelphia the other day; the average age of a school building in Philadelphia is sixty-five years of age. Now, a lot of those schools are very well built, but they're in poor repair. And there are a lot of school districts that simply don't have the property tax base and simply don't have a high enough percentage of parents living in the school district as property owners to do everything they need to do to rebuild these buildings.[55]

Other issues that Carol championed during her Senate term included student loan interest deduction, a bill to defeat the school voucher program and affirmative action. On March 30, 1995, Carol rose to speak on the floor of the senate about affirmative action and specifically addressed the Glass Ceiling Initiative. Her main goal was to convince her colleagues that affirmative action must continue and that it has been beneficial not only for women and minorities but that it is important for the country's economic growth.

She used narrative discourse when she described the need for continued action. She said:

> What we are debating is whether the majority of America's people—and that is what you get if you count our nation's 51 percent women and 10 percent non-white males—will have a shot, a chance to participate on an equal footing in America's economic affairs. Last month, I met with a group of young schoolchildren. I talked with them about the historic nature of the 104th Con-

gress, and how we had come so far in the seventy-five years the women's suffrage amendment became part of our Constitution. I pointed out to them that there are now eight women in the U.S Senate. I spoke of this as if it were a great accomplishment. The children looked at me in confusion—one little girl looked at me and said: "Is that all?" What that young girl is telling us, is that we need to look at the whole picture. And when we do, we know without a doubt that much work remains to be done.[56]

Many of her actions brought positive attention to her. One vote, however, preserved a legal loophole that would result in giving the drug company Glaxo Wellcome an extra two years on its patent for Zantac, the best-selling drug used to treat ulcers. Without the patent, Zantac could have been made generically, saving consumers millions of dollars. Carol was criticized because she knew the CEO of Glaxo from when she was a state legislator and he was a lobbyist. Glaxo also contributed money to Moseley Braun's senate campaign.

When she was up for re-election, she faced a multi-millionaire Republican, state Senator Peter Fitzgerald. Although Fitzgerald kept a low profile in the campaign, he benefited from the negative press that Moseley Braun's financial handlings and trip to Nigeria brought. Fitzgerald said, "The most important qualification for United States Senator is that people be able to have faith in the ethics and judgment of their U.S. Senator. I think she is vulnerable to questions of ethics and judgment."[57] Although she had been a strong voice for a number of important issues in the Senate, Moseley Braun's image was tarnished by repeated mentions in the press about her withholding some of her mother's money from Medicaid and running up a $544,000 debt in her first senate race. Other negative press reported that she backed her campaign manager, also her boyfriend, Kgosie Matthews, against sexual harassment charges. When she was elected to the Senate in 1992, she and her son, along with her Matthews took a twenty-six-day trip to Africa, instead of spending time thanking constituents for support and tackling the many details of setting up her Senate office. And in 1996 she took a trip to Nigeria, and met with the country's military ruler, General Sani Abacha. Abacha is thought to have murdered his political opponents and stolen over $1 million from Nigeria. To make matters worse, Carol Moseley Braun did not meet any pro-democracy leaders while she was there.

When Fitzgerald won the race, with 51 percent of the vote, he became the first Republican to win a Senate race in Illinois in eight previous elections.

After she lost her bid for re-election to the Senate, President Clinton appointed her as a consultant for the Department of Education and then nominated her to be the Ambassador to New Zealand, which she describes as her favorite position, often referring to it as "Ambassador to Paradise." In 2001, Moseley Braun became a professor of politics at Morris Brown College in Atlanta, Georgia.

TAKE THE 'MEN ONLY' SIGN OFF THE WHITE HOUSE: CAROL MOSELEY BRAUN FOR PRESIDENT

Carol Moseley Braun first started to think about running for president in January 2003 when she told Democratic Party Chairman Terry McAuliffe of her idea.[58] Then, in mid-February, she filed papers to form an exploratory bid. She said, "I'm not unaware that I'm trying to do what no woman has done before."[59] She campaigned in the early primary states of Iowa, New Hampshire, and South Carolina the weekend before filing her [exploratory bid] papers, she drew meager audiences—just one old college friend made it through a snowstorm to the first campaign event of her presidential race in Des Moines. Undaunted, she moved on to New Hampshire, where she had "about fifteen people" in her audience.[60] Asked about her failed Senate re-election bid, Carol told the *Washington Post*, "The people of Illinois saw through that. I've won fifteen elections and lost only one. I have every confidence I will be able to do the fundraising necessary. We'll know in the next few months whether the support is out there."[61] Some pundits described her as a spoiler, taking votes away from Al Sharpton. A *USA Today* article said she faced "seemingly insurmountable odds" and Moseley Braun countered their criticisms by pointing out "that one of her opponents, Senator John Edwards of North Carolina, has yet to stand for re-election; another, Dr. [Howard] Dean, led a state with fewer residents than Cook County; and a third, Rev. [Al] Sharpton, has never held elective office. She says she is the only candidate with experience in local, state, national and international government."[62] Donna Brazile, who managed Al Gore's 2000 presidential campaign commented on Moseley Braun's presidential bid. She said, "She's intelligent, she's charming. She knows how to talk about farm issues. She'll be good in the South." Brazile also noted that while Carol would "start out as an asterisk" she would likely build support.[63] But many press reports discounted her chances for a successful race less than a month after she started her exploratory bid. *USA Today* noted that, "Of the eight candidates currently vying for the Democratic presidential nomination, a good case can be made that Carol Moseley Braun is the least likely to end up as the party's standard bearer. The former Illinois senator has two politically fatal flaws: She is black and female."[64] Columnist Ellen Goodman noted that Carol Moseley Braun's presidential bid "didn't get the requisite seven-second sound bite on the evening news. CBS used her announcement to lead in a story on bottom-tier candidates, asking 'Why are they running?' And Diane Sawyer opened her 'Good Morning America' interview asking, 'Why don't you work for another candidate who has a real shot at victory?"[65] Although her candidacy was described as a way to put herself back into the national spotlight, she insisted that hers was neither a vanity nor a spoiler candidacy. And she repeatedly told reporters that, "I'm in it to win."[66] A Quinnipiac University poll late February found she had 7 percent of the Democratic vote, placing her ahead of Senator Bob Graham (D-Fla.), Reverend Al Sharpton (who had 5 percent), Dean, and Representative Dennis Kucinich (D-Ohio).[67] *Christian Science Monitor* noted, that "Moseley Braun's Democratic rivals in the race treat her with a polite deference, which in political circles is tantamount to being dismissed. She's raised so little money she often drives herself to events in a rented car."[68] While she's lauded for her articulate, well-reasoned responses, she's usually no more than a footnote in news coverage, an "also ran," if she's mentioned at all. "Of the three who have no chance at all, she has been by far the most appealing," said political analyst Larry Sabato, "But she has absolutely no chance whatsoever."[69]

Her presidential bid, though repeatedly described as a long shot, also received positive attention. The *Chicago Defender* described her as "Illinois' favorite daughter and the first lady in the community."[70] She was honored by the Women's Campaign School at Yale University during the presidential campaign as a notable woman in politics. Women who attended the event described her as "inspirational" and a sign that "women can do anything."[71]

In May, she debated along with the other eight Democratic presidential candidates. Moderator George Stephanopoulos asked her, as she had been asked before, if she was in the race just to undermine Al Sharpton's bid, and Carol explained that her candidacy was to defeat all the other contenders, not just Sharpton. In her closing statement she used a narrative style when she talked about how her mother used to say that whether you came to this country on the Mayflower, on slave ships, across the Rio Grande or through Ellis Island, "we're all in the same boat now." With passion, she said,

I believe that the challenge for all of us is to work to make certain that Americans come together to transform this nation, so that we can live up to our promise of democracy. We have a sacred responsibility to leave the next generation with no less than what we inherited from the last. The last generation gave us all opportunity, they gave us liberty and a hopefulness that I believe has been lost.[72]

Her exploratory bid continued until she made a formal announcement at Howard University in September. Carol began with thanking Howard University, her audience, her many supporters, including the National Organization for Women and the National Women's Political Caucus, which both endorsed her candidacy. She stated her reason for declaring her candidacy:

> I am running for the Democratic nomination because I believe this party ought to stand for inclusion, hope, and new ways to resolve old problems. I am fighting for the nomination because I am determined to move our party in the direction of our nation's most noble ideals, and live up to our generation's duty to leave the next generation no less freedom, no less opportunity, no less optimism than we inherited from our ancestors.[73]

In late fall, Patricia Ireland, President of the National Organization for Women, became campaign manager for Moseley Braun's presidential campaign. At the time, the campaign was working on raising enough money to qualify for matching funds. She said that while the campaign did not meet the matching funds' goal it had set for itself, it would still have enough money to continue. And while some of the frontrunners were buying spots on television, Moseley Braun's campaign was working on radio ads in South Carolina. In November, Carol participated, along with the other Democratic candidates in the "Rock the Vote" debate held in Boston's Faneuil Hall. In response to Howard Dean's recent remark that he wanted to be the candidate for "guys with Confederate flags on their pickup trucks," Moseley Braun said,

> In the Senate I opened myself up to the venom of the right-wing conspiracy by battling Jesse Helms over the Confederate flag. We have to as Democrats begin to engage a civil conversation how we can get past that racist strategy that the Republicans have foisted upon this country, how we can bring Southern whites and blacks and northern blacks and whites together, how we can come together to reclaim this country—and Latinos, and Asians, and Christians and Muslims and Jews and Protestants.[74]

In December, the campaign suffered a blow when it was 700 signatures short of making the Virginia Democratic primary ballot. Although Virginia is a fairly conservative state, the campaign expected to get the 10,000 names required by the State Board of Elections; the other eight candidates were able to get the needed signatures.

On January 15th, after Moseley Braun appeared as a guest on the Daily Show with Jon Stewart, she announced her withdrawal from the race, although during the show she gave no clue of her decision. When she made her announcement she said:

I want to thank everybody for your kindness to me, and for allowing me to participate as a candidate for the Democratic nomination for president of the United States. The campaign has been a wonderful learning experience for me, one that restored my faith in the political process and renewed my belief in the goodness of the American people. I am here today to thank those Iowans who were prepared to stand for me in Monday's caucuses, and to ask that you stand instead for Howard Dean.[75]

With this speech, Carol Moseley Braun ended her bid for the presidency.

CAROL MOSELEY BRAUN'S PRESIDENTIAL OBSTACLES

One of the most obvious obstacles facing Moseley Braun was the consistent mentions in the press that she was a long shot for the nomination. Voters are unlikely to back, financially or otherwise, a candidate who doesn't seem to have any chance of winning. The suggestion that Democrats asked her to join the race to be a spoiler for Rev. Al Sharpton, and the articles that insinuated that Sharpton was her main competitor, implied that blacks would only vote for black candidates. Moseley Braun recognized this and repeatedly bristled at the suggestions that she was competition only to Sharpton. Typical of her response was the one she offered a *Daily News* reporter:

The black community is not a monolith, and to suggest that black voters have to be [in] lockstep and have to get behind a single black candidate seems to take that community for granted. And to suggest that somehow I am competitive with Al Sharpton and not competitive with [ex-Vermont Gov. Howard] Dean, [North Carolina Sen. John] Edwards, [Missouri Rep. Richard] Gephardt [Connecticut Sen. Joseph] Lieberman or [Massachusetts Sen. John] Kerry is to really relegate me to an unfortunate corner. I hope to reach out to all people.[76]

Another disadvantage was her lack of funds. She commented in her withdrawal from the race and endorsement of Howard Dean that: "the funding and organizational disadvantages of a nontraditional campaign could not be overcome, and so this campaign was unable to compete effectively or support your hard work as it should."

Although she had been endorsed by two influential women's group—the National Organization for Women and the National Women's Political Caucus—that support failed to translate into financial support. Braun struggled to raise money while running up thousands of dollars in debt. She also missed the deadline to file paperwork for the initial round of federal campaign money, delaying for several weeks the receipt of any federal matching funds, expected to amount to several hundred thousand dollars.[77]

The negative press that dogged her Senate races followed her into her presidential bid. Rarely was she described as simply "former Illinois Senator." More likely, the explanation of who she is included the words "alleged misuse of campaign money" and "ethics" and those terms further dampened her chances, especially in the "sound bite" nature of political messages. Carol Moseley Braun has spent a good part of her career fending off criticism and accusations. In fact, a Federal Election Campaign audit in 1996 found sloppy accounting practices in Ms. Moseley Braun's campaign organization, but the commission levied no fines. The case was dropped in 1997.[78]

Because she was a Senator for one term, and even though it catapulted her to national fame, it is possible that many people did not remember who she was when she ran for president, five years after her Senate term ended.

CAROL MOSELEY BRAUN'S COMMUNICATION STYLE

Carol Moseley Braun has gained a reputation as an engaging and warm communicator. When speaking in public, she has a stage presence and exudes "high wattage."[79] Moseley Braun enjoys speaking and seems to gain energy from expressing herself. The *New York Times* described her as "commanding and ebullient, a den mother with a cheerleader's smile."[80] Carol Moseley Braun has never taken a public speaking course and has not been coached on her skills. She commented: "I still feel I'm grappling with my public speaking. I write my own speeches and I try to speak in ways that engage the listener."[81] Her statement on the floor of the Senate against the use of the Confederate flag was extemporaneous. Her first speech was more reasoned and her second speech was impassioned. It was perhaps at that moment that Moseley Braun learned well that to convince her audience she needs a measure of both reason and emotion, two elements that have become hallmarks of her communication. As a communicator, Carol Moseley Braun is friendly and warm, exuding an optimistic, no-nonsense approach to issues. Characteristic of her bluntness was: "The Government has no more role in telling a woman what to do with her body than it would a man."[82]

INVENTION

Carol Moseley Braun speaks about concerns that face average Americans and her speeches reflect that goal. When she campaigned in 1992 for the Illinois Senate seat, she told constituents:

> I'm an ordinary person. I'm not a millionairess. I'm not part of the 'In'-crowd. I can bring the concerns of people who know what it's like to have to balance

a checkbook and pay the mortgage and go to the grocery store. And those are the voices that need to be heard in the Senate.[83]

Her colloquial, down-to-earth style helps her to relate with average citizens. She described her disdain for the Iraq wars by saying that "If you pick a fight with somebody that's smaller than you and you beat them, where's the honor in that?"[84]

DISPOSITION

Carol Moseley Braun organizes most of her speeches by using narratives to explain a problem, as she did in this speech:

> Last month, I met with a group of young schoolchildren. I talked with them about the historic nature of the 104th Congress, and how we had come so far in the seventy-five years the women's suffrage amendment became part of our Constitution. I pointed out to them that there are now eight women in the U.S Senate. I spoke of this as if it were a great accomplishment. The children looked at me in confusion—one little girl looked at me and said: "Is that all?"[85]

She often tells a short, humorous story at the beginning of her speech to warm up the audience and orient them to her topic. When she spoke at the President's Day commemoration of American Women Presidents in Des Moines, Iowa on February 15, 2003, she said:

> I want to thank all of you for coming out today and braving the cold. I want to thank all of you for coming today, and for braving this snow. When I was Ambassador to New Zealand, I had the privilege of going up to the South Pole, which is about 10,000 feet in altitude. When I got off the plane, I couldn't breathe because of the height, and the pilot, offering me oxygen said, "oh, is it too cold for you to breathe?" I instinctively answered, "no, I'm from Chicago; this is nothing." Thanks, again, for ignoring the weather to come here today.[86]

MEMORIA

Carol Moseley Braun writes her own speeches. She speaks sometimes from main points listed on paper and at other times from a prepared text. The formality of the occasion and the advance time to prepare, dictates the choice. For example, on the floor of the Senate she frequently spoke with main points listed and when she spoke as a candidate for president, she most often had entire texts prepared. Regardless of her method, she appears energized by the occasion to speak and genuinely happy to share her views.

AFTER HER PRESIDENTIAL BID

Immediately after her presidential bid, Carol campaigned for the Democratic party. First, she endorsed Howard Dean and then, when John Kerry won the nomination, she campaigned for him. The highest profile speech was at the Democratic National Convention in 2004. Since then, Carol continues her work on behalf of the Democratic party, by speaking about issues she championed during her Senate term and presidential bid.

Carol Moseley Braun was a featured speaker at the 2004 Democratic Convention in Boston in July 2004. She began her speech with a narrative about her own life, and then she described her experience working with the Democratic nominee, John Kerry. She said:

> I am honored to have this chance to say thank you to you delegates to the 44th Democratic convention. Thank you for your activism. Thank you for making this convention a turning point for America. Thank you for working to elect John Kerry as the next President of the United States.
>
> I come to you as the granddaughter of Edna and Thomas Davie. He was a patriot who served his country in WWI, who was prepared to make the ultimate sacrifice for America. He did not have the right to vote. In fact, he had no rights. Yet his patriotism survived the hard rock of segregation because he believed that his sacrifice would help to make things better for the next generation, and that the future he sought to create would be better than the past he could not change.
>
> In the US Senate, (I) worked with John Kerry for six years, and had the chance to get to know him as only a colleague can. Based on that experience, I can stand here and say to you without reservation that in him we have a chance to put a patriot in the White House who will save our great country, and put us on a path of peace, prosperity and progress. We have the opportunity to give our great country a great President.
>
> You will leave this convention with a nominee and a message that can inspire the American people, and revitalize their faith that this country can work for them. You can assure them that Democrats will reward the sacrifice and contributions of millions of everyday people by restoring the greatest values of the greatest country in the world. Your effort will guarantee that this economy will work for working people. You will give our country better leadership than we have today. You are the patriots who will inspire every voter to go to the polls and then make sure that every vote is counted.
>
> You are the hope of our nation.

While she was at the Democratic National Convention, she was also a speaker at the Revolutionary Women's Rally. She told her audience: "I thought I'd get right to the point why Revolutionary Women are important, and why I think it would be a good thing to build support for the concept of Every Open Seat A Woman's' Seat."[87]

During her term as a senator from Illinois, Carol Moseley Braun made a reputation for herself as an advocate for education and civil rights. She lost re-election amidst speculation that she withheld some of her mother's money from Medicaid, ran up over a half million dollars of campaign debt, and backed her campaign manager against sexual harassment charges. She was ready to explain her position with respect to the allegations. As a former Ambassador to New Zealand, a country that has had two women Prime Ministers, Carol Moseley Braun's goal was to run for president so that America could join the ranks of countries that have women at the top. She said "Ours is the greatest nation in the world not because we have the biggest military or the most money. America's greatness lies in the spirit of her people. That spirit of hope defines and under girds the American Dream. Now is the time for Democrats to renew hope that we will leave that dream for the next generation in even better shape than we found it. And a woman can lead the way."[88] African American Barack Obama was elected to the senate in 2004—also from Illinois—and the only black senator since Carol Moseley Braun. There are now fourteen women who serve as United States senators.

NOTES

1. Wayne D'Orio. *Carol Moseley Braun.* (Philadelphia: Chelsea House Publishers, 2004), 99.

2. Carol Moseley Braun, speech to announce presidential candidacy, September 22, 2003. www.carolforpresident.com. (accessed February 5, 2005).

3. www.npr.org (accessed April 22, 2005).

4. Ibid.

5. Biographical information for this section was culled from the following sources: Wayne D'Orio, *Carol Moseley-Braun.* (Philadelphia: Chelsea House Publishers), 2004; Mellonee Carrigan, *Carol Moseley-Braun: Breaking Barriers.* (Chicago: Childrens Press), 1993 and from carolforpresident.com. (accessed April 23, 2005).

6. Carol Moseley Braun, "Between W. E. B. DuBois and B. T. Washington." *Ebony,* November 1995, 58.

7. Ibid.

8. www.nationalcenter.org/brown.html. (accessed June 5, 2006).

9. Carol Moseley Braun, interview with Nichola D. Gutgold, May 6, 2005.

10. Ibid.

11. Jean Latz. "California Goes to the Head of Class in School Reform." *Chicago Tribune.* April 21, 1985, 10.

12. Bonita Brodt. "School Reform's Achilles' Heel: The Parents." *Chicago Tribune,* November 20, 1988, 1.

13. Lillian Williams. "Carol Braun: Experienced, Productive." *Chicago Sun Times,* November 6, 1988, 60.

14. Steve Neal. "Stone's Tactics Unlikely to Dim Braun's Rising Star." *Chicago Sun Times*, November 7, 1988.

15. R. Bruce Dodd. "Stone Campaign Brochure Called Divisive." *Chicago Tribune*, October 21, 1988, 4.

16. "We Endorse Representative Braun." *Chicago Sun Times*, October 18, 1988, 37.

17. Carol Moseley Braun. "Between W. E. B. DuBois and B. T. Washington," *Ebony*, November 1995, 58–59.

18. "Good Deeds from the New Recorder." *Chicago Tribune*, June 24, 1989, 8.

19. Carole Ashkinaze. "Political Party for Women No Longer Just Talk." *Chicago Sun Times*, June 28, 1992, 33.

20. Catherine Crier. "Carol Moseley Braun Reacts to Senate Campaign Victory." CNN, November 4, 1992.

21. Carol Moseley Braun, interview with Nichola D. Gutgold, May 6, 2005.

22. "Kulp's Column." *Chicago Sun Times*, March 18, 1992, 62.

23. Lynn Sweet. "A Braun Upset; First Defeat for Dixon in 42 Years." *Chicago Sun Times*, March 18, 1992, 1.

24. Isabel Wilkerson. "Black Woman's Senate Race Is Acquiring a Celebrity Aura." *New York Times*, July 29, 1992, A1.

25. Steve Neal. "Brady Backs Braun Over Ex-Colleague." *Chicago Sun Times*, September 18, 1992, 31.

26. "Braun for the Senate—with Big Reservations." *Crain's Chicago Business*. October 19, 1992, 14.

27. Lynn Sweet. "Charisma Wrapped Up in Many Questions." *Chicago Sun Times*, October 25, 1992, 18.

28. "Carol Moseley Braun for U.S. Senate." *Chicago Sun Times*, October 19, 1992.

29. Lynn Sweet. "Braun Bus Tour Takes Road Not Yet Traveled." *Chicago Sun Times*, September 12, 1992, 9.

30. Mark Black. "Braun Takes Heat on Funds; Says She's Carrying Out Mom's Wishes." *Chicago Sun Times*, October 1, 1992, 5.

31. Ibid.

32. R. Bruce Dodd. "Stone Campaign Brochure Called Divisive." *Chicago Tribune*, October 21, 1988, 4.

33. Thomas Hardy and Steve Johnson. "Debate Has Familiar Ring: Williamson Chides Braun in Final Forum." *Chicago Tribune*, October 23, 1992, 1.

34. Lynn Sweet. "Braun Ad Slams Williamson." *Chicago Sun Times*, May 15, 1992, 24.

35. Don Thompson. "Williamson, Braun Debate Issues, Beliefs." *Pantagraph* (Bloomington, IL), October 23, 1992, A1.

36. Ibid.

37. Hardy and Johnson. "Debate Has Familiar Ring."

38. Chris Black. "Four Women, Including First Black, Elected to U.S. Senate." *Boston Globe*, November 4, 1992, 1.

39. "1992 Elections: State by State." *Washington Post*, November 5, 1992, A39.

40. Isabel Wilkerson. "Milestone for Black Woman in Gaining U.S. Senate Seat." *New York Times*, November 4, 1992, B7.

41. Judi Hasson. "Senate's New-Look Class of '92 Learns Ropes." *USA Today*, November 10, 1992, 5A.

42. Steve Daley. "Senator Braun Takes Her Place in History: Illinoisan is the First Black Woman in the Senate." *Chicago Tribune*, January 6, 1993, 1.

43. "Carol Moseley Braun Is Sworn in as First Black U.S. Senator." *Jet*, January 25, 1993, Volume 83, Issue 13, 5.

44. L. Michelle Stewart. "Year of the Black Woman." *Ebony*, January 1993.

45. Isabel Wilkerson. "Milestone for Black Woman in Gaining U.S. Senate Seat." *New York Times*, November 4, 1992, B7.

46. Wayne D'Orio. *Carol Moseley Braun*. (Philadelphia: Chelsea House Publishers, 2004), 51.

47. Adam Clymer. "Daughter of Slavery Hushes Senate." *New York Times*, July 23, 1993, B6.

48. John Masheck. "Moseley Braun Spurs Senate Debate," *Boston Globe*, July 23, 1993, 3.

49. "Ms. Moseley Braun's Majestic Moment," *New York Times*, July 24, 1993, 18.

50. Celeste M. Walls. "You Ain't Just Whistling Dixie: How Carol Moseley Braun Used Rhetorical Status to Change Jesse Helms' Tune." *Western Communication Journal*, June 22, 2004. Volume 68, Issue 3, 343.

51. John Butler. *Argumentation and Advocacy*. River Falls, Wisc.: Fall 1995. Volume 32, Issue 2, 62.

52. Carol Moseley Braun, interview with Nichola D. Gutgold, May 6, 2005.

53. Lizatte Alvarez. "Confirmation 'Courtesy' Not Given for Ex-Senator." *New York Times*, November 5, 1999, A28.

54. James Bennet. "Clinton Raises Money for Senator in Illinois." *New York Times*, June 26, 1997, D27.

55. "Remarks at a Dinner for Senator Carol Moseley-Braun in Chicago." *Weekly Compilation of Presidential Documents* (Newsletter) June 30, 1997 U.S. Government Printing, v33, n26.

56. Carol Moseley Braun. "Affirmative Action and the Glass Ceiling." *Black Scholar*. (San Francisco, CA: 1995), Volume 25, Issue 3, 7.

57. Pete Falcone. "Senate Candidate Fitzgerald Speaks in Twin Cities." *The Pantagraph* (Bloomington, Ill.) November 18, 1997, A4.

58. Jeff Zeleny. "Eyes on the Presidency: Moseley Braun encouraged to run for White House." *Chicago Tribune*, January 17, 2003, 10.

59. "Carol Moseley-Braun to Run for President." *Ms. Magazine On Line*, February 13, 2003.

60. "Crowd of One Greets Moseley Braun." *Human Events*, February 24, 2003, Vol. 29, Issue 7, 1.

61. David Von Drehle and Kari Lydersen. "Moseley Braun Joins Democratic Presidential Field." *Washington Post*, February 19, 2003, 1.

62. Jodi Wilgoren. "Past Triumphs and Debacles." *New York Times*, March 14, 2003, 19.

63. Jill Lawrence. "Senate Pioneer Has Eyes on White House Prize; Moseley Braun Targets Blacks and Women." *USA Today*, February 20, 2003, 6.

64. DeWayne Wickham. "Black, Female: Both Impair Moseley Braun's Chances." *USA Today*, February 25, 2003, 3.

65. Ellen Goodman. "Braun Injects Women's Issues into Campaign." *Boston Globe*, September 25, 2003, A23.

66. Joel Siegel. "In the Prez Race to Win She Says." *Daily News* (New York), March 11, 2003, 24.

67. Ibid.

68. Alexandra Marks. "The Quest of Carol Moseley Braun," *Christian Science Monitor*, November 20, 2003, 1.

69. Ibid.

70. "Carol Moseley Braun: Illinois' Favorite Daughter and the First Lady of the Community." *Chicago Defender*, February 25, 2004, 11.

71. Rita Lazzaroni. "Women Candidates Hail Moseley Braun as One of Their Own." *Connecticut Post*. April 25, 2003.

72. Herb Boyd. "Sharpton and Braun Steadfast in Debate." *New York Amsterdam News* (New York, NY), May 8, 2003, 4.

73. Carol Moseley Braun, speech to announce presidential candidacy, September 22, 2003. www.carolforpresident.com. (accessed February 5, 2005).

74. www.issues2000.org/archive/Rock_The_Vote_Carol_Moseley-Braun.htm (accessed April 30, 2005).

75. www.carolforpresident.com (accessed April 30, 2005).

76. Joel Siegel. "In the Prez Race to Win She Says," *Daily News* (New York), March 11, 2003, 24.

77. *St. Petersburg Times*, January 16, 2004 www.sptimesru/archive/times/935/ (accessed July 21, 2005).

78. Lizette Alvarez. "Confirmation 'Courtesy' Not Given for Ex-Senator." *New York Times*, November 5, 1999, A28.

79. Eleanor Clift and Tom Brazaitis. *Madam President: Women Blazing the Leadership Trail.* (New York: Routledge), 2003, 320.

80. Isabel Wilkerson. "Black Woman's Senate Race Is Acquiring Celebrity Aura." *New York Times*. July 29, 1992, A1.

81. Carol Moseley Braun, interview with Nichola D. Gutgold, May 6, 2005.

82. Isabel Wilkerson. "Black Woman's Senate Race Is Acquiring a Celebrity Aura." *New York Times*, July 29, 1992, A1.

83. Donald Sevener. "Carol Moseley Braun, Democratic candidate for U.S. Senate." *Illinois Periodicals Online*. www.lib.niu.edu/iop/aboutipo.html (accessed May 1, 2005).

84. Ibid.

85. Carol Moseley Braun. "Affirmative Action and the Glass Ceiling." *Black Scholar*. (San Francisco, CA: 1995), Volume 25, Issue 3, 7.

86. Carol Moseley Braun, speech on President's Day commemoration of American Women Presidents in Des Moines, Iowa, February 15, 2003. www.carolforpresident.com (accessed June 15, 2005).

87. Ibid.

88. Ibid., 101.

6

Continuing on the Trail

"To Make the Way Easier for Her"[1]

All public speakers recognize that in any speech situation there are
both long- and short-terms goals. A theme that emerges from these
remarkable women's quests for the presidency, which could be described
as a long-term goal of their campaign speaking, is that at the very least
they were making the way easier for the next woman who traveled in
their footsteps and the generations of women to follow. The same sentiment is reflected in this excerpt about an overworked female executive
trying to balance home and work:

> The way I look at it, women in the City are like first-generation immigrants.
> You get off the boat, you keep your eyes down, work as hard as you can and
> do your damnedest to ignore the taunts of ignorant natives who hate you just
> because you look different and you smell different and because one day you
> may take their job. And you hope. You know it's probably not going to get
> that much better in your own lifetime, but just the fact that you occupy the
> space . . . all makes it easier for the women who come after you. Years ago,
> when I was still at school, I read this book about a cathedral by William Gold-
> ing. It took several generations to build a medieval cathedral, and the men
> who drew up the plans knew that not their sons but their grandsons, or even
> great-grandsons, would be around for the crowning of the spire they had
> dreamed of. It's the same for the women in the City, I think. We are the foun-
> dation stones. The females who come after us scarcely give us a second
> thought, but they will walk on our bones.[2]

These five women metaphorically are the foundation stones for future generations of women who will occupy a larger percentage of elected offices—including the presidency of the United States. In the future women will be working in the cathedrals, metaphorically speaking, now only being built, by the efforts of women including Margaret Chase Smith, Shirley Chisholm, Patricia Schroeder, Elizabeth Dole, and Carol Moseley Braun.

Being "first" to do anything marks a person as a trailblazer and someone likely to be able to give advice to future generations. Sandra Day O'Connor, the first female Supreme Court justice, offered this formula in a speech to Barnard College, "Women who have been particularly successful tend to be intelligent and open minded and I would say friendly."[3] Besides these personality traits, for women to achieve parity in the political world, they need to consider the following constraints.

CRITICAL MASS

Currently there are fourteen women in the United States Senate, sixty-seven women in the United States House of Representatives and eight women governors. When the percentages are closer to fifty percent male and female, then there will be less of the spectacle aspect of women candidates.

While we cannot dispute the pioneering characteristics of the five women profiled in this book, none was the first to run for president. Yet, perhaps because of the novelty of women in the political pipeline, the press each woman received when she ran accentuated her uniqueness as a candidate. For example, Margaret Chase Smith was called "first" to serve both in the House and Senate; Shirley Chisholm was the "first" African American; Patricia Schroeder was the "first" candidate with children; Elizabeth Dole was the "first" spouse of a presidential nominee turned candidate; and Carol Moseley Braun was the "first" female African American senator to run for president. Continuing to call each woman who runs for president, "the first" accentuates their novelty and may have hindered each of their campaigns. By framing [their] candidacies as a "first" instead of a continuation or extension of a long history of political activism and involvement among women in politics, the press may have promoted the idea that women were less normal and more risky in the political sphere.[4] They may be "first" in specific categories, such as "first" to be elected to Congress or "first" African American, but even these designations may restrict the freedom of these women to move about their campaign without the burden of a special designation. As women continue to run in larger numbers, the goal of critical mass will become realized, thus reducing the "first" designation that stigmatizes instead of elevates the candidates.

FAIR MEDIA COVERAGE AND
HISTORICAL ACKNOWLEDGMENT

In 1990, when Dianne Feinstein and Pete Wilson were engaging in a hotly contested race for governor of California, the two candidates were featured in a televised debate. While the *Los Angeles Times* declared the debate a "virtual tie" in the following day's paper, it gave Wilson a slight edge because he "looked" more like a governor.[5] Although Feinstein had established a lofty résumé of political experience by 1990, the media did not acknowledge it. Instead, they chose to focus on her image and appearance at the expense of her credentials and political positions.

The implications of this type of media coverage can impede a female candidate's ability for success. Given that voters may be uncertain about the policy capabilities of women candidates, the consistent difference in issue or experience coverage could lead voters to develop less favorable images of women candidates.[6] When these "less favorable images" translate into a fewer number of votes for female candidates, it becomes difficult to circumvent the media barrier and win elections. According to Kim Fridkin Kahn, the media's coverage of campaigns may present an important obstacle for women candidates.[7] Because of the news media's influential role in shaping politician's images, it is important for women candidates to remind journalists, perhaps only by their increasing numbers on the political scene, that accentuating their gender, and not their political agendas, undermines the continued growth of women in politics and does not a news story make.

In addition, history books need to reflect the efforts of women candidates. If children read about the efforts of women they are more likely to become adults with broader perspectives than their ancestors have held about the leadership capabilities of both men and women. In the book, *Campaigns: A Century of Presidential Races*, none of the women candidates for president are mentioned.[8] This type of exclusion by history books perpetuates the lack of acknowledgment of women candidates.

CULTURAL ACCEPTANCE

Geert Hofstede's finding that the United States is a highly masculine country is especially important to the prospects of a woman American president. Hofstede notes that "Femininity stands for a society in which social gender roles overlap: both men and women are supposed to be modest, tender, and concerned with the quality of life. Masculinity, on the other hand, stands for a society in which social gender roles are clearly distinct: men are supposed to be assertive, tough and focused on material success."[9] The United States ranks relatively high on measures of masculinity, ranking 15th out of fifty-three countries.[10] Despite being traditionally a highly masculine country, this is changing slowly, as evidenced by the more and more women in the political pipeline as state representatives, senators, cabinet members, and governors. How women candidates express their femininity and power at the same time is likely to be important to the image of a successful woman leader.

WOMEN IN THE PIPELINE

2008—Will there be a woman candidate? On March 12, 2005, Secretary of State Condoleezza Rice told *Washington Times* editor Wesley Pruden that she doesn't want to be president. "I never wanted to run for anything—I don't think I even ran for anything when I was in school." The website, www.americanforrice.org urges visitors to support Condoleeza Rice for president for several reasons, including "she has the President's ear." Despite Rice's adamant rejections of any presidential aspiration, Republicans are still hopeful that there will be a Rice and Clinton face off in 2008. Former Clinton administration strategist Dick Morris and his wife Eileen McGann argue in a book titled *Condi vs. Hillary: The Next Great Presidential Race* that America may be poised for a presidential face off between Condoleezza Rice, whom they argue is better than Hillary Clinton. Web sites that want to "Draft Condi" and "Draft Hillary"[11] are already posted on the Internet. A poll conducted by the Siena College Institute found six out of ten people surveyed would vote for a woman president. Fifty-three percent said they'd vote for Senator Hillary Clinton and 42 percent of the voters would cast their vote for Condoleezza Rice.[12]

FROM GOVERNOR TO PRESIDENT

Barbara Lee, president of the Barbara Lee Foundation created a guide, titled "Keys to the Governor's Office" to help women running for governor. At first, her interest was focused on women and the presidency, but she notes that "as I understood more about the paths to power, it was clear that electing a woman president would become a reality only after we unraveled voters' complex reactions to a woman seeking full executive authority."[13] Marie Wilson, president of the White House Project also noted the importance of the role of governor to increase women's participation on the national political stage. "Look at governors from large states,"[14] she advised when contemplating who may win the presidency. Brenda DeVore Marshall and Molly A. Mayhead, editors of *Navigating Boundaries: The Rhetoric of Women Governors*, note, "the increasing importance of the state governor throughout the history of the country, coupled with women's steadily expanding role in that office, demonstrates that the face of the governorship *has* changed."[15] It also indicates that examining the women who are governors in America is a good place to start when identifying women most likely to make successful bids for the presidency.

CURRENT WOMEN GOVERNORS

Janet Napolitano, Democrat, Arizona

Janet Napolitano was sworn into office in January 2003, faced with a billion-dollar state budget deficit and the spiraling price of prescription drugs. She won approval for a budget that erased a billion-dollar state deficit without raising taxes. Described as highly intelligent, extremely hard-working, open, forthright, and courageous, she spoke at the Democratic National Convention in 2004 on behalf of Democratic presidential hopeful John Kerry.

Napolitano graduated summa cum laude from Santa Clara University in Santa Clara, California with a degree in political science. She received a law degree from the University of Virginia Law School in 1983. In 1992 she served as co-council to Anita Hill when the United States Judiciary Committee questioned charges Hill made concerning Clarence Thomas. In 1993 Napolitano was appointed U.S. attorney for the District of Arizona and in 1998 she won the election for attorney general.

M. Jodi Rell, Republican, Connecticut

M. Jodi Rell was sworn in as Connecticut's 87th governor in 2004. Prior to that, she was Lieutenant Governor for more than nine years. She was also a member of the House of Representatives for ten years as a representative for the 107th assembly district. She ran and won the office of governor after former Republican Governor John G. Rowland resigned amid scandals involving bribes, bid-rigging, favors, and hundreds of millions of allegedly squandered taxpayer dollars. One of her first initiatives as governor was to issue an executive order and appoint a Special Counsel for Ethics Compliance to advise her and all state agencies, departments, and boards and commissions on issues of public integrity. Rell is the second woman to serve as governor of Connecticut. In 1974 Ella Grasso was elected governor. Rell is running for re-election in 2006. Born in Norfolk, Va., Rell initially aspired to become an English teacher. Instead she dropped out of Old Dominion University to get married. Soon after, she moved to Connecticut, gave birth to two children and put aside her education for a while. Her second attempt at college, at Western Connecticut

State University, was interrupted in 1984 when friends took note of her activism in the parent-teacher association and the Republican Women's Club in her home town of Brookfield and persuaded her to run for state representative. She received an honorary degree from the University of Hartford in 2001.

Ruth Ann Minner, Democrat, Delaware

Ruth Ann Minner was sworn in as governor of Delaware in 2001. A no-nonsense, self-educated businesswoman, she took over her family's towing business after the death of her husband in order to raise her three sons. She has championed a comprehensive fight against high cancer rates by budgeting funding for increased education, screening, and treatment and the creation of a cancer registry to identify cancer case "hot spots" or environmental causes. She spearheaded the first in the country's program to pay for cancer treatment for those who can't afford it.

Linda Lingle, Republican, Hawaii

Linda Lingle was elected governor of Hawaii in 2002. Since then she reversed the $200,000 deficit that she inherited when she took office. A publisher, she moved to Hawaii to serve as publisher of the Moloka'I Free Press after receiving her journalism degree from California State University at Northridge.

Kathleen Sebelius, Democrat, Kansas

Kathleen Sebelius has the unique distinction of being the first daughter of a governor to be elected to the same position. Her father, John Gilligan, was governor of Ohio from 1971 to 1975. She became governor in 2002 and targeted two major areas of commitment: fiscal responsibility and improving Kansas's public schools. Prior to becoming governor, Ms. Sebelius served for eight years in the Kansas state legislature and prior to that was an insurance commissioner for eight years.

Kathleen Blanco, Democrat, Louisiana

Kathleen Blanco became governor of Louisiana on January 12, 2004. Before becoming governor, she completed two terms as lieutenant governor. As governor, her top priorities include providing affordable, accessible healthcare, improving education, and creating a strong economy. Before becoming governor, Blanco was a teacher. She received a Bachelor of Science degree from the University of Louisiana at Lafayette. Her articulate advocacy for her state during the tragic aftermath of Hurricane Katrina, which destroyed many areas of Louisiana, propelled her to national attention.

Jennifer Granholm, Democrat, Michigan

In November 2002, Canadian born Jennifer Granholm became the 47th governor of the state of Michigan. Despite difficult fiscal times, Granholm has received high marks for her ability to communicate effectively, even in the face of a high jobless rate and a huge deficit. Her leadership ability has even drawn interest in her as a presidential candidate, although her Canadian roots disqualify her. Laura Liswood, Secretary-General, Council of Women World Leaders suggested, "The U.S. is a nation of immigrants; we might want to re-look at this requirement of a natural born citizen. Maybe we should change it to that if you've been here ten years, or it you have been raised and educated here [you could run for president]."[16] Granholm has telegenic looks and an articulate speaking style and she is a frequent guest on national television political news programs.

Granholm began her career in public service as a clerk for United States Judge Damon Keith on the Sixth Circuit Court of Appeals. In 1990 she became a federal prosecutor in Detroit, where is maintained a 98 percent conviction rate. In 1994 Graholm was appointed Wayne County Corporation Counsel. In 1998 she was elected Michigan's first female attorney general. She is a graduate of the University of California at Berkeley and Harvard Law School.

Christine Gregoire, Democrat, Washington

Christine Gregoire was sworn in on January 12, 2005, after winning in the closest-ever race for governor in the history of Washington. In 1992, she was the first woman elected attorney general in Washington. During her first term she focused on children's issues and led a comprehensive reform of the state's juvenile system. She was re-elected in 1996 and again in 2000. In the wake of the Enron scandal, she worked to protect consumers and investors and in 2002 she filed a complaint with the United States District Court in Houston seeking to recoup $97.5 million lost by the state in Enron bonds. She has also investigated and sued several drug companies for violating anti-trust laws by illegally manipulating the price and availability of drugs. As governor, her main initiatives include education, healthcare, the environment, and veteran's defense. Raised in Auburn, Washington, Gregoire graduated from the University of Washington in 1969 with a teaching certificate and Bachelor of Arts degree in speech and sociology. In 1977, she received a Juris Doctor degree.

None of the eight women governors have said that they have intentions to run for president in 2008. Six of the nation's forty-two male governors say they may run and ten of the eighty-six male senators have taken steps toward presidential campaigns; Hillary Clinton is the only one of the fourteen female senators positioned to run.[17]

WILL HILLARY RUN?

Time featured a cover photo of John McCain and Hillary Clinton with the headline: "Is this the face-off for '08"? According to the article, polls show the former first lady winning every conceivable Democratic primary match up, even over 2004 nominee John Kerry.[18] A website, www.hillarynow.com describes itself as "a national and international grassroots draft Hillary Clinton campaign out of Florida, the scene of the stolen election of 2000." It urges supporters to sign the petition to endorse Hillary "because she is the only democrat capable of defeating the Republican machine." Yet, nationwide, four in ten Democrats and those who lean Democratic in a USA Today/CNN/Gallup Poll say they would support her for their party's nomination. Majorities of 53 percent to 68 percent of adults in the survey say she is strong, decisive, likable, caring, and honest.[19] Since her entrance onto the national stage as first lady, Hillary Rodham Clinton has been a polarizing figure. She knows what it feels like to be a scrutinized public figure from her experience as first lady and from her hard-fought battle to win a senate seat. If she vies for the presidency she will be more scrutinized than ever and, as she has stretched the perceptions of what people can expect from a first lady, she will move the debate about gender and power further along if she makes a presidential bid, regardless of the outcome.

This book has told the stories of the five most prominent women who have run for president. It isn't certain which women will throw their hats into the presidential ring in the future. Whoever that first woman president will be owes gratitude to her sisters who went before her.

NOTES

1. From Margaret Chase Smith's announcement for president speech, January 27, 1964. Margaret Chase Smith with William C. Lewis, Jr., *Declaration of Conscience*. (New York: Doubleday, 1972), 369.

2. Allison Pearson. *I Don't Know How She Does It: The Life of Kate Reddy, Working Mother*. (New York: Random House, 2002), 121–122.

3. Evan Thomas and Stuart Taylor, Jr. "Queen of the Center." *Newsweek*, July 11, 2005, 29.

4. Erika Falk and Kathleen Hall Jamieson. "Changing the Climate of Expectations." In Robert P. Watson and Ann Gordon, eds., *Anticipating Madam President*. (Boulder, CO: Lynne Rienner Publishers, 2003), 49.

5. Dianne Feinstein, Kay Bailey-Hutchison, Barbara Boxer, Susan Collins, Mary Landrieu, Blanche L. Lincoln, Barbara Mikulski, Patty Murray, Olympia Snowe, and Catherine Whitney. *Nine and Counting: The Women of the Senate*. (New York: Perennial, 2001), 53.

6. Kim Fridkin Kahn. *The Political Consequences of Being a Woman*. (New York: Columbia: University Press, 1996), 135.

7. Ibid.

8. Alan Brinkley and Ted Widmer. *Campaigns: A Century of Presidential Races*. (New York: DK Publishing, 2001).

9. Geert Hofstede, *Cultures and Organizations: Software of the Mind* (London: McGraw-Hill, 1991), 14.

10. Ibid., 262.

11. Two websites that are drafting women for president are: www.rice2008.com (for Condoleezza Rice) www.clinton.com (for Hillary Clinton). (accessed March 15, 2005).

12. www.outsidethebeltway.com/archives/9359 (accessed March 16, 2005).

13. *Keys to the Governor's Office*, The Barbara Lee Foundation, 2001.

14. Marie C. Wilson, interview with Nichola Gutgold, August 23, 2004.

15. Brenda DeVore Marshall and Molly A. Mayhead "Changing the Face of the Governorship." In Brenda DeVore Marshall and Molly A. Mayhead (eds.) *Navigating the Boundaries: The Rhetoric of Women Governors*. (Westport: Praeger, 2000), 14.

16. Laura Liswood. Interview with Nichola Gutgold, June 5, 2005.

17. Susan Page. "Call her Madame President." *USA Today*, October 10, 2005 www.usatoday.comlife/2005-10-10-woman-president_x.htm (accessed October 18, 2005).

18. Karen Tumulty. "Is This the Race for 2008?" *Newsweek*, August 29, 2005, 27.

19. Jill Lawrence. "DA Says She Plans to Run for Senate in New York Next Year." *USA Today*, August 8, 2005, www.usatoday.com/news/washington/2005-08-08-pirro-clinton-race_x.htm (accessed September 9, 2005).

Bibliography

"1992 Elections: State by State." *Washington Post*, November 5, 1992, A-39.

"ABC News This Week." *ABC News*, April 18, 1999, 11:30 A.M., transcript #99041803-j12.

Alexander, Paul. "Vice Can Be Nice." *Mirabella*, September 2000, 66–69.

Alvarez, Lizatte. "Confirmation 'Courtesy' Not Given for Ex-Senator." *New York Times*, November 5, 1999, A-28.

American Profile Interview. "Life and Career of Patricia Schroeder." December 23, 1988. Obtained from www.cspan.org.

Arnold, Lorin. "Can She Win?" *Bangor Daily News*, January 28, 1964, 1.

Ashkinaze, Carole. "Political Party for Women No Longer Just Talk." *Chicago Sun Times*, June 28, 1992, 33.

Bennett, W. Lance. "Storytelling in Criminal Trials: A Model of Social Judgment." *Quarterly Journal of Speech*, February 1978, vol. 64, 1–22.

Berke, Richard L. "As Political Spouse, Bob Dole Strays from Campaign Script." *New York Times*, May 17, 1999, A-1.

Black, Chris. "Four Women, Including First Black, Elected to U.S. Senate." *Boston Globe*, November 4, 1992, 1.

Black, Mark. "Braun Takes Heat on Funds; Says She's Carrying Out Mom's Wishes." *Chicago Sun Times*, October 1, 1992, 5.

Blankenship, Jane. "Geraldine Ann Ferraro." In Karlyn Kohrs Campbell, ed. *Women Public Speakers in the United States, 1925–1936: A Bio-Critical Sourcebook*, (Westport, Conn.: Greenwood Press, 1994), 199.

Blankenship, Jane and Deborah C. Robson. "A 'Feminine Style' in Women's Political Discourse: An Exploratory Essay." *Communication Quarterly*, Summer 1995, Volume 43, Issue 3, 353.

Blyth, Myrna. "One Smart Lady." *Ladies Home Journal*, August 1999, 44.

Bomann, Mieke H. "Newspaper Reporting on Women Candidates Differs from That on Men." *Times Union* (Albany, NY), October 22, 2000, A-5.

Boyd, Herb. "Sharpton and Braun Steadfast in Debate." *New York Amsterdam News* (New York, NY), May 8, 2003, 4.

Braden, Maria. *Women Politicians and the Media*. (Lexington: University Press of Kentucky, 1996), 186.

"Braun for the Senate—with Big Reservations." *Crain's Chicago Business*, October 19, 1992, 14.

Braun, Carol Moseley. "Affirmative Action and the Glass Ceiling." *Black Scholar*, (San Francisco, CA: 1995), Volume 25, Issue 3, 7.

Braun, Carol Moseley. "Between W. E. B. DuBois and B. T. Washington." *Ebony*, November 1995, 58.

Brinkley, Alan and Ted Widmer. *Campaigns: A Century of Presidential Races from the Photo Archives of the New York Times*. (New York: DK Publishing, 2001), 307.

Brinson, Claudia Smith. "Woman of the Year: Pat Schroeder." *Ms. Arlington*. January/February 1997, 56.

Brodt, Bonita. "School Reform's Achilles' Heel: The Parents." *Chicago Tribune*. November 20, 1988, 1.

Brownmiller, Susan. "This Is Fighting Shirley Chisholm." *New York Times*, April 13, 1969, SM32.

Brownmiller, Susan. *Shirley Chisholm*. (New York: Archway Paperback, 1972).

CNN Morning News. "Elizabeth Dole Bows Out of the Presidential Race: What Was Behind the Decision Not to Run?" October 20, 1999, 11:00 A.M. ET, Transcript #99102010V09.

Campbell, Karlyn Kohrs. "The Rhetoric of Women's Liberation: An Oxymoron Revisited." *Communication Studies*, 50 (1999), 139.

Campbell, Steve. "Daffron to run Elizabeth Dole's Exploratory Campaign." *Portland Press Herald*, (Maine), March 7, 1999, 2-C.

"Carol Moseley Braun for U.S. Senate." *Chicago Sun Times*, October 19, 1992.

"Carol Moseley Braun: Illinois' Favorite Daughter and the First Lady of the Community." *Chicago Defender*, February 25, 2004, 11.

"Carol Moseley Braun Is Sworn in as First Black U.S. Senator." *Jet*, January 25, 1993, Volume 83, Issue 13, 5.

"Carol Moseley-Braun to Run for President." *Ms. Magazine On Line*, February 13, 2003.

Carroll, Susan J., Carol Heldman, and Stephanie Olson. "She Brought Only a Skirt: Gender Bias in Newspaper Coverage of Elizabeth Dole's Campaign for the Republican Nomination." Unpublished paper, White House Project Conference, Washington, D.C., February 20, 2000.

Chisholm, Shirley. *The Good Fight*. (New York: Harper and Row, 1973).

Chisholm, Shirley. *Unbought and Unbossed*. (Boston, MA: Houghton-Mifflin, 1970).

Clift, Eleanor and Tom Brazaitis. *Madam President: Women Blazing the Leadership Trail*. (New York: Routledge, 2003).

Clymer, Adam. "Daughter of Slavery Hushes Senate." *New York Times*, July 23, 1993, B-6.

"Coalition Rebuffed by Margaret Smith." *New York Times*, May 21, 1964, 23.

Collins, Gail. "Politics: Taking the 'Help' Out of 'Helpmate.'" *New York Times*, May 18, 1999, A-22.

"The Communist Party in the U.S." *Newsweek*, June 2, 1947, 22–26 and J. Edgar Hoover, "How to Fight Communism." *Newsweek*, June 9, 1947, 30.

Crier, Catherine. "Carol Moseley Braun Reacts to Senate Campaign Victory." CNN, November 4, 1992.

"Crowd of One Greets Moseley Braun." *Human Events*, February 24, 2003, Vol. 29, Issue 7, 1.

Cuniberti, Betty. "Dole's Decision: Why She's Quitting to Hit the Campaign Trail." *Los Angeles Times*, September 18, 1987, D-10.

Daley, Steve. "Senator Braun Takes Her Place in History: Illinoisan Is the First Black Woman in the Senate." *Chicago Tribune*, January 6, 1993, 1.

Danzinger, N. "Sex Related Differences in the Aspirations of High School Students." *Sex Roles, A Journal of Research*, September 1983, 683–684.

Diaz, Amy. "Dole: Milosevic Must Be Defeated 'Absolutely.'" *Union Leader*, (Manchester, NH), May 25, 1999, A-13.

Dickerson, John F. and Nancy Gibbs. "Elizabeth Unplugged." *Time*, May 10, 1999. www.time.com (accessed February 22, 2004).

Dold, R. Bruce. "Stone Campaign Brochure Called Divisive." *Chicago Tribune*, October 21, 1988, 4.

"Dole Drops Out; Her Poor Showing Wasn't Just a Money Problem." *Pittsburgh Post Gazette*, October 22, 1999, A-22.

"Dole Pushes Fundraising and Garners Endorsement." *Boston Globe*, April 28, 1999, A-13.

Dole, Robert, Elizabeth Dole, Richard Norton Smith, and Kerry Tymchuk. *Unlimited Partners, Our American Story*. (New York: Simon and Schuster, 1996).

D'Orio, Wayne. *Carol Moseley Braun*. (Philadelphia: Chelsea House Publishers, 2004).

Dow, Bonnie J. and Mari Boor Tonn. "Feminine Style and Political Judgment in the Rhetoric of Ann Richards." *Quarterly Journal of Speech*, 79 (1993), 286–302.

Dowd, Maureen. "Schroeder at Ease with Femininity and Issues." *New York Times*, August 23, 1987.

Duffy, Bernard K. and Halford R. Ryan. *American Orators of the Twentieth Century*. (Westport, Conn.: Greenwood Press, 1987).

Eccles, Jacqueline S. "Why Doesn't Jane Run? Sex Differences in Educational and Occupational Patterns." In R. D. Horowitz and M. O'Brien (eds.) *The Gifted and Talented: Developmental Perspectives* (Washington, D.C.: American Psychological Association, 1985), 251–295.

"Elizabeth Dole Outlines Abortion Stance." *Patriot Ledger*, (Quincy, MA), April 10, 1999, 8.

"Elizabeth Dole Resigns Red Cross Post, May Test Presidential Waters." www.cnn .com/allpolitics/stories/1999/01/04/presiodent.2000/dole/ (accessed April 14, 2005).

"Exploratory Essay." *Communication Quarterly*, Summer 1995, Volume 43, Issue 3, 353.

"Face the Nation." as broadcast over the CBS Television Network and the CBS Radio Network. February 2, 1964, 12:30–1:00 P.M. EST. MCS Library and Museum.

Falk, Erika and Kathleen Hall Jamieson. "Changing the Climate of Expectations." In Robert P. Watson and Ann Gordon, eds., *Anticipating Madam President*, (Boulder, Colo.: Lynne Reinner Publishing, 2003).

Farrell, John Aloysius. "The Once and Future Candidate Pat Schroeder Still Has Her Eye on a White House Run." *Boston Globe*, November 28, 1987. www.infoweb .newsbank.com (accessed March 21, 2005).

Farrell, John Aloysius. "Schroeder Tests Waters in New Hampshire for a Presidential Bid." *Boston Globe*, June 16, 1987, 1.

Fehr, Stephen C. "Dole Resignation Revives 'Stand by your Man' Debate." *Kansas City Times*, September 20, 1987, B-1.

Feldmann, Linda. "Dole's Candidacy Had Historic Impact." *Christian Science Monitor*, October 21, 1999, 1.

Ferraro, Geraldine A. with Linda Bird Francke. *Ferraro: My Story*. (New York: Bantam Books, 1985).

Ferree, Myra Marx. "A Woman for President? Changing Responses 1958–1972." *Public Opinion Quarterly*, Fall 1974, Volume 38, Issue 3, 390–400.

Fineman, Howard and Matthew Cooper. "Back in the Amen Corner." *Newsweek*, March 22, 1999, 33.

Fireside, Bryna J. *Is There a Woman in the House . . . or Senate?* (Morton Grove, Ill.: Albert Whitman and Company, 1994).

Fournier, Ron. "Dole Leaving Read Cross, Eyeing White House." *Morning Call*, (Allentown, PA), January 5, 1999, A-3.

Fournier, Ron. "President Dole? Some See Elizabeth as a Hot Prospect." *Morning Call* (Allentown, PA), May 20, 1998, A-14.

Frazier, Amy. "Dole Welcomed with Down-home Dinner." *Winston Salem Journal*, April 3, 2002. www.elizabethdole.org (accessed March 5, 2004).

Friedan, Betty. *The Feminine Mystique*. (New York: Dell Publishing, 1963).

"From Telephone Operator to President of the U.S.?" *Ohio Bell News*, March 18, 1964, Number 6, 1.

Gailey, Phil. "Schroeder Considers Running for President." *New York Times*, June 6, 1987, 1, 33.

Gardner, Marilyn. "Schroeder Sees Void in Campaign of Family Issues." *Christian Science Monitor*, November 30, 1987.

Gates, Henry Louis Jr. "The Next President Dole 2000." *The New Yorker*, October 20 and 27, 1997, 228.

Gilligan, Carol and Lyn Mikel Brower. *Meeting at the Crossroads*. (New York: Random House, 1992).

Glover, Mike. Associated Press, March 10, 1999. www.lexis.nexis.com (accessed April 10, 2005).

Glover, Mike. "Dole Joins Exploratory Offering 'Better Nature.'" Associated Press, March 10, 1999. www.lexis.nexis.com (accessed April 10, 2005).

Goldman, Peter L., Tony Fuller, and Thomas DeFrank. *The Quest for the Presidency 1984*. (New York: Bantam Books, 1985), 330.

"Good Deeds from the New Recorder." *Chicago Tribune*, June 24, 1989, 8.

Goodman, Ellen. "Braun Injects Women's Issues into Campaign." *Boston Globe*, September 25, 2003, A-23.

Goodman, Ellen. "A Dole on the National Ticket?" *Boston Globe*, April 5, 1988, 10-A.

Goodman, Ellen. "Gender Spotlight Cuts Both Ways." *Boston Globe*, October 24, 1999, E-7.

Gootman, Elisa. "Patsy Mink, Veteran Hawaii Congresswoman, Dies at 74." *New York Times*, September 30, 2002, 10.

Graham, Frank, Jr. *Margaret Chase Smith: Woman of Courage*. (New York: John Day Company, 1964), 35.

Greenberg, Bridgette. "Dole Pushes Gun Control in Commencement Speech." *Standard-Speaker* (Hazleton, PA), May 25, 1999, 2.

Hardy, Thomas and Steve Johnson. "Debate Has Familiar Ring: Williamson Chides Braun in Final Forum." *Chicago Tribune*, October 23, 1992, 1.

Hartman, Mary S. *Talking Leadership: Conversations with Powerful Women.* (New Brunswick, N.J.: Rutgers University Press, 1999).

Hasson, Judi. "Senate's New Look: Class of '92 Learns Ropes." *USA Today*, November 10, 1992, 5-A.

Hawley, Peggy. "What Women Think Men Think: Does it Affect Their Career Choice?" *Journal of Counseling Psychology*, 18, 193–199.

Hayward, Ed. "Elizabeth Dole Denies Presidential Goal." *Boston Herald*, May 9, 1997, 14.

Hofstede, Geert. *Cultures and Organizations: Software of the Mind* (London: McGraw-Hill, 1991).

Hollihan, Thomas. *Uncivil Wars: Political Campaigns in a Media Age.* (New York: Bedford/St. Martin's, 2001).

Horgan, John. *Mary Robinson.* (Niwot, Colo.: Roberts Reinhart Publishing, 1998).

Hunter, Marjorie. "Margaret Chase Smith Seeks Presidency." *New York Times*, January 28, 1964, 1.

"I Did Not Plan to Be Emotional." *San Francisco Chronicle*, September 30, 1987, A-21.

Jamieson, Kathleen Hall. *Beyond the Double Bind.* (New York: Oxford University Press, 1995).

Jamieson, Kathleen Hall. *Eloquence in an Electronic Age.* (New York: Oxford University Press, 1988).

Jerry, E. Claire and Michael Spangle. "Patricia Scott Schroeder." In *Women Public Speakers in the United States: A Bio-Critical Sourcebook.* Karlyn Kohrs Campbell, ed. (Wesport, Conn.: Greenwood Press, 1994).

Johnson, Thomas A. "Representative Chisholm Declares That She May Run for President in 1972." *New York Times*, August 1, 1971, 40.

Kahn, Kim Fridkin. *The Political Consequences of Being a Woman.* (New York: Columbia University Press, 1996).

Kern, Montague. "Pat Schroeder's Real Tears." *Washington Post*, November 7, 1987.

Kirchofer, Tom. "Dole's Education Platform Urges Locker, Backpack Searches." *Daily Collegian*, (Penn State), September 23, 1999, 10.

Koplinski, Brad. *Hats in the Ring: Conversations with Presidential Candidates.* (Bethesda, Md.: Presidential Publishing, 2000).

Kozar, Richard. *Elizabeth Dole.* (Philadelphia: Chelsea House Publishers, 2000).

Kramer, Michael. "Liddy Without Tears." *Daily News*, (New York), October 24, 1999, 47.

"Kulp's Column." *Chicago Sun Times*, March 18, 1992, 62.

Latz, Jean. "California Goes to the Head of Class in School Reform." *Chicago Tribune*, April 21, 1985, 10.

Lawler, Peter Augustine and Robert Martin Schaefer, eds. *American Political Rhetoric, A Reader*, fifth edition. (Lanham, Md.: Rowman and Littlefield, 2005).

Lawrence, Jill. "DA Says She Plans to Run for Senate in New York Next Year." *USA Today*, August 8, 2005.

Lawrence, Jill. "Senate Pioneer has Eyes on White House Prize: Moseley Braun Targets Blacks and Women." *USA Today*, February 20, 2003, 6.

Lazzara, Marie. "Mr. Schroeder Goes to Washington." *Elmhurst Press*, January 20, 1999.

Lazzaroni, Rita. "Women Candidates Hail Moseley Braun as One of Their Own." *Connecticut Post*, April 25, 2003.

Leishman, Katie. "A Very Private Person." *McCalls*, April 1988, 135.

Leonard, Mary. "A Life in Politics; Liddy's Way; In Elizabeth Dole's Formative Years, Hints of Her Drive to Challenge, Compete." *Boston Globe*, May 9, 1999, A-1.

Lewiston Evening Journal, November 26, 1951, 10.

Liswood, Laura A. *Women World Leaders: Fifteen Great Politicians Tell Their Stories.* (San Francisco: Pandora, 1995).

Loth, Renee. "The Immigrants of the Political System. Patricia Schroeder's Exploratory Campaign Crystallized the Deep Conflicts Among Women in the Political Process Not the Least of These Is Whether to Play the Political Fame by Its often Exclusionary Rules—Or Change the Rules." *Boston Globe*, November 1, 1987. www.infoweb.newsbank.com (accessed March 21, 2005).

Lynn, Frank. "New Hat in Ring: Mrs. Chisholm's." *New York Times*, January 26, 1972, 1.

MacPherson, Myra. "Woman's Day: With Tears and Hope, Democratic Women Hail Their Heroine." *Washington Post*, July 19, 1984, D1.

Maddens, Richard L. "Mrs. Chisholm Gets Off House Farm Committee." *New York Times*, January 30, 1969, A-16.

Mandel, Ruth B. and Mary S. Hartman. "Patricia Schroeder." in *Talking Leadership: Conversations with Powerful Women*. Hartman, Mary S., ed. (New Brunswick, NJ: Rutgers University Press, 1999).

Mann, Judy. "Schroeder for President." *Washington Post*, June 10, 1987, D-3.

Mann, Judy. "Tears, Idle Tears." *Washington Post*, October 2, 1987, B-3.

Mann, Judy. "Who Says a Woman Can't Be President? We Do." *New York Times*, January 29, 2000, 11.

Marks, Alexandra. "The Quest of Carol Moseley Braun." *Christian Science Monitor*, November 20, 2003, 1.

Marshall Brenda DeVore and Molly A. Mayhead, eds. *Navigating the Boundaries: The Rhetoric of Women Governors*. (Westport, Conn.: Praeger, 2000).

Masheck, John. "Moseley Braun Spurs Senate Debate." *Boston Globe*, July 23, 1993, 3.

McAllister, Bill. "Schroeder's Political Humor Leaves National Archives Crowd in Stitches." *Denver Post*, March 19, 2000, A-10.

McFeatters, Ann. "Presidential Candidates Saying Something of Values; Religious References Fill Slates of GOP, Democratic Hopefuls." *Pittsburgh Post-Gazette*, May 30, 1999, A-11.

McMahon, Mary and Wendy Patton. "Gender Differences in Children's and Adolescents' Perceptions of Influences on Their Career Development." *School Counselor*, 44, 368–376.

Mead, Margaret. *Continuities in Cultural Evolution*. (New Haven: Yale University Press, 1964).

Means, Howard. "At Least Pat Schroeder's Teary Adieu Has a Human Quality." *Orlando Sentinel*, October 4, 1987. www.infoweb.newsbank.com (accessed March 21, 2005).

Mehren, Elizabeth. "Representative Schroeder Tests Presidential Waters; Congresswoman in Iowa to Study Entry into Democratic Race." *Los Angeles Times*, June 13, 1987, 22.

"The Monitor's View." *Christian Science Monitor*, April 19, 1999, 8.

Mooneyham, Scott. "Dole's Celebrity Risky Campaign Asset." *Morning Call*, (Allentown, PA), February 10, 2002, A-21.

"Mrs. Chisholm Declares Two Rivals are Mediocre." *New York Times*, April 21, 1972, 44.

"Mrs. Smith Says Her Age Is No Bar to Presidency." *New York Times*, February 7, 1964, 14.

"Mrs. Chisholm Says Support Is Growing." *New York Times*, October 4, 1971, 22.

"Ms. Moseley Braun's Majestic Moment." *New York Times*, July 24, 1993, 18.

Neal, Steve. "Brady Backs Braun Over Ex-Colleague." *Chicago Sun Times*, September 18, 1992, 31.

Neal, Steve. "Stone's Tactics Unlikely to Dim Braun's Rising Star." *Chicago Sun Times*, November 7, 1988.

Neuffer, Elizabeth. "Elizabeth Dole Said to Be Interested in Envoy, Decision Hangs on Whether Position Is in the Cabinet." *Boston Globe*, January 17, 2001, A-8.

New York Times, January 26, 1972, A-1.

Novak, Robert. "Strategists Need to Decontrol Elizabeth Dole." *Standard Speaker*, (Hazleton, PA), April 27, 1999, 16.

O'Reilly, Jane and Gloria Jacobs. "Watch Pat Run." *Ms.*, February 16, 1988, 44–51.

Page, Susan. "Call Her Madame President." *USA Today*, October 10, 2005.

Pearson, Allison. *I Don't Know How She Does It: The Life of Kate Redding, Working Mother*. (New York: Random House, 2002).

"People on the Cover." *Newsweek*, November 1973, 4.

Perlex, Jane. "Ferraro the Campaigner." *New York Times*, September 30, 1984, 22.

Polman, Dick. "Female Faces in the 2000 Race?" *Philadelphia Inquirer*, April 12, 1998, E-4.

Post, Rose. "Effort to Have Dole on Bush's Ticket Getting Under Way." *Salisbury Post*, March 19, 2000. www.salisburypost.com/2000march/031900c.htm (accessed April 4, 2005).

Putnam, Eileen. "Mrs. Dole Acknowledges Gender Gap, Asks Women to Have an Open Mind." Associated Press, August 16, 1988.

"Red Cross Wonder Woman?" *Business Week*, January 25, 1999, 81.

"Remarks at a Dinner for Senator Carol Moseley-Braun in Chicago." *Weekly Compilation of Presidential Documents*, (Newsletter), June 30, 1997, U.S. Government Printing vol. 33 no. 26.

Representative American Speeches. (New York: H. W. Wilson, 1994–1995), Volume 21.

"Representative Patricia Schroeder Sees the Military as 'King of the Hill' Not in Washington." *Los Angeles Times*, March 3, 1991, B-3.

Ripley, Josephine. "Women and the Convention." *Christian Science Monitor*, July 25, 1964, 2.

Ronan, Thomas P. "Shirley Chisholm Gives McGovern Drive a Push." *New York Times*, October 20, 1972, 20.

Rule, Wilma. "Women's Under-representation and Electoral Systems." *Political Science and Politics*, 27: 4 P.S., December 1994, 689–692.

Ryan, Halford Ross, (ed), *American Rhetoric from Roosevelt to Reagan*, 2nd edition. (Prospect Heights, Ill.: Waveland Press, 1987).

Schemo, Diana Jean. "Curiosity in Dole Exceeds Support." *New York Times*, October 6, 1999, A-28.

Schmidt, Patricia L. *Margaret Chase Smith: Beyond Convention*. (Orono: The University of Maine Press, 1996).

Schroeder, Pat. *Champion of the Great American Family*. (New York: Random House, 1989).

Schroeder, Pat. *24 Years of Housework and the Place Is Still a Mess: My Life in Politics*. (Kansas City: Andrew McMeel Publishing, 1998), 93, 94.

"Schroeder Says United States Is Ready for Woman President: Eyes Bid." *Houston Chronicle*, July 19, 1987, 12. www.HoustonChronicle.com (accessed March 23, 2005).

"Schroeder Tests Water in New Hampshire for a Presidential Bid." *Boston Globe*, June 16, 1987, 1.

"Schroeder Toe in Water." *Washington Post*, June 7, 1987, A-6.

"Schroeder: Female Candidates Trivialized." *Orlando Sentinel*, November 23, 1987. www.infoweb.newsbank.com (accessed March 21, 2005).

Seelye, Katherine Q. "The Dole Candidacy: The Overview." *New York Times*, October 21, 1999, A-1.

Sevener Donald. "Carol Moseley Braun, Democratic Candidate for U.S. Senate." *Illinois Periodicals Online*. www.lib.niu.edu/iop/aboutipo.html (accessed May 1, 2005).

"Senator Smith Arrives on Coast, 'Still in Race.'" *New York Times*, July 13, 1964, 16.

"She Didn't Win, But She Blazed a Political Trail." *Bangor Daily News*, July 17, 1964.

Sheeler, Kristina Horn. "Marginalizing Metaphors of the Feminine." In Brenda DeVore Marshall and Molly A. Mayhead (eds.) *Navigating the Boundaries: The Rhetoric of Women Governors*. (Westport, Conn.: Praeger, 2000).

Sherman, Janann. *No Place for a Woman: The Life of Senator Margaret Chase Smith*. (New Brunswick, N.J.: Rutgers University Press, 2000).

Siegel, Joel. "In the Prez Race to Win She Says." *Daily News*, (New York), March 11, 2003, 24.

Smith, Adrienne Yvette. *Trailblazers on the Hill: The First African-American Women in Washington (Shirley Chisholm, New York, Barbara Jordan, Texas, Carol Moseley Braun, Illinois)*. Unpublished thesis, Regent University, 1999.

Smith, Bruce. "Elizabeth Dole Pledges to Rebuild U.S. Military Might." *Morning Call*, (Allentown, PA), September 28, 1999, A-4.

Smith, Margaret Chase with William C. Lewis, Jr. *Declaration of Conscience*. (New York: Doubleday, 1972).

"Smith Showing in Illinois Almost Overshadows Barry." *Fort Worth Star Telegram*, April 15, 1964.

Smith, Marie. "Maine Lady Eyes Maine Event." *Washington Post*, August 16, 1963, D-1.

"A Softer Look, A Strong Appeal." *Newsweek*, August 30, 1999, 4.

Steinem, Gloria. "The Ticket That Might Have Been. . . ." *Ms.*, January 1973, 13.

St. Petersburg Times, January 16, 2004 www.sptimesru/archive/times/935/ (accessed July 21, 2005).

Stewart, L. Michelle. "Year of the Black Woman." *Ebony*, January 1993.

Swartz, Kirsten Lee. "Women's Conference Knows No Limits Cal Lutheran: Keynote Speaker Representative Patricia Schroeder sees the military as 'king of the hill' not in Washington." *Los Angeles Times*, March 3, 1991, B3.

Sweet, Lynn. "Braun Ad Slams Williamson." *Chicago Sun Times*, May 15, 1992, 24.

Sweet, Lynn. "Braun Bus Tour Takes Road Not Yet Traveled." *Chicago Sun Times*, September 12, 1992, 9.

Sweet, Lynn. "A Braun Upset; First Defeat for Dixon in Forty-two Years." *Chicago Sun Times*, March 18, 1992, 1.

Sweet, Lynn. "Charisma Wrapped Up in Many Questions." *Chicago Sun Times*, October 25, 1992, 18.

"That's Madam Vice President." *Morning Call*, (Allentown, PA), November 1, 1998, A-2.

Thomas, Evan and Stuart Taylor, Jr. "Queen of the Center." *Newsweek*, July 11, 2005, 29.

Thompson, Don. "Williamson, Braun Debate Issues, Beliefs." *Pantagraph*, (Bloomington, IL), October 23, 1992, A-1.

Time, February 7, 1964, 23.

Trent, Judith S. and Robert V. Friedenberg. *Political Campaign Communication.* (Westport, Conn.: Praeger, 2000), 67.

Tumulty, Karen. "Is This the Race for 2008?" *Newsweek*, August 29, 2005, 27.

Vallin, Marlene Boyd. *Margaret Chase Smith: Model Public Servant.* (Westport, Conn.: Greenwood Press, 1998), 207–213.

Verba, Sidney. "Women in American Politics." In Louise A. Tilly and Patricia Gurin, eds., *Women, Politics and Change.* (New York: Russell Sage Foundation, 1990).

Vital Speeches of the Day, January 1, 2003, 162–167.

Von Drehle, David and Kari Lydersen. "Moseley Braun Joins Democratic Presidential Field." *Washington Post*, February 19, 2003, 1.

Vorst, Judith. "Congresswoman Pat Schroeder: The Woman Who Has a Bear by the Tail." *Newsweek*, November 1973, 7.

Wallace, Patricia Ward. *Politics of Conscience: A Biography of Margaret Chase Smith.* (Westport, Conn.: Praeger Press, 1995).

Walls, Celeste M. "You Ain't Just Whistling Dixie: How Carol Moseley Braun Used Rhetorical Status to Change Jesse Helms' Tune." *Western Communication Journal*, June 22, 2004, Volume 68, Issue 3, 343.

Warren, Richard. *Evening Star*, February 3, 1964.

Washington, Shirley. *Outstanding Women Members of Congress.* (Washington, D.C: United States Capital Historical Society, 1995), 17.

Watson, Cary M. "Career Aspirations of Adolescent Girls: Effects of Achievement Level, Grade, and Single-Sex School Environment." *Sex Roles: A Journal of Research*, May 2002, 323–342.

"We Endorse Representative Braun." *Chicago Sun Times*, October 18, 1988, 37.

Wehrwein, Austin C. "Mrs. Smith Ran Well in the Suburbs." *New York Times*, April 19, 1964, 81.

Wertheimer, Molly Meijer and Nichola D. Gutgold. *Elizabeth Hanford Dole, Speaking from the Heart.* (Westport, Conn.: Praeger Press, 2004).

Wickham, DeWayne. "Black, Female: Both Impair Moseley Braun's Chances." *USA Today*, February 25, 2003, 3.

Widmer, Ted. *Campaigns: A Century of Presidential Races from the Photo Archives of The New York Times*. (London: DK Publishing, 2001).

Wilgoren, Jodi. "Past Triumphs and Debacles." *New York Times*, March 14, 2003, 19.

Wilkerson, Isabel. "Black Woman's Senate Race Is Acquiring a Celebrity Aura." *New York Times*, July 29, 1992, A-1.

Wilkerson, Isabel. "Milestone for Black Woman In Gaining U.S. Senate Seat." *New York Times*, November 4, 1992, B-7.

Williams, Lillian. "Carol Braun: Experienced, Productive." *Chicago Sun Times*, November 6, 1988, 60.

Williams, Marjorie. "Bob and Liddy Dole, Doing the Town: On the Run with a Well-Oiled Political Act." *Washington Post*, August 16, 1988, E-1.

Wineka, Mark. "Dole Returns to Salisbury." *Salisbury Post*, October 3, 1999, 1.

Witt, Linda, Karen M. Paget, and Glenna Matthews. *Running as a Woman: Gender and Power in American Politics*. (New York: The Free Press, 1994).

Wolbrecht, Christina and David E. Campbell. "Do Women Politicians Lead Girls to Be More Politically Engaged? A Cross-National Study of Political Role Models." A paper presented at the 2005 American Political Science Association Conference, September 1–4, 2005.

"Woman: Bold Move in Choice of Running Mate Holds Risk for Mondale." *Los Angeles Times*, July 8, 1984, 21.

Zeleny, Jeff. "Eyes on the Presidency: Moseley Braun Encouraged to Run for White House." *Chicago Tribune*, January 17, 2003, 10.

Index

About the Author

Nichola D. Gutgold is Associate Professor of Communication Arts and Sciences at Penn State Lehigh Valley where she also coordinates communication across the curriculum and the first year seminar experience. Dr. Gutgold enjoys teaching the introductory public speaking course as well as honor's courses, media, and film. She is author of numerous articles as well as co-author of the book *Elizabeth Hanford Dole: Speaking from the Heart* (2004).